D1589678

Ontario
for Free
(and Almost Free)

Ontario for Free

(and Almost Free)

DAVID E. SCOTT

Whitecap Books
Vancouver / Toronto

Copyright © 1992 by David E. Scott
Whitecap Books
Vancouver/Toronto

All rights reserved. No part of this publication may be reproduced, stored in a retrieval system or transmitted in any form or by any means, electronic, mechanical, photocopying, recording or otherwise, without prior written permission of the publisher.

Edited by Clifford Maynes
Cover design and illustration by Warren Clark
Interior design by Carolyn Deby
Maps by Wendy Reid
Typography by CompuType, Vancouver, B.C.

Printed and bound in Canada by
  D.W. Friesen and Sons Ltd., Altona, Manitoba

Canadian Cataloguing in Publication Data

Scott, David E., 1939-
  Ontario for free

  Includes index.
  ISBN 1-55110-039-8

  1. Ontario–Guidebooks. I. Title.
FC3057.S36 1992   917.1304′4   C92-091534-5
F1057.S36 1992

Table of Contents

Preface

This book lists more than 600 free attractions throughout the Province of Ontario.

There are major museums and exhibitions which offer free admission during specific times on certain days; there are smaller ones which are free whenever they are open. There are free guided tours of historic areas, enormous wood product mills and even wineries, distilleries and breweries that include a free sample of the product after the tour.

There are also some oddball superlatives, like the world's largest culvert, the world's shortest covered bridge and the world's largest Christmas tree. A surprising number of people delight in the trivia of such superlatives—or, in some cases, diminutives.

Some entries in this book are just plain oddball—a shrinking building, a million dollar bridge at the end of a road which goes nowhere and a house built entirely from empty liquor bottles. There's a public elevator for boats, a railway for boats and a four-storey castle built of one-ton logs by a lone man in his mid-fifties.

If you live in Ontario you may be surprised to learn what's fascinating—and free—in your own back yard, just off your beaten track, or in a part of the province you plan to visit "one of these days."

If you're a visitor to Ontario I hope this book helps to add fond memories of your visit with us.

That's the good news. Now, here's the bad news.

This book originally was also going to contain comprehensive listings of free special events and festivals as well as year-round and seasonal attractions. But when information about these celebrations started flooding in from the hundred-plus sources to which I had appealed, it was soon apparent that a book containing all the free attractions *and* festivals and special events would be very thick—and very expensive.

As a result, this compilation includes only a scanty listing at the start of each chapter of some major events—just enough information to pique your interest. If you want to know more, Ontario's Ministry of Tourism and Recreation publishes two free books that list special events, one for summer and one for winter. (See More Ontario For Free for details on how to get those books.)

Every single entry in this book was painstakingly double-checked immediately prior to my editorial deadline, but changes are bound to have occurred in times, dates and perhaps even the free admission policy. Before travelling any distance to visit any of the attractions, only to find locked doors or gates, please make a quick telephone check. It will save you time and disappointment and it will spare me from angry letters and phone calls.

If I've overlooked anything which deserves to be included in a subsequent edition of this book, please share it through me with others.

My sincere thanks for the kind assistance of Tracey Arial, Information Officer, Ontario Ministry of Tourism and Recreation, staff of the twelve regional MTR offices, dozens of visitor and convention bureaux and chambers of commerce and scores of private owners and operators of attractions, museums, industries, manufacturers, retailers and others in the tourism sector of Ontario.

Happy travels!

David E. Scott
P.O. Box 131
Ailsa Craig, Ont.
N0M 1A0

Finding your way around this book

Ontario is such an enormous area—over one million km²
(412,000 sq. mi.)—that the provincial Ministry of Tourism has
broken the province into twelve regions. Despite signposting on
all major highways, these regions, often arbitrarily divided along
county boundaries, can be confusing to the traveller trying to co-
ordinate travel plans with the tourism literature.

The system isn't perfect, but Ontario has to be divided into
smaller areas somehow, so this book adopts the Ministry's twelve
regions. In hopes of making the regions easier to grasp, we've added
at the start of each chapter, the names of major towns and cities
within the region.

A map is also included, with place names marked of all the
listings in the chapter.

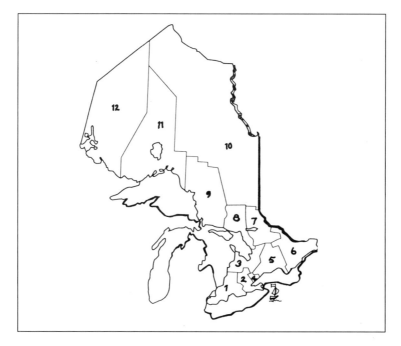

Southwest

Includes: Chatham, Goderich, Grand Bend, London, Pelee Island, Sarnia, St. Thomas, Stratford, Wallaceburg, Windsor, Woodstock and their environs.

The small cities in this region are for the most part compact, with well defined boundaries. Within minutes, residents can drive into the countryside and savour its therapeutically quieter lifestyle.

Some of Ontario's most popular summer resorts are found in this region, on the shores of lakes Erie, St. Clair and Huron. Spring weather arrives in southwestern Ontario a few days before any other part of the province.

Festivals, Carnivals, Celebrations, Special Events:

JANUARY: Ska-Nah-Doht Indian Village, Longwoods Road, *Winter Heritage Carnival* (husky dogs, native crafts).

FEBRUARY: Grand Bend, *Winter Carnival* (snow-sculpting, dog team races); Goderich, *Snow Blitz Winter Weekend;* London, *Ski Club Winter Carnival.*

MARCH: Harrietsville, *A Maple Syrup Experience;* Ilderton, *Maple Magic;* Colchester, *First Taste of Spring;* St. Thomas-

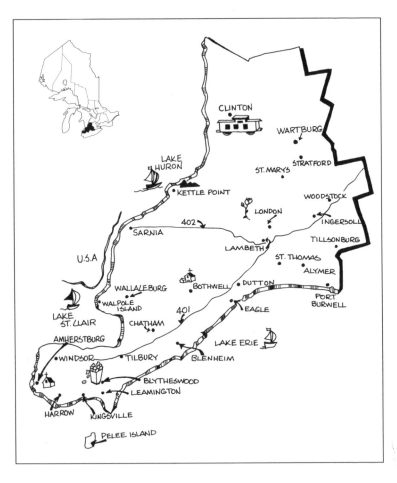

Aylmer, *Springwater Maple Syrup Festival* (wagon rides); Alvinston, *Maple Syrup Festival* (log-sawing); Watford, *Sugarfest* (pancakes and sausages); Sweaburg, *Annual Maple Syrup Festival;* Aylmer Wildlife Management Area, *Return of the Tundra Swans;* Grand Bend, *Return of the Swans, Ducks, Geese;* Sarnia, Wawanosh Wetlands, *Waterfowl Viewing Day.*

APRIL: Ruthven, Colasanti's, *Easter Celebration* (Easter Egg Hunt); Delaware, Sharon Creek Conservation Area, *Plant a Baby Tree.*

MAY: Oil Springs, *Kite Fly;* Kingsville, Colasanti Farms, *Mother's*

Day Celebration; London, *N'Amerind Native Art Festival* (storytelling, Native regalia fashion show); Clinton, *Klompenfest* (Dutch barbecue, parade); Amherstburg, Park House Museum, *Victorian Tea;* Woodstock, *Victoria Day Parade;* Grand Bend, *Spring Heritage Day* (steam engines); Walpole Island, *Mnookimi Arts Festival;* Stratford, *Stratford Festival City Days;* Amherstburg, *Spring Fest* (garden tour); Delaware, *Battle of Longwoods Re-enactment;* Chatham, *Fitnic* (bicycle tours, river cruises).

JUNE: St. Thomas, *St. Anne's Festival* (cabaret); Stratford, *Southwestern Ontario Fiddle and Step Championships;* Windsor, *Voyageur Village and Canoe Race* (tomahawk throw, frying pan toss); London, *Eldon House Garden Party;* Corunna, *Fireman's Field Day;* La Salle, *Strawberry Festival;* London, *Musicfest* (Native musicians from North, South and Central America); Sarnia, *Chippewa Indian Pow Wow;* London, N'Amerind Friendship Centre, *Native Heritage Celebration;* Windsor, *Carousel of the Nations* (multicultural festival); Ruthven, *Essex County Wine and Food Tasting Festival;* Blyth, *Rutabaga Festival* (gong show); Windsor, *International Freedom Festival* (rope tug across the Detroit River); London, *Royal Canadian Big Band Music Festival; Strathroy Lions Annual Turkey Festival.*

JULY: Ailsa Craig, *Gala Days* (non pari-mutuel turtle races); Essex, *Fun Fest* (citizenship court); Kettle Point and Stony Point, *Pow Wow;* Petrolia, *Hard Oil Festival of Country Music;* Walpole Island, *Pow Wow;* Ridgetown, *Summerfest;* Goderich, *Kinsmen Summerfest Carnival and Beach Blow-Out;* Mount Brydges, Longwoods Road Conservation Area, *Night Walk with the Spirits;* Thamesville, *Threshing Festival* (frog jumping); Petrolia, *Old Town Picnic;* Mount Brydges, *Longwoods Road Summer Festival;* Embro, *Highland Games;* London, *Home County Folk Festival;* Chatham, *Highland Games;* Wheatley, *Fish Festival* (moto-cross bicycle race).

AUGUST: London, *Molson Canadian Light Hot Air Balloon Fiesta* (country and western show); Corunna, *Captain Kidd Days;* Sarnia, *Highland Games;* Amherstburg, *Fort Malden Military Field Day;* Thamesville, *Moraviantown Pow Wow;* Windsor, *Annual Commemoration of Surrender of Detroit;* Lucknow, *Point*

Clark Old Tyme Fiddler's Jamboree; Port Burwell, *Tub Daze* (tub races); Port Burwell, *Discovery Week* (sand sculptures); Warwick, *Festival Day;* Watford, *Cornfest* (corn-eating contest); Leamington, *Tomato Festival* (tomato stomping); St. Marys, *Teddy Bear Reunion;* Tecumseh, *Green Giant Corn Festival;* Zurich, *Bean Festival* (frog jumping); Sarnia, *Festival by the Bay;* St. Thomas, *Firemuster.*

SEPTEMBER: Kingsville, Happy Acres and Colasanti's, *M.D. Festival;* Norwich, *Harvest Festival* (antique farm machinery demonstrations); London, *Panorama Multicultural Festival* (foods of the world); Walpole Island, *Annual Fall Fair;* Ruthven, *Apple Festival;* Sarnia, *Labour Day Parade.*

OCTOBER: Kingsville, *Migration Festival* (birdcarving show, parade); London, *Harvest Festival.*

NOVEMBER: Walpole Island, *Quilt Show and Sale;* Delaware, Longwoods Road Conservation Area, *Feeding the Winter Birds;* London, Tillsonburg, Wallaceburg, Goderich, Woodstock, Leamington, *Santa Claus parades.*

DECEMBER: Ailsa Craig, Alvinston, Forest, Petrolia, Ridgetown, Sarnia, Watford, Stratford, *Santa Claus parades.*

More detailed information on the festivals, carnivals, celebrations and other attractions of Southwestern Ontario is available from: Southwestern Ontario Travel Association, 920 Commissioners Rd., London, Ontario N5Z 3J1, Tel. 519-649-7075.

Amberstburg

Christ Church

WHERE: 317 Ramsay St.

WHEN: Open year round.

WHAT: Christ Church, one of the earliest Anglican churches in the province, served the garrison of nearby Fort Malden prior to the War of 1812. The present building was constructed in 1819.

Fort Malden

WHERE: 100 Laird Ave., one block west of Hwy. 18.

WHEN: Open year round, daily. Labour Day through May, open 10 a.m. to 5 p.m. June through Labour Day, open 10 a.m. to 6 p.m. Closed December 25, 26, January 1, Remembrance Day and Easter.

WHAT: This national historic site includes barracks dating from 1819 and part of the Fort Malden earthworks dating from about 1841. The original fortification was built in 1796 as a successor to Fort Lernoult in Detroit and played an important role in the War of 1812. In the early stages of the war, General Brock led his British regulars from Fort Malden to capture Detroit with the assistance of Tecumseh and his Native warriors. Two buildings contain artifacts and displays relating to the War of 1812 and the 1837-1838 Rebellion. Picnic tables, wheelchair-accessible washrooms. Pets are not allowed in the buildings but dog kennels are provided on site.

CONTACT: 519-736-5416, Fort Malden National Historic Site.

Aylmer

Aylmer and District Museum

WHERE: 14 East St., east end of Aylmer, just off Talbot St.

WHEN: Open year round. Labour Day to Victoria Day open Monday to Friday, 9 a.m. to 5 p.m. Victoria Day to Labour Day also open Saturdays, 10 a.m. to 4 p.m. Admission by donation.

WHAT: A small community museum features changing exhibits and local artifacts. Gift Shop. Washroom. Wheelchair accessible with assistance.

CONTACT: 519-773-9723, Aylmer and District Museum.

Uplands Pheasantry

WHERE: 8 km (5 mi.) south of Aylmer on Hwy. 73.

WHEN: Open year round. May through August, open daily, 8 a.m. to 5 p.m. Rest of the year, open Monday to Friday, 8 a.m. to 5 p.m.

WHAT: You can view 8,000 to 30,000 birds at various stages of maturity at Canada's largest pheasant hatchery. Chicks are hatched twice weekly from May through July and may be seen in full plumage from September through November in outdoor enclosures. Hatchery and washrooms are wheelchair accessible.

CONTACT: 519-773-8151, Uplands Pheasantry.

Blenheim

London Winery (formerly Charal Winery)

WHERE: On Hwy. 3, 5 km (3 mi.) west of Blenheim, 27 km (17 mi.) south of Chatham.

WHEN: Open year round. May to November, open Monday to Saturday, 10 a.m. to 6 p.m., with tours at 2 p.m. May to September, also open Sunday. Closed December 25, 26 and January 1.

WHAT: The tour includes a tasting in the barrel room. Retail shop. Wheelchair-accessible washrooms.

CONTACT: 519-676-8008, London Winery.

Blytheswood

Russell Jones Popcorn

WHERE: Blytheswood, 8 km (5 mi.) north of Leamington on the 8th Concession, east of Hwy. 77.

WHEN: Open year round, Monday to Saturday, 8 a.m. to 5 p.m. Open Sunday by appointment only.

WHAT: On this farm, popcorn is grown from seed, harvested and marketed. Also for sale is Jones' line of coconut oil and salt. Wash-

---

rooms. Wheelchair accessible with assistance (one step into barn). CONTACT: 519-326-7128, Russell Jones Popcorn.

Bothwell

The Avenue of Peace,
1848 Church and Fairfield Museum

WHERE: On the south side of Hwy. 2 between Bothwell and Thamesville.

WHEN: Open year round, 10 a.m. to 5 p.m. Closed Mondays. Donations accepted at museum.

WHAT: In 1792 a group of Moravian missionaries and converted Delaware Indians settled on land along the Thames River, granted to them by the Upper Canada government. Fairfield, the first Christian Indian town in Canada, boasted fifty homes, a two-storey church, two schools, carpenters' shops and barns. The Indians farmed many hectares and sold their produce in Detroit. During the War of 1812, the Indian chief Tecumseh was killed by American soldiers in the nearby Battle of the Thames, and the peaceful Indians fled. The Americans pillaged Fairfield and razed it, sending seventeen raft loads of plunder down the Thames River to Detroit. The village site was excavated during the 1940s, yielding artifacts that are displayed in a small museum on the site of the original village. Behind the museum you will find The Avenue of Peace, a tree-lined path where the main street of Fairfield once ran. A monument and plaques note the years of peace between Canada and the U.S. The mission was re-established across the Thames River and its church, dating from 1848, still stands. Washrooms. Wheelchair accessible with help. (One step into museum).

CONTACT: 519-692-4397, Fairfield Museum.

Chatham

Chatham Cultural Centre

WHERE: 75 William St. N., north of King St. W., opposite Tecumseh Park.

WHEN: Open year round, Tuesday to Sunday, 1 p.m. to 5 p.m. Closed Good Friday, Christmas Day and between exhibitions.

WHAT: The Centre houses the Thames Art Gallery, the 700-seat Kiwanis Theatre and the Chatham-Kent Museum (see listing below). The Gallery offers changing exhibits of local, national and international art work. Admission is charged to plays, music festivals, concerts and films at the Kiwanis Theatre. Wheelchair-accessible washrooms.

CONTACT: 519-354-8338, Chatham Cultural Centre.

Chatham-Kent Museum

WHERE: In Chatham Cultural Centre (see listing above), 75 William St. N. and the Milner House, 59 William St. N.

WHEN: Open year round, Tuesday to Sunday, 1 p.m. to 5 p.m. Closed Christmas and Boxing Day, New Year's Day and Good Friday. The Milner House is open from Victoria Day weekend to Labour Day, Tuesday to Sunday, 1 p.m. to 5 p.m.; Saturday, 10 a.m. to 5 p.m.

WHAT: Five galleries display the history of Chatham, including early transportation, collections from Chatham's world travellers, and changing contemporary exhibits. The Milner House, partially restored to 1910 vintage, offers educational and participatory programmes. Wheelchair-accessible washrooms.

CONTACT: 519-354-8338, Chatham-Kent Museum.

Clinton

School on Wheels #15089

WHERE: At Sloman Park, signposted off Hwy. 4 at south side of Clinton.

WHEN: Victoria Day to Labour Day, open Monday to Friday, 2 p.m. to 5 p.m.; Saturday, Sunday, and holidays, 11 a.m. to 7 p.m. Off-season, open by appointment. Donations welcome.

WHAT: This restored Canadian National Railway car is one of seven which travelled throughout Northern Ontario providing conventional schooling to children in isolated areas. Teachers Fred and Cela Sloman of Clinton raised their own five children in the mobile school. No washroom. Not wheelchair accessible.

CONTACT: 519-482-3180, School on Wheels #15089; 519-482-3997, Town of Clinton Municipal Office.

Dutton

The Village Pride Shop—Art Gallery

WHERE: 168 Main St., Dutton.

WHEN: Open year round, Monday to Saturday, 9 a.m. to 5 p.m.; Sunday, 1 p.m. to 4 p.m. Donations welcome.

WHAT: A retail gallery-studio features working artists, local works of art in oils, drawings, acrylics, weaving, pottery, and carving. Washroom. Store only accessible to wheelchairs with assistance.

CONTACT: 519-762-3496, The Village Pride Shop.

Eagle

Swain Greenhouses Ltd.

WHERE: At Eagle, Hwy. 3 and Hwy. 76, 6 km (4 mi.) south of Hwy. 401 from Exit 137, 36 km (22 mi.) west of St. Thomas.

WHEN: Open year round, Monday to Saturday, 9 a.m. to 5:30 p.m.; Sunday, 10 a.m. to 6 p.m. Closed December 25 and 26 and January 1.

WHAT: Greenhouses and shops covering 1.8 ha (4.5 a.) are filled with house plants, cacti, succulents, seasonal plants and flowers. Guided tours available. Restaurant, washrooms, nursery, gift shop, wheelchair accessible.

CONTACT: 519-768-1116, Swain Greenhouses Ltd.

Harrow

Harrow Agricultural Research Station

WHERE: Village of Harrow, 15 km (9 mi.) west of Kingsville on Hwy. 18.

WHEN: All tours by appointment only. July to September, inside and outdoor tours offered Tuesday and Thursday, 2 p.m. October to April, inside tours only offered at 8:15 a.m. No tours in May and June. Tours take approximately one hour outside and one hour inside.

WHAT: This facility develops methods of improving farm productivity for various crops, including vegetables, oilseed and protein seeds, soft white winter wheat, grain corn and tree fruits. Tour wagons provide rides through the grounds. Washrooms and the inside portion of the tour are wheelchair accessible.

CONTACT: 519-738-2251, Harrow Agricultural Research Station.

Winery tour, Colio Wines

WHERE: Colio Dr., Harrow, 47 km (29 mi.) south of Windsor.

WHEN: Open year round. Public tours offered Wednesday, 1 p.m.; Saturday, every hour between noon and 4 p.m. Retail outlet open Monday to Saturday, 10 a.m. to 5 p.m. Closed holidays.

WHAT: Visitors can tour this small winery and taste both wines and non-alcoholic sparkling grape juices. Wheelchair-accessible washrooms.

CONTACT: 519-726-5317 or 519-738-2241, Colio Wines.

Ingersoll

Ingersoll Cheese Factory Museums and Sports Hall of Fame

WHERE: Centennial Park off Hwy. 19, 1.5 km (1 mi.) north of Hwy. 401 at Exit 218.

WHEN: Victoria Day weekend to mid-June, open weekends, 1 p.m. to 5 p.m. Mid-June through Labour Day, open daily, 10 a.m. to 6 p.m. Labour Day to Thanksgiving, open weekends, 1 p.m. to 5 p.m. Donations appreciated.

WHAT: Early cheese-making equipment is housed in a replica of an Oxford County Cheese Factory, 1860 vintage. Guides explain the cheese-making process. Two reconstructed barns house early farm machinery, tools and a blacksmith shop. The Sports Hall of Fame recalls area sports highlights, including the sporting achievements of a surprising number of area residents. Washrooms, picnic tables, playground, tourist information centre, gift shop, all wheelchair accessible. Small charge for overnight camping and water and electrical hookups when the museum is operating; no reservations for campsites.

CONTACT: 519-485-4930, Ingersoll Cheese Factory Museums and Sports Hall of Fame.

Kettle Point

Kettles

WHERE: Along the shoreline of Kettle Point, about 10 km (6 mi.) north of Forest at the west end of Ipperwash Beach.

WHEN: Spring through fall.

WHAT: The wave action of Lake Huron formed these strange, kettle-shaped rock formations of varying sizes, which dot the shore.

Kingsville

Colasanti Tropical Gardens and Petting Farm

WHERE: 3rd Concession, Ruthven. West off Hwy. 3 or 5 km (3 mi.) east of Jack Miner's Bird Sanctuary (see following listing).

WHEN: Open year round, Monday to Thursday, 8 a.m. to 5 p.m.; Friday to Sunday, 8 a.m. to 7 p.m. Closed December 25, January 1.

WHAT: Large tropical greenhouses feature a wide range of cactus species. A petting farm includes goats, a llama and an emu. Hundreds of exotic (and often loud) birds are displayed in cages. Restaurant, banquet room, retail store, wheelchair-accessible washrooms.

CONTACT: 519-322-2301, Colasanti Tropical Gardens and Petting Farm.

Jack Miner's Bird Sanctuary

WHERE: North of Kingsville, west of Division Rd., well signposted.

WHEN: Year round. Museum open Monday to Saturday, 9 a.m. to 5 p.m. Peak migration periods are March, the first week of April and the last two weeks of October and November. During migration times, best seen from 3:30 p.m. to sundown; "Air Show" held at 4 p.m. In summer, waterfowl nest in the Hudson Bay region.

WHAT: The sanctuary is a resting area and feeding ground for large flights of geese and other wildfowl. At a pond beside the Miner home visitors can feed far-from-shy geese and ducks. Free feed is available from a bin just outside the fenced enclosure. A two-storey museum in the former stables contains a wealth of memorabilia about Jack Miner, a conservationist who lectured around the world from 1910 to 1940. Miner earned the Order of the British Empire "for the greatest achievement in conservation in the British Empire."

CONTACT: 519-733-4034, Jack Miner's Bird Sanctuary.

Lambeth

Bygone Babies Doll and Teddy Bear Museum and Gift Shop

WHERE: 48 Main St., Lambeth, about 10 km (6 mi.) southwest of London City Hall.

WHEN: Open year round, Monday to Saturday, 10 a.m. to 5 p.m. In November, December, July and August, also open Sunday 1 p.m. to 5 p.m. Free admission to Museum during December. Admission charged rest of year.

WHAT: The collection includes dolls and buggies dating from the 1840s, dolls from around the world and teddy bears dating from the early 1900s. Retail store.

CONTACT: 519-652-9240, Bygone Babies Doll and Teddy Bear Museum and Gift Shop.

Leamington

Leamington Regional Art Gallery

WHERE: 11 Queens Ave.

WHEN: Year round. Early September to late June, open Wednesday to Saturday, noon to 5 p.m.; Sunday, 1 p.m. to 4 p.m. Late June to early September, open Monday to Saturday, 9 a.m. to 5 p.m.; Sunday, 1 p.m. to 4 p.m. Closed December 24 to January 2.

WHAT: The Art Gallery, in a former church with stained glass windows, showcases the work of numerous local artists. Not wheelchair accessible.

CONTACT: 519-326-3634, Leamington Regional Art Gallery.

Our Lady of Lebanon Shrine

WHERE: North of Leamington on the west side of Hwy. 77, between the 4th and 5th concessions.

WHEN: Always open.

WHAT: The shrine is a reproduction in miniature of a shrine in Lebanon. Eighty-five steps ascend a 13.7-m (45-ft.) cone-shaped tower to a 4.6-m (15-ft.) statue in Italian marble. The tower contains a small chapel. Picnic tables and washrooms.

CONTACT: 519-326-3883, Leamington Lebanese Club.

London

Archival Teaching and Research Museum

WHERE: London Psychiatric Hospital, 850 Highbury Ave.

WHEN: Tours by appointment.

WHAT: The Museum depicts the history of mental health accomplishments since 1870. It includes a reproduction of the original superintendent's office, two bedrooms, a hydrotherapy room and many historical artifacts. A replica of the original telephone used in the region is on loan from the Bell Canada Museum. Wheelchair-accessible washrooms.

CONTACT: 519-455-5110, Ext. 2155, Archival Teaching and Research Museum.

Blackfriars Bridge

WHERE: Blackfriars St.

WHEN: Year round.

WHAT: The oldest known wrought-iron bridge in Ontario was built in 1875 to replace a wooden structure. The bowstring arch bridge is a fine example of cross construction.

Covent Garden Market

WHERE: 130 King St. (one-way east).

WHEN: Open Monday to Saturday, 8 a.m. to 6 p.m.

WHAT: A London fixture for well over a century, this is one of the few Ontario farmers markets that is open six days a week, year round. Wheelchair-accessible washrooms.

CONTACT: 519-439-3921, Covent Garden Market.

Eldon House

WHERE: 481 Ridout St. N. between Fullarton St. and Dufferin Ave.

WHEN: Open year round. Free Tuesdays, except for groups, noon to 5 p.m. Admission is charged Wednesday to Sunday and holidays, noon to 5 p.m.

WHAT: London's oldest surviving private dwelling was built by John Harris in 1834. The house is filled with heirloom furnishings, some of which are 300 years old, and which reflect the family's world-wide travels. Wheelchair access to first floor and washrooms.

CONTACT: 519-661-5165, Eldon House.

1st Hussars Museum

WHERE: 399 Ridout St. N.

WHEN: Open year round. Tours available Monday to Friday, 1:30 p.m. to 3:30 p.m. Closed weekends and holidays.

WHAT: Exhibits include equipment, uniforms and photographs that depict the history of the London-based Cavalry and Armoured Regiment, which dates from 1856. Wheelchair-accessible washrooms.

CONTACT: 519-434-7321, curator; 519-471-1538.

Labatt's Pioneer Museum

WHERE: 150 Simcoe St.

WHEN: Open Victoria Day to Labour Day, Monday to Saturday, 11 a.m. to 5 p.m.

WHAT: This small, very well done replica of Labatt's original distillery offers a self-guided, walk-through tour. No product samples.

CONTACT: 519-667-7308, Labatt's Pioneer Museum.

London Regional Art and Historical Museum

WHERE: 421 Ridout St. N.

WHEN: Open year round, Tuesday to Sunday and holidays, noon to 5 p.m. Closed Mondays.

WHAT: The Museum houses changing exhibitions and a permanent collection of 2,700 art works. The modern building consists of six joined, glass-covered structures whose ends are the shape of rounded croquet hoops. Wheelchair access to all three floors and washrooms.

CONTACT: 519-672-4580, London Regional Art and Historical Museum.

McIntosh Gallery

WHERE: University of Western Ontario Campus, north of University

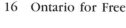

College and south of the Medical Sciences Building.

WHEN: Open year round, Tuesday to Thursday, noon to 7 p.m.; Friday to Sunday, noon to 4 p.m.

WHAT: The Gallery displays a continuous and changing programme of historical and contemporary art exhibitions, with a programme of films on art, lectures, artists' workshops, concerts and guided tours. Washroom. Gallery not wheelchair accessible.

CONTACT: 519-661-3181, McIntosh Gallery.

Medical Museum

WHERE: University Hospital, 339 Windermere Rd.

WHEN: Open year round, by appointment.

WHAT: The Museum illustrates the state of medicine over the last century and a half in a recreated Victorian doctor's office. Another exhibition area displays medical technology, including antique microscopes, stethoscopes, surgical kits and pharmaceutical items. Not wheelchair accessible.

CONTACT: 519-663-3120, Medical Museum, University Hospital.

Old Courthouse and Gaol

WHERE: 399 Ridout St. N.

WHEN: Open Monday to Friday. One-hour tour available at 1:30 p.m. Closed holidays and weekends.

WHAT: London's oldest building, modelled after Malahide Castle in England, is now the home of Middlesex County Council. The courthouse was built between 1827 and 1829, with additions in 1878 and 1911. It was restored in 1980. The jail was built in 1846. On the tour you'll see old furniture, pictures, early maps and an 1840s cell block. Wheelchair-accessible washroom.

CONTACT: 519-434-7321; from the 519 area, 1-800-265-5939.

Memorial Gardens

WHERE: Springbank Dr. at Wonderland Rd. (west side of city).

WHEN: Spring through fall.

WHAT: Formal rose gardens, in a 3.2-ha (8-a.) setting, are dedicated to the memory of London musician Melvin Rayner. An adjacent grove of trees provides a backdrop for the formal display beds of the Elmo Curtis Memorial Gardens.

The Royal Canadian Regiment Museum

WHERE: Wolseley Hall, Canadian Forces Base London, corner of Oxford St. and Elizabeth St.

WHEN: Open Tuesday to Friday, 10 a.m. to 4 p.m.; Saturday and Sunday, noon to 4 p.m. Closed on Mondays and holidays.

WHAT: The first floor contains a gallery honouring the Regiment's colonels and honorary colonels, a library, war memorials and a military souvenir shop. The second floor contains displays of uniforms, medals, decorations, scale models of tanks, war memorabilia, sports trophies, weapons and captured enemy equipment. Wheelchair-accessible washrooms.

CONTACT: 519-660-5102, The Royal Canadian Regiment Museum.

Second City ''improvs''

WHERE: Second City dinner theatre, 340 Wellington St.

WHEN: Monday to Thursday, 10 p.m. to 10:45 p.m.; Friday, 10:45 p.m. to 11:15 p.m.

WHAT: Following their regular shows, the actors offer impromptu sketches inspired by audience suggestions. There is no admission to this portion of the shows.

CONTACT: 519-439-0521, Second City.

Sifton Bog

WHERE: Bounded by Oxford St. on the north and Hyde Park Rd. on the east, on the west side of the city. Accessible from Oxford St. W.

WHEN: Year round.

WHAT: The most southerly large acid bog in Canada, formed when a huge chunk of glacial ice created a deep, undrained depression. A trail follows the perimeter and a boardwalk takes you to the edge of Redmond's Pond in the middle of the bog. You can see numerous flowers, plants, shrubs, trees, insects and reptiles unique to southern Ontario. In summer come prepared for clouds of mosquitoes and black flies.

Springbank Park

WHERE: In west London off Springbank Dr.

WHEN: Year round.

WHAT: A beautifully landscaped park borders the Thames River, with picnic tables, washroom facilities, winding pathways and bicycle and jogging paths. Admission is charged to Storybook Gardens inside the park, and to ride the miniature train and London Princess cruise boat.

Pelee Island

Pelee Island Pheasant Farm

WHERE: Near West Dock on Pelee Island.

WHEN: Open year round, daily, 8 a.m. to 5 p.m.

WHAT: The island has raised pheasant on a commercial basis since 1932 and profits from the annual October pheasant hunts continue to keep municipal taxes low. The hunt draws 700 hunters who fire buckshot at 18,000 pheasant. A guide is usually available to show visitors through the pheasant farm operation where a dozen species are on display. No washrooms, wheelchair accessible.

CONTACT: 519-724-2931, Township Clerk, Pelee Island.

Vin Villa

WHERE: Between Scudder and West Dock on Pelee Island.

WHEN: Year round.

WHAT: In 1865, three Kentuckians discovered that Pelee Island's moderate climate was conducive to growing grapes. They founded a winery, cut two 12.2- by 18.3-m (40- by 60-ft.) vaults in the rock for storing wine and built a pretentious stone manor house they called Vin Villa. Prohibition eventually closed the winery, Vin Villa burned down and islanders who had grown grapes switched back to wheat, corn and tobacco. There's a scale model of Vin Villa at the intersection of East-West Rd. and Centre Dike Rd., near the Pheasant Farm, and you can visit the site where a couple of walls still stand, overgrown by wild grape vines. You can also scramble down into the vaults to admire the high, curved stone ceilings. None of the snakes you're very likely to encounter are poisonous.

Port Burwell

Port Burwell Lighthouse

WHERE: Village of Port Burwell, 25 km (15.5 mi.) south of Tillsonburg on Hwy. 19.

WHEN: Open early May to Labour Day, daily, 10 a.m. to 6 p.m. There is no charge to walk around the lighthouse, but there's a small fee to enter it and climb 19.8 m (65 ft.) to the top.

WHAT: This lighthouse was built in 1840. Parking, picnic area.

CONTACT: 519-874-4343, Village of Port Burwell office.

St. Marys

Canada's largest outdoor swimming pool

WHERE: St. Marys.

WHEN: Last weekend of May through Labour Day, public swimming offered 1:30 p.m. to dusk.

WHAT: Canada's largest swimming pool is located in a former limestone quarry of the St. Marys Cement Company, which has been made suitable for swimming. Life guards, change rooms, washrooms.

CONTACT: 519-284-3500, St. Marys Visitor Information.

St. Marys Museum

WHERE: 177 Church St.

WHEN: Year round. April and May and from September 1 to Thanksgiving, open weekdays, 10 a.m. to noon and 1 p.m. to 4 p.m. Thanksgiving to Christmas, open weekdays, 1 p.m. to 4 p.m. June through August, open Monday to Friday, 9 a.m. to 5 p.m.; weekends, 1 p.m. to 5 p.m. Donations welcome.

WHAT: One of southwestern Ontario's better museums is housed in an 1850s stone mansion, with ten rooms of exhibits. There are community artifacts and a fine collection of stuffed birds. A barn is filled with antique farm machinery. No washrooms. Not wheelchair accessible.

CONTACT: 519-284-3556, St. Marys Museum; 519-284-3500, St. Marys Visitor Information.

Sir Arthur Meighen Statue

WHERE: Corner of Church St. and Jones St.

WHEN: Year round.

WHAT: Arthur Meighen, who grew up in St. Marys, was prime minister of Canada in 1920, 1921 and 1926. Meighen was a brilliant debater who achieved the passage of much controversial legislation, including the Conscription Bill of 1917. An impressionistic statue of him, commissioned in 1967, was not well received by his family. (It was described by former Prime Minister John Diefenbaker as a cross between Ichabod Crane and daddy-longlegs.) The statue sat in an Ottawa warehouse until local citizens effected its release in 1987 and erected it in a place of honour in Meighen's home town.

St. Thomas

Art Gallery St. Thomas-Elgin

WHERE: 301 Talbot St.

WHEN: Open year round, Tuesday to Saturday, 10 a.m. to 5 p.m.; Sunday, noon to 5 p.m. Closed Mondays.

WHAT: Exhibitions that range from historical paintings to experimental works by contemporary artists are changed monthly. Washrooms, wheelchair accessible.

CONTACT: 519-631-4040, Art Gallery St. Thomas-Elgin.

Guildhouse Gallery Inc. and Centre of Contemporary Art

WHERE: 180 Talbot St.

WHEN: Open year round, daily, 10 a.m. to 6 p.m. Closed Christmas and Easter.

WHAT: The top three floors of this former 1910-vintage shoe factory are occupied by sixty-four artists who work in all media. Their work is exhibited. The fourth floor houses the Centre of Contemporary Art, a non-profit gallery that features rotating art and sculpture exhibits. On the lower floors, visitors can watch weavers, potters, sculptors, artists and artisans at work, and browse their finished works. Snack bar. Wheelchair accessible.

CONTACT: 519-637-2450, Guildhouse Gallery Inc.

Jumbo Monument

WHERE: West entrance to St. Thomas.

WHEN: Year round.

WHAT: This statue of the largest elephant ever in captivity improves on reality: it's 10 per cent larger than life. Jumbo, who travelled with the Barnum and Bailey Circus, was killed by a train on his second visit to St. Thomas in 1885. The monument excited considerable opposition when it was erected in 1985. Since then, however, it has drawn up to 101,500 visitors a year. An old railway caboose adjacent to the monument sells Jumbo kitsch.

CONTACT: 519-631-1981, St. Thomas and District Chamber of Commerce.

St. Thomas' Church

WHERE: 55 Walnut St.

WHEN: Year round.

WHAT: The church, dated 1824, was one of the earliest built in the Talbot Settlement. It is considered one of the finest remaining examples of Early English Gothic Revival architecture in the province.

Technicolour house

WHERE: 14 Lydia St.

WHEN: Year round, most striking in sunlight.

WHAT: In the late 1940s, tinsmith Frank Melbourne decided to brick over his two-storey frame home. He made the bricks himself, and as they were hardening he embedded broken glass, china and other bits of colourful whimsy he found around the neighborhood. For five summers he added the eye-catching bricks until the walls of the house were completely covered.

Sarnia

Canatara Park

WHERE: Take Front St. Exit from Hwy. 402, north to Michigan Ave., east to Christina, then north to entrance at Cathcart Blvd.

WHEN: Open year round, daily. Animal farm open May 24 through October, daily, 8 a.m. to 7:30 p.m. Rest of the year, open 8 a.m. to 4 p.m.

WHAT: A 75-ha (185-a.) park features a children's animal farm and historic log cabin, beach and picnic areas. Special events include an Easter egg hunt and egg and bonnet contests, Christmas on the farm with sleigh rides, crafts, baking and a parade and ethnic food booths on Canada Day. Picnic area, ball diamond, playground, refreshments, bandshell, beach with bathhouse and lifeguards, launching ramp for centreboard sailboats, wheelchair-accessible washrooms and parking areas, nature trail, fitness trail, frisbee golf course. No alcohol allowed in the park.

CONTACT: 519-332-0330, Ext. 201, City of Sarnia, Parks and Recreation Dept.

Celebration of Lights

WHERE: Throughout Sarnia. The focal point is Centennial Park.

WHEN: Late November through the first week of January.

WHAT: Each Christmas, homes, businesses, industry and parks are adorned with tens of thousands of Christmas lights.

CONTACT: 519-336-3232, Sarnia/Lambton Visitor and Convention Bureau.

Dow Chemical Canada Inc. plant tour

WHERE: In Chemical Valley, south of Sarnia on Vidal St. S.

WHEN: Tours offered year round for groups; June through September for individuals, by appointment.

WHAT: Dow offers two-hour conducted tours of its billion dollar chemical complex.

CONTACT: 519-339-5232, Dow Chemical Canada.

Gallery Lambton

WHERE: 124 Christina St. S.

WHEN: From the first Sunday after Thanksgiving to the end of May, open weekdays, 9 a.m. to 9 p.m.; Saturday, 9 a.m. to 5:30 p.m.; Sunday, 2 p.m. to 5 p.m. Closed during summer.

WHAT: The second floor of this building is a gallery of works by Canadian artists that is changed every six weeks by the Sarnia Branch of Lambton County Library. The Library also operates the Lawrence House-Suncor Centre across the street at 127 Christina St. S. The public may visit the restored Victorian mansion during the same hours as the Gallery is open. The house has been restored to the era in which it was built, but it is not furnished, and some rooms are closed to the public.

CONTACT: 519-337-3291, Lambton County Library, Sarnia Branch.

St. Clair Parkway

WHERE: Between Sarnia and Mitchell's Bay.

WHEN: Year round.

WHAT: This scenic drive for 70 km (43.5 mi.) along the St. Clair River passes twenty-one parks fronting on the busy waterway. The parks aren't large, but most have parking areas and picnic facilities. They're great spots from which to watch shore birds, and business and pleasure traffic on the river.

CONTACT: 519-332-1820, Tourism Division Sarnia/Lambton Economic Development Commission.

Stratford

Art in the Park

WHERE: Along the Avon River near Island Bridge.

WHEN: Open June to mid-September, Wednesday, Saturday and Sunday, all day.

WHAT: Artists display their wares in the shade of the willows along the riverbank near the Festival Theatre.

CONTACT: 519-271-5140, Tourism Stratford.

Farmers Market

WHERE: Stratford Fairgrounds.

WHEN: Operates year round, Saturday, 6:30 a.m. to noon.

WHAT: Stalls sell fresh produce, baked goods, fish, cheese, flowers and handcrafts.

CONTACT: 519-271-5140, Tourism Stratford.

Shakespeare Gardens

WHERE: Downtown Stratford near the tourist information booth at 40 York St. Follow the path from the tourist booth under Huron St. and climb flagstone steps to the left, just beyond the bridge. The gardens are well marked.

WHEN: Year round. Best seen mid-June through September.

WHAT: The gardens contain all the herbs and flowers mentioned in the plays of William Shakespeare.

CONTACT: 519-273-5140, Tourism Stratford.

The Gallery/Stratford

WHERE: 54 Romeo St.

WHEN: Year round. November to May, open Tuesday to Friday and

Sunday, 1 p.m. to 5 p.m.; Saturday, 10 a.m. to 5 p.m. June through October, open Tuesday to Sunday, 9 a.m. to 6 p.m. Admission is charged in summer.

WHAT: Exhibits include costumes, designs and props from Festival productions. Washrooms not wheelchair accessible.

CONTACT: 519-271-5271, The Gallery/Stratford.

Walking tour

WHERE: Downtown Stratford.

WHEN: Year round. Ninety-minute guided tours held July and August, Monday to Saturday, 9:30 a.m. Tours start at the tourist information booth at 40 York St., where copies of a free self-guided tour map are available. In the off-season, when the booth is closed, free copies of the tour map are available at Tourism Stratford, 88 Wellington St.

WHAT: Twenty-one points of historic or architectural significance are included in this tour.

CONTACT: 519-273-5140, Tourism Stratford.

Tilbury

Tilbury West Agricultural Museum

WHERE: On Hwy. 77, 10 km (6 mi.) southwest of Tilbury, 38 km (24 mi.) southwest of Chatham.

WHEN: June to September, open Thursday to Monday, 1 p.m. to 5 p.m. Donations accepted.

WHAT: The Museum displays agricultural tools and household artifacts dating from 1880. Washrooms wheelchair accessible.

CONTACT: 519-687-2240, Tilbury West Agricultural Museum.

Tillsonburg

Tillsonburg Museum and Annandale House

WHERE: 30 Tillson Ave.

WHEN: Open year round, Monday to Friday, 9 a.m. to 4 p.m.; Sunday, 1 p.m. to 4 p.m. Closed Saturday. Admission by donation.

WHAT: The Tillsonburg Museum has recently been moved to the late Victorian Annandale House, which has unique painted ceilings. Washrooms, wheelchair accessible.

CONTACT: 519-842-2294, Tillsonburg Museum and Annandale House.

Coyle's

WHERE: Hwy. 19, 3 km (2 mi.) north of Tillsonburg, 18 km (11 mi.) south of Hwy. 401.

WHEN: Open year round, Monday to Saturday, 9:30 a.m. to 5 p.m.; Friday to 8 p.m.; Sunday and holidays, 12:30 p.m. to 5 p.m. Closed Easter Sunday, December 25 and 26, January 1.

WHAT: This large country store specializes in confectionery and baking supplies, party and cake decorations, fresh roasted nuts, Canadian-made gifts and souvenirs and a year-round stock of Christmas supplies. Picnic tables. Washrooms not wheelchair accessible.

CONTACT: 519-842-5945, Coyle's.

Tillsonburg District Craft Guild— The Great Western Railway Station

WHERE: In Tillsonburg, corner of Bridge St. and Bidwell St.

WHEN: Open year round, Monday to Saturday, 10 a.m. to 5 p.m. Farmers market open summer only, Saturday, 8 a.m. to noon.

WHAT: The Great Western Railway Station, built in 1887, was restored in 1982-83 by the Tillsonburg District Craft Guild. It now

---

houses the Guild's craft shop, the Baggage Room, and the Station Gallery, which displays the multi-media works of artists and craftspeople from the area. In summer an outdoor market features fresh produce from local farmers and the Mennonite community. Washrooms wheelchair accessible.

CONTACT: 519-842-6151, Tillsonburg and District Craft Guild.

Wallaceburg

Libbey-St. Clair Glass Factory Outlet

WHERE: Beside the factory, Forhan St.

WHEN: Open year round, Thursday to Saturday, 9:30 a.m. to 5:30 p.m. Closed on statutory holidays.

WHAT: Factory outlet sells an assortment of glassware, stemware, terrariums and cannisters. No tours of factory. Wheelchair accessible.

CONTACT: 519-627-2271, Ext. 5260, Libbey-St. Clair Glass Factory Outlet.

Walpole Island

Walpole Island Heritage Centre

WHERE: Highbanks Park at the junction of the St. Clair River and Chenal Ecarte.

WHEN: Open year round, Monday to Friday, 8:30 a.m. to 4:30 p.m. Other times by appointment.

WHAT: The Centre offers historical, archaeological and environmental displays. Washrooms, reading room, resource library. Souvenir counter. Washrooms and exhibits on the first floor are wheelchair accessible.

CONTACT: 519-627-1475, Walpole Island Heritage Centre.

Wartburg

Brickman's Botanical Gardens

WHERE: About 2 km (1.2 mi.) northwest of Wartburg, about 12 km (7.5 mi.) northwest of Stratford.

WHEN: Year round. April to mid-June, open daily, 8 a.m. to 9 p.m. Mid-June to March, open Monday to Saturday, 8 a.m. to 5 p.m. Open holiday Mondays. Perennials are at their peak on July 1 weekend.

WHAT: In spring (April to June) over 10,000 spring bulbs are in bloom, followed by 2,000 perennials in old English gardens.

CONTACT: 519-393-6223, Brickman's Botanical Gardens.

Windsor

Art Gallery of Windsor

WHERE: 445 Riverside Dr. W., between Church Ave. and Bruce Ave., overlooking the Detroit River.

WHEN: Open year round, Tuesday, Wednesday and Saturday, 11 a.m. to 5 p.m.; Thursday and Friday, 11 a.m. to 9 p.m.; Sunday, 11:30 a.m. to 5 p.m. Closed holidays.

WHAT: Three floors of galleries feature touring exhibitions and changing installations from an extensive permanent collection of works by Canadian artists, from the nineteenth century to the present. Children's gallery, resource centre, restaurant, gift shop with Canadian Inuit and Native arts and crafts, wheelchair accessible.

CONTACT: 519-258-7111, art gallery; 519-258-7115, gift shop; 519-255-7511, restaurant.

Coventry Gardens

WHERE: On Riverside Dr. E. at Pillette Rd., 3 km (2 mi.) east of downtown Windsor.

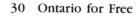

WHEN: Open May to October daily, 11 a.m. to 11 p.m.

WHAT: North America's largest floating fountain, the Peace Fountain, presents a selection of three-dimensional water displays. The fountain is set in .8 ha (2 a.) of floral gardens with decorative night lighting. Concession, free parking, wheelchair-accessible washrooms.

CONTACT: 519-255-6276, City of Windsor Dept. of Parks and Recreation.

Hiram Walker Distillery Tour

WHERE: Walker Rd. and Riverside Dr.

WHEN: Open year round, weather permitting, days and evenings. Telephone reservation required. Minimum age, nineteen years. Tours Monday to Friday, 2 p.m.

WHAT: A tour of Hiram Walker's Canadian Club Distillery covers the distilling, blending and bottling departments when they are in production. The ninety-minute tour covers 2.4 km (1.5 mi.) through three buildings. A cocktail is offered after the tour.

CONTACT: 519-254-5171, Ext. 499, Hiram Walker Distillery.

Hiram Walker Historical Museum

WHERE: 254 Pitt St. W., one block from Riverside Dr., two blocks west of Ouellette Ave.

WHEN: Open year round, Tuesday to Saturday, 10 a.m. to 5 p.m.; Sunday, 2 p.m. to 5 p.m. Closed Easter weekend and holidays.

WHAT: This local history museum with changing exhibits relates the development of the City of Windsor and Essex County from prehistoric times to the present. The Museum is located in the former Francois Baby House, a building of historical significance that was occupied by both British and American forces during the War of 1812. The Francois Baby farm was also the site of the Battle of Windsor, which marked the end of the Upper Canada Rebellion. Gift counter for souvenirs. Main floor wheelchair accessible, but washrooms are not.

CONTACT: 519-253-1812, Hiram Walker Historical Museum.

Jackson Park Queen Elizabeth II Garden

WHERE: Tecumseh Rd. and Ouellette Ave.

WHEN: Year round, daily.

WHAT: This sunken garden is illuminated at night by over 400 ornamental lights set among flower beds and shrubs. Fountains, accented by underwater lights, are enhanced by a large sculpture. Immediately adjacent is found the Lancaster Memorial Rose Test Garden. A mounted Second World War Lancaster bomber is surrounded by a rose test garden in the form of a compass that consists of 12,000 rose bushes representing over 500 varieties from around the world. Wheelchair access to the park and concession at south end, picnic areas, bowling greens, tennis courts, lighted stadium, bandshell, ball park, free parking.

CONTACT: 519-255-6276, City of Windsor, Dept. of Parks and Recreation.

Mackenzie Hall Cultural Community Centre

WHERE: 3277 Sandwich St. From downtown, follow Riverside Dr. west to Old Sandwich Town.

WHEN: Year round. Public areas open Tuesday to Thursday, 10 a.m. to 5 p.m.; Friday 10 a.m. to 9 p.m.; Saturday, 10 a.m. to 5 p.m.; Sunday, 11 a.m. to 4 p.m. Closed Monday. Conducted tours by reservation. Admission is charged to special events.

WHAT: This former courthouse was built in 1855 by Alexander Mackenzie, later Canada's second prime minister. One of the area's most significant architectural landmarks, it is now a showplace for cultural activities, exhibitions, performances and other events. Function rooms, cafe bookstore, galleries, arts and craft shops, printmaking studio. Fully accessible by wheelchair.

CONTACT: 519-255-7600, Mackenzie Hall Cultural Community Centre.

Ojibway Park and Nature Centre

WHERE: From downtown, take Riverside Dr. west. Turn left on Broadway to Matchette Rd.

WHEN: Year round. The park is open daily, 5 a.m. to midnight. The Nature Centre is open daily, 10 a.m. to 5 p.m.

WHAT: Visitors can take a self-guided hike on trails through deep oak forest and sunny prairie glades. See Ontario's finest display of wild flowers from late July to mid-September. The 120-ha (300-a.) park contains the largest tall-grass prairie in Ontario. Picnic tables, charcoal grills, cross-country skiing, 66.4-ha (164-a.) Nature Centre with wildlife exhibits. The Centre and one nature trail are accessible by wheelchair. Washrooms. Small gift shop.

CONTACT: 519-966-5852, Ojibway Park Nature Centre.

The Serbian Heritage Museum

WHERE: 6770 Tecumseh Rd. E.

WHEN: Open year round, Monday to Friday, 10 a.m. to 4 p.m.; Sunday, 2 p.m. to 4 p.m. Closed Saturday.

WHAT: The Museum collects, preserves, and exhibits artifacts related to the Serbian culture and traditions. The gift shop features jewelry, paintings and handcrafted items from Yugoslavia. Wheelchair-accessible washrooms.

CONTACT: 519-944-4884, The Serbian Heritage Museum.

University of Windsor Campus tours

WHERE: 440 Sunset Ave., between University St. and Wyandotte St.

WHEN: Tours available by appointment two weeks in advance, year round, Monday to Friday, 10 a.m. to 3 p.m.

WHAT: The tour is wheelchair accessible, but not the office at 440 Sunset Ave. Cafeteria.

CONTACT: 519-973-7014, Liaison Office, University of Windsor.

Windsor City Market

WHERE: Chatham St. E. between McDougall St. and Mercator St.

WHEN: Open year round, Monday to Thursday, 7 a.m. to 4 p.m.; Friday, 7 a.m. to 6 p.m.; Saturday, 5:30 a.m. to 4 p.m. At Monday's market, only produce is sold.

WHAT: More than a hundred permanent vendors sell fresh produce, handcrafts and baked goods. This market deserves to be called a farmers market more than most in Ontario because so many farmers are in evidence. Washrooms. Accessible to powered wheelchairs (steep ramp).

CONTACT: 519-255-6260, Windsor City Market.

Woodstock

Woodstock Museum

WHERE: City Square, 466 Dundas St.

WHEN: Year round. May to August, open Monday to Saturday, 10 a.m. to 5 p.m.; Sunday, 1 p.m. to 5 p.m. September to April, open Tuesday to Saturday, 10 a.m. to 5 p.m. Admission is by donation.

WHAT: The Museum is housed in the 1852 Old Town Hall, designated a national historic site. The original council chambers have been restored to the 1879 era. In the Old Oxford Gallery visitors can walk through a representation of an Oxford forest and enter an Indian longhouse and a First World War trench. Gift shop. Wheelchair-accessible washrooms as of 1993.

CONTACT: 519-537-8411, Curator, Woodstock Museum.

Woodstock Public Art Gallery

WHERE: 447 Hunter St.

WHEN: Open year round, Tuesday to Saturday, 10 a.m. to 5 p.m. Mid-September to mid-May, also open Sunday, 1 p.m. to 4:30 p.m. Closed Monday.

WHAT: This gallery has changing monthly exhibitions, a permanent collection, adult and children's classes, workshops, a gift shop, and washrooms. The washrooms and the first floor are wheelchair accessible.

CONTACT: 519-539-6761, Woodstock Public Art Gallery.

Festival Country

Includes: Ancaster, Brantford, Burlington, Cambridge, Dundas, Dunnville, Fergus, Fort Erie, Grimsby, Guelph, Hamilton, Harriston, Kitchener, Niagara Falls, Oakville, Port Colborne, St. Catharines, Thorold, Shelburne, Simcoe, Waterloo, Welland.

Festival Country extends from the roar of Niagara Falls through peaceful vineyards and orchards and from the mighty steel mills of history-steeped Hamilton to quiet sideroads in Wellington and Waterloo counties where the Mennonites' black, horse-drawn carriages often outnumber motorized vehicles.

True to its name, this region offers a plethora of festivals, some of which are listed below.

Festivals, Carnivals, Celebrations, Special Events:

JANUARY: Niagara Falls, *Winter Festival of Lights,* (starts late November); Burlington, *Family Winter Carnival;* Hamilton, *Winterfest;* Welland, *Winter Carnival.*

FEBRUARY: Oakville, *Winter on the Escarpment* (longhouse tours, snowsnake demonstrations); Campbellville, *Valentine Magic,* (card-making); Selkirk, *Heritage Day* (bread- and rope-making demonstrations); Fergus, *Heritage Day;* Dunnville and District,

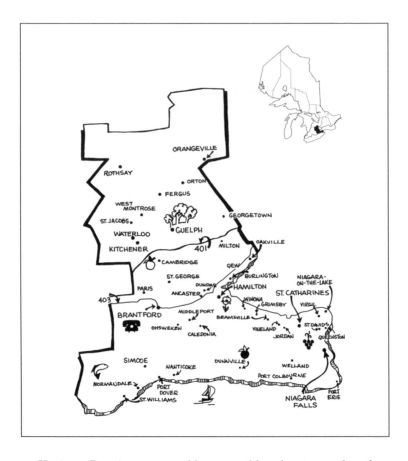

Heritage Day (sausage- and butter-making, hunters and anglers game food sampling); St. George, *Birthday of Adelaide Hunter Hoodless* (displays and music at homestead); Brantford, Woodland Cultural Centre, *Snowsnake Tournament* (Native people compete in hurling short and long snakes).

MARCH: Delhi, *Multicultural Day* (Parade of Nations in costume); Stoney Creek at Battlefield House, *March School Break Program* (candle-making, quill writing, tin punching); Oakville, *Sweet Water Day* (demonstrations of Native people's methods of maple syrup production); Burlington, *March Break at Bronte Creek Provincial Park* (spinning, weaving, soap making);

Elmira, *Maple Syrup Festival.*

APRIL: Niagara Falls, *Children's Festival* (educational and scientific exhibits); Shelburne, *Pioneer Spring Festival;* Oakville, Mountsberg and Crawford Lake Conservation areas, *Earth Day* (games, displays).

MAY: Guelph, *Spring Festival;* Niagara Falls, *Children's Festival* (educational and scientific exhibits); Brantford, *Festival of the Arts;* Carlisle, *May 24 Party Weekend* (rock concert); St. Catharines, *Folk Arts Festival;* Niagara Falls, *Blossom Festival Parade;* Fergus, *Great Teddy Bear Caper;* St. Catharines, *Music Celebration* (town crier competition); Virgil, *Stampede;* Hamilton, *Tulip Festival* and *Festival of Flowering Trees;* Hamilton, *Lilac Festival;* Cambridge, *Kinsmen Carnival;* Kitchener, Doon Heritage Crossroads, *Working The Land* (villagers perform farm chores as they were done in 1914); Brantford, *Riverfest;* Milton, *Spring Celebration and Environmental Fair* (demonstrations of gardening, composting and energy-saving ideas); Brantford, *Rubber Duck Derby;* Kitchener, *Teddy Bear's Picnic;* Hagersville, *Haldimand Agricultural Day.*

JUNE: Stoney Creek, *Flag Week* (Battle of Stoney Creek Re-enactment); Brantford, *Glenhyrst Family Day;* Dunnville, *Mudcat Festival;* Carlisle, *Bluegrass Canada* (banjo and fiddle contest); Welland, *Rose Festival;* Ridgeway, *Re-enactment of the Battle of Ridgeway;* Ohsweken, *Grand River Days* (native dancers); Mount Forest, *Medieval Festival and Market;* Cambridge, *Grand Riverfest;* Kitchener, *Father's Day at Sports World;* Burlington, *Sound of Music Festival* (big band, jazz, rhythm and blues and rock and roll); Beamsville, *Strawberry Festival;* St. Catharines, *Soap Box Derby;* St. Catharines, *Strawberryfest;* Port Dalhousie (St. Catharines) *Lions Club Carnival;* St. Catharines, *Annual Ontario Sausage Festival;* Port Colborne, *Pioneer Demonstrations at Museum;* Hamilton, *It's Your Festival;* Georgetown, *Highland Games; Ridgeway Fest;* Kitchener, *Multicultural Festival;* Fort Erie, *Highland Games;* Hamilton, *International Peony Society Show;* Hamilton, *Canadian Iris Society Show;* Hamilton, *Gatsby in the Gardens Croquet Tournament;* Crieff Hills,

Covenanter's Service (seventeenth-century Covenanter's outdoor worship service protected by the Scottish pipers); Hamilton and Burlington, *Rose Society Show.*

JULY: Port Colborne, *Lions Club Carnival;* Milton, *Springridge Strawberry Festival;* Brantford, *International Villages Festival* (folklore of various cultures); Orangeville, *Founder's Day Celebrations;* Ohsweken, *Grand River Champion of Champions Pow Wow;* Cambridge, *Highland Games;* St. Catharines, *Grantham Lions Club Carnival;* Hamilton, *Ontario Regional Lily Society Show;* Fisherville, *Lions Fun Day;* Acton, *Children's Carnival;* Oakville, *Midnight Madness;* Fergus, *Sheep Focus* (sheep shows, sales, sheep dog trials, shearing competition); Cayuga, *Lions Fun Day;* Port Colborne, *Minifest;* Jordan, *Cherry Festival* (cherry spitting contest); Port Dover, *Great Lakes Fisherman's Exhibition* (fishing industry contests, tug boat pull); Port Colborne, *Annual Ethnic Day;* Port Colborne, *International Week Parade;* Hamilton, *Open House at the Teaching Garden;* Guelph, *Hillside Festival; Greater Hamilton Aquafest* (Mex-Tex Fiesta, bellyflop contest).

AUGUST: *Elora Festival;* Carlisle, *Country Jamboree;* Port Colborne, *Canal Days* (model boat fun run); Shelburne, *Canadian Open Old Time Fiddler's Contest;* Burlington, *Joseph Brant Day* (Native dances); Simcoe, *Friendship Festival* (soap box derby, bathtub race, tug-o-war); Fergus, *Highland Games;* Drayton, *Annual Old Tyme Jamboree;* Brantford, *Old Tyme Family Picnic;* Fort Erie, *Annual Re-enactment of Siege of Fort Erie;* Ohsweken, *Six Nations Native Pageant* (plays based on Native history performed by Native cast); Oakville, *Mayor's Picnic;* Selkirk, *Sports Day;* Brantford, *International Celebrity Haggis Contest;* Dundas, *Cactus Festival;* Brantford, *Highland Games;* Grimsby, *Festival at the Forty;* Dunnville, *Lions Carnival;* Hamilton, *Cari-Can Festival* (steel band music); Brantford, *Scottish Festival;* Port Dover, *Summer Festival;* Welland, *Folklore Festival;* Fort Erie, *Fire Station #1 Carnival;* Merriton, *Lions Carnival;* Port Rowan, *Tomato Fest* (turtle races, frog jumping); Wainfleet, *Marshville Heritage Festival* (demonstrations of farm activities, barbershop quartet, country and western concert); Hamilton, *Opening of the Plant Lovers' Garden;* Hamilton, *Magic and Medicine, a Child's Visit to the Herb Garden;* Hamilton, *The Scarecrow's Picnic.*

SEPTEMBER: Delhi, *Harvest Festival* (tobacco priming-tying contest, pet dress-up contest, soap box derby); Aberfoyle, *Fall Fair and Old Tyme Fiddler's Contest;* St. Catharines, *Niagara Grape and Wine Festival* (grape stomping); Hamilton, *Chrysanthemum and Dahlia Society Show;* Port Rowan, Backus Heritage Conservation Area, *Re-enactment of War of 1812;* Hamilton, *Ikenobo Ikebana Japanese Flower Show;* St. George, *Apple Harvest Weekend;* Hamilton, *Garden Clubs of Ontario Show;* Wellesley, *Apple Butter and Cheese Festival* (toy tractor pull, regatta, apple pies); Fergus, *Harvest Festival* (poor man's dinner, fall foliage tours).

OCTOBER: Fort Erie, *Annual Heritage Day;* Kitchener-Waterloo, *Oktoberfest;* Brantford, *Harvest Day at Alexander Graham Bell Homestead;* Milton, *Harvest Craft Fair* (haystack jumping, scarecrow building, pumpkin carving); Waterford, *Pumpkin Festival* (1,000 carved and lighted pumpkins); Delhi, *Oktoberfest;* St. Catharines, *Oktoberfest.*

NOVEMBER: Hamilton, *Mum Show;* Kitchener, Joseph Schneider House, *Butchering Bee;* Kitchener, Woodside National Historic Site, *Victorian Christmas Celebration;* Hamilton, Royal Botanical Gardens, *Annual Great Bird Feeding Bonanza* (family bird watching hikes, Great Sun Flower Seed Shell Off); Port Rowan, Backus Heritage Conservation Area, *Winter Birds* (demonstrations of feeders and seed types); Hamilton, Royal Botanical Gardens, *Auxiliary Christmas Sale and Show;* Brantford, *Independent Indian Handcrafters Bazaar;* Hamilton, Cambridge, Orangeville, Milton, Fort Erie, Oakville, Niagara Falls, Brantford, *Santa Claus parades.*

DECEMBER: Hamilton, *Day Without Art* (part of World Health Day); Rockwood, *Christmas Fiesta* (ride vintage electric railway vehicles); Milton, Halton Region Museum, *Christmas Tea;* Burlington, New Hamburg, Cambridge, Cayuga, Dunnville,

Paris, Port Rowan, Niagara-on-the-Lake, *Santa Claus parades.*

More detailed information on the festivals, carnivals, celebrations and other attractions of Festival Country is available from: Niagara and Mid-Western Ontario Travel Association, 38 Darling St., Suite 102, Brantford, Ontario N3T 6A8, Tel. 519-756-3230.

Ancaster

The Hermitage Gatehouse Museum

WHERE: Dundas Valley Conservation Area, 3 km (2 mi.) west of Ancaster on Sulphur Springs Rd.

WHEN: Open Victoria Day weekend to Thanksgiving, Sunday and holiday Mondays, 11 a.m. to 6 p.m., or by appointment.

WHAT: The Hermitage was a magnificent estate built in the Dundas Valley around 1856 by George Leith, second son of a Scottish baronet. A fire in 1938 left only the ruins of the main house and outbuildings. However, the former gatehouse has been developed as a museum depicting the life and times of the Leith family and their estate. The estate is now part of the Dundas Valley Conservation Area, which is laced with scenic hiking trails. The Trail Centre is located in Sulphur Springs Station, a reproduction of a Victorian railway station which has been featured in various films, notably *Anne of Green Gables.* Grounds are wheelchair accessible. Outhouse.

CONTACT: 416-525-2181, Hamilton Region Conservation Authority.

Beamsville

Ninavik—The Native Arts Place

WHERE: North of the Queen Elizabeth Way on Tufford Rd., and the North Service Rd. Take Exit 56 (Victoria Ave.) in Vineland or the Ontario St. Exit in Beamsville.

WHEN: Year round. May through September, open Tuesday to Saturday, 9 a.m. to 6 p.m. October through April, open Wednesday to Saturday, 9 a.m. to 6 p.m. or by appointment.

WHAT: More than 600 Inuit and Indian artifacts and handcrafts are displayed and offered for sale. Washrooms, wheelchair accessible. No smoking.

CONTACT: 416-563-4274, The Native Arts Place.

Brantford

Bell Homestead

WHERE: 94 Tutela Heights Rd., between Cockshutt Rd. and Mt. Pleasant Rd. Well signposted from downtown.

WHEN: Year round. Labour Day to mid-June, open Tuesday to Sunday and holiday Mondays, 10 a.m. to 6 p.m. Mid-June through Labour Day, open daily 10 a.m. to 6 p.m. Closed December 25, 26 and January 1.

WHAT: Alexander Graham Bell and his parents lived in this house between 1870 and 1881. It was here, in the summer of 1874, that Bell conceived the principle of the telephone. And it was here, in August of 1876, that the world's first long distance call was made. The home is furnished with period pieces, including many original items. Next door you will find the restored Henderson House (moved from downtown), which was the first telephone office in Canada. This building contains displays of telephone technology and telephone artifacts (not including Bell's original telephone, which is in the Smithsonian Institute in Washington, D.C.). Wheelchair-accessible washrooms.

CONTACT: 519-756-6220, Bell Homestead.

Farmers Market

WHERE: 79 The Ring Rd.

WHEN: Open year round, Thursday, 9 a.m. to 2 p.m.; Friday, 9 a.m. to 6 p.m.; Saturday 6 a.m. to 2 p.m.

WHAT: About thirty vendors sell produce, baked goods, crafts and refrigerated goods. During garden season another fifteen to twenty vendors bring their produce to outdoor stalls.

CONTACT: 519-752-8824, Farmers Market.

Glenhyrst Art Gallery of Brant

WHERE: 20 Ava Rd.

WHEN: Open year round, Tuesday to Friday, 10 a.m. to 5 p.m.; Saturday and Sunday, 1 p.m. to 5 p.m. Gardens open all year, daily. Gallery closed December 25, 26, January 1, and Easter.

WHAT: Rotating exhibitions and a permanent collection of paintings, graphics, sculpture and photography are on view. The gallery is located in the Main House on the Glenhyrst estate, which includes spacious gardens and a nature trail overlooking the Grand River. Only the first-floor galleries and the washrooms are wheelchair accessible.

CONTACT: 519-756-5932, Glenhyrst Art Gallery of Brant.

Her Majesty's Royal Chapel of the Mohawks

WHERE: 291 Mohawk St.

WHEN: Victoria Day through June, open daily, 1 p.m. to 5 p.m. June through Labour Day, open daily, 10 a.m. to 6 p.m. Labour Day to Thanksgiving, open weekends only, 1 p.m. to 5 p.m., or for groups by reservation. Gardens open daily all year. Donations accepted.

WHAT: Built in 1785, this is the only Royal Chapel in the world belonging to Native People. It is also the first Protestant church in Ontario. The Chapel was a gift from George III, who was grateful for the assistance of the Six Nations Indians in the American Revolutionary War. Eight stained-glass windows depict the interesting history of the Six Nations people and the interior woodwork is a study in precision carpentry. The simple white-painted frame building is known as the Mohawk Church. In 1904, by Royal assent, it was given the name His Majesty's Chapel of the Mohawks, (now changed to Her Majesty's). Wheelchair accessible. No washrooms.

CONTACT: 519-445-4528, Her Majesty's Royal Chapel of the Mohawks, Six Nations Reserve office.

Historical Walking Tour

WHERE: Downtown Brantford.

WHEN: Year round.

WHAT: A free brochure with a good map, called *Stroll,* includes numerous buildings of historic or architectural interest. Parking lots are marked on the map, which outlines a loop-shaped tour that can be started at any point. The walking tour takes about ninety minutes.

CONTACT: 1-800-563-9999 or 519-759-4150, City of Brantford Department of Economic Development, City Hall, 100 Wellington Sq.

Murals

WHERE: On the building opposite the Sanderson Centre on Dalhousie St. in downtown Brantford.

WHEN: Year round.

WHAT: The colourful murals on this building depict five famous people associated with Brantford and the nearby Six Nations reserve: Jay Silverheels, Wayne Gretzky, Joseph Brant, Alexander Graham Bell and E. Pauline Johnson.

Six Nations Council House

WHERE: Six Nations Reserve, Village of Ohsweken, Fourth Line, 14 km (9 mi.) southeast of Brantford.

WHEN: Open year round, Tuesday to Friday, 1 p.m. to 5 p.m.; Saturday, 10 a.m. to 2 p.m.

WHAT: The yellow brick building, erected in 1863, was the first permanent Council House, home of the traditional Iroquois government. It is now the Six Nations Public Library, a fund of information on First Nations people. Original furnishings from the 1800s and many historic photographs are on display. No washrooms. Not wheelchair accessible.

CONTACT: 519-445-4528, Six Nations Council House.

Sports Hall of Recognition

WHERE: North Park St.

WHEN: Open year round, Monday to Friday, 4 p.m. to 9:30 p.m.; Saturday and Sunday, 10 a.m. to 6 p.m.

WHAT: The Hall features a collection of memorabilia from famous local athletes and actors such as Wayne Gretzky, Tom Longboat, Todd Brooker, Jay Silverheels (Tonto) and more. The Sports Hall of Recognition is part of the Wayne Gretzky Sports Centre. Washrooms. Wheelchair accessible.

CONTACT: 519-756-9900, Sports Hall of Recognition.

Burlington

Burlington Cultural Centre

WHERE: 425 Brock Ave. (across from Spencer Smith Park).

WHEN: Open year round, Tuesday to Saturday, 10 a.m. to 5 p.m.; Tuesday to Thursday, 7 p.m. to 10 p.m.; Sunday, noon to 5 p.m.

WHAT: Visitors can watch local artists and artisans at work in this gallery, which also houses a major collection of contemporary ceramic art.

CONTACT: 416-632-7796, Burlington Cultural Centre.

Driving and walking tours of Burlington

WHERE: In and around Burlington.

WHEN: Year round.

WHAT: Burlington's Local Architectural Conservation Advisory Committee has prepared free, full colour brochures with maps showing the routes for a driving tour and a walking tour of Burlington. The brochures include photographs of the most architecturally significant among the thirty-three buildings on the driving tour and eleven buildings on the walking tour. Copies of the brochures are available from the Regional Municipality of Halton, 1151 Bronte Rd., the Burlington Visitor and Convention Bureau, 1340 Lakeshore Rd., or City Hall, 426 Brant St.

CONTACT: 416-825-6300, Business Development Department, Regional Municipality of Halton; 416-634-5594, Burlington Visitor and Convention Bureau.

Royal Botanical Gardens: *See Hamilton section*

Caledonia

Edinburgh Square Heritage and Cultural Centre

WHERE: In the old town hall building at 80 Caithness St. E., corner of Edinburgh and Caithness, along Hwy. 54 and the Grand River.

WHEN: Open year round, Tuesday to Friday, 11 a.m. to 3 p.m.; Saturday, noon to 4 p.m. Special events on weekends, or visit by appointment. Admission by donation.

WHAT: Changing exhibits of historical records and area artifacts emphasize the regional gypsum industry. Telephone for additional information.

CONTACT: 416-765-3134, Edinburgh Square Heritage and Cultural Centre.

Cambridge

Cambridge Farmers Market

WHERE: Corner of Dickson St. and Ainslie St.

WHEN: Year round. In summer, market operates Saturday and Wednesday. Rest of the year, open Saturday only, 5:45 a.m. to 1 p.m.

WHAT: Fresh produce, flowers, meats, cheeses and baked goods are offered.

CONTACT: 519-623-1340, City of Cambridge.

The Gallery

WHERE: The Library and Gallery, 20 Grand Ave. N.

WHEN: Open year round, Monday to Thursday, 9:30 a.m. to 8:30 p.m.; Friday and Saturday, 9:30 a.m. to 5:30 p.m. September to May, also open Sunday, 1 p.m. to 5 p.m. Closed statutory holidays.

WHAT: Changing and permanent exhibits are mounted that include local, national and international works of art. Lectures, art courses and Sunday afternoon concerts are offered. Wheelchair-accessible washrooms.

CONTACT: 519-621-0460, The Gallery.

Landreth Gallery

WHERE: 84 Water St. S.

WHEN: Open year round, Wednesday to Sunday, noon to 4 p.m.

WHAT: Art and pottery are displayed in a stone cottage on the banks of the Grand River. Washroom. Not wheelchair accessible.

CONTACT: 519-740-1894, Landreth Gallery.

Walking tours of Old Galt

WHERE: Downtown Cambridge. Tours start from Lutz House, 60 Water St. N.

WHEN: Tours available June through September, Sunday, 2 p.m.

WHAT: The City of Cambridge was formed in 1972 with the amalgamation of the towns of Galt, Preston and Hespeler. A free brochure, Old Galt Walking Tours, is available at downtown stores and the Cambridge Visitor and Convention Bureau, 531 King St. E. Included in the tour is the 1880 Gothic and Romanesque Central Presbyterian Church, with its unique octagonal mosaic tile spire.

CONTACT: 519-653-1424, Cambridge Visitor and Convention Bureau.

Dundas

Ben Veldhuis Greenhouses

WHERE: 154 King St. E. Take Hwy. 403 to the Main St. W. Exit, turn left on Main St. Just past McMaster University turn right on Cootes Dr. Turn right on Olympic Dr., and immediately left on King St. E.

WHEN: Open year round, Monday to Saturday, 9 a.m. to 5 p.m.; Sunday, 10 a.m. to 5 p.m. Closed December 25 and January 1.

WHAT: Two greenhouses which cover .8 ha (2 a.) contain thousands of varieties of cacti, succulents and exotic plants. The Earth Store sells a wide range of exotic plants. Picnic area. Wheelchair-accessible washrooms.

CONTACT: 416-628-6307, Ben Veldhuis Greenhouses.

Dundas Historical Society Museum

WHERE: Park St. and Albert St.

WHEN: Year round, open Monday to Friday, 10 a.m. to 4 p.m. May to October, also open Sunday, 2 p.m. to 5 p.m. Closed all holidays. Evening tours by appointment.

WHAT: The Museum displays a diversified collection of community exhibits and artifacts. A Children's Corner offers a variety of toys, including a large doll collection. Washrooms. Not wheelchair accessible.

CONTACT: 416-627-7412, Dundas Historical Society Museum.

Dunnville

Farmers Market

WHERE: Market Square.

WHEN: Operates May through November, Tuesday and Saturday, 8 a.m. to noon.

WHAT: Area farmers sell local produce and meats.

Historical walking tour

WHERE: Downtown Dunnville.

WHEN: Year round.

WHAT: Fifty-two points of historic, architectural or general interest are included in this tour, which starts from the Chamber of Commerce at 106 Main St. W., between Pine St. and Cedar St. Each point is described in a free booklet available at the Chamber office.

CONTACT: 416-774-3183, Dunnville Chamber of Commerce.

Fergus

Bicycle tours

WHERE: A 32-km (20-mi.) tour around Lake Belwood. A 40-km (25 mi.) tour around Eramosa Township

WHEN: Year round, best in summer.

WHAT: There is little traffic on these paved roads, which are recommended for a day's bicycle outing. Get a local restaurant to pack you a lunch since restaurants along the way are few and far between.

CONTACT: 519-843-5140, Fergus and District Chamber of Commerce.

Drunkard's Grave

WHERE: St. Andrew's Church.

WHEN: Year round.

WHAT: The pauper's grave of drunkard George Clephane draws visitors from around the world. Clephane was a Scottish remittance man who settled on a small farm just north of Fergus in 1842 and did more drinking than farming. In 1851, while intoxicated and riding into Fergus, he was crossing a wooden bridge when his horse reared and threw him into a ditch. He died of his injuries. His young sister Elizabeth believed her brother was the lost sheep who would be rescued by the love of God. In her grief she wrote a poem. Five years after her death in 1869 visiting American evangelists Dwight Moody and Ira Sankey read Elizabeth's poem in a Glasgow newspaper. That night Moody preached to a crowd and asked Sankey to sing a hymn. Unfolding the newspaper, Sankey began playing the organ and singing. Note by note the tune came to him as he began the gospel song now known throughout the English-speaking world as "The Ninety and Nine."

Fergus Farmers Market

WHERE: Corner of Queen St. and St. David St. W.

WHEN: Open year round, Saturday, 8 a.m. to 5 p.m.; Sunday, 9 a.m. to 5 p.m.

WHAT: This farmers market is located in a century-old limestone building, a former foundry, on the bank of the Grand River. Fergus boasts that its market is "the friendliest in Ontario." On sale are the usual fresh meats and veggies plus handcrafts, candies,

---

clothing, jewelry, toys, baked goods, antiques, bedding, gifts and other items. Inside the market complex you will find the Scottish Shop, which sells all manner of Scottish merchandise and is open seven days a week.

CONTACT: 519-843-5221, Fergus Farmers Market.

Ghosts

WHERE: Information available at Chamber of Commerce office, Fergus Market Building, corner of Queen St. and St. David St. W.

WHEN: Year round.

WHAT: Fergus has earned a reputation for its ghosts. A pamphlet, available from the Chamber of Commerce, describes some phantasmagoric sightings and offers advice to receptive souls who wish to encounter ghosts for themselves.

CONTACT: 519-843-5140, Fergus and District Chamber of Commerce. Since not everyone at the Chamber office believes in ghosts or wants to talk about them ask for someone who is a believer in supernatural phenomena.)

Grand River Gorge

WHERE: The gorge starts in Fergus and may be followed downstream by canoe or pathway to Elora, a distance of about 5 km (3 mi.).

WHEN: Year round. Best seen in summer.

WHAT: Along the gorge in Fergus you can visit a whirlpool at Templin Gardens, a restored English garden. At Mirror Basin a pedestrian bridge across the gorge offers excellent views up and down the river.

CONTACT: 519-843-5140, Fergus and District Chamber of Commerce.

Historical walking tour

WHERE: In Fergus.

WHEN: Year round.

WHAT: Fergus boasts dozens of historic buildings, many beautifully crafted of limestone. Those with particularly interesting histories bear plaques telling when they were built and the names and occupations of the original owners. A free brochure is available for the self-guided tour, which takes about two hours if you want to visit all the properties.

CONTACT: 519-843-5140, Fergus and District Chamber of Commerce.

Fort Erie

Fort Erie LaFrance Association Museum

WHERE: 233 Concession Rd. Take the Queen Elizabeth Way to Bertie St., east to Concession Rd., turn right. Museum is on left side, behind McDonald's Restaurant.

WHEN: Open Canada Day weekend to Labour Day, Wednesday to Sunday, 10 a.m. to 5 p.m., and holiday Mondays, 10 a.m. to 5 p.m.

WHAT: This collection of antique fire-fighting equipment includes five fire trucks and a 1915 fire chief's car. The kids will love Sparky, a remote-control dog.

CONTACT: 416-871-1271, Fort Erie LaFrance Association.

Niagara River Recreation Trail:
See Niagara-on-the-Lake section.

Georgetown

The Canadian Military Studies Museum

WHERE: Near the hamlet of Limehouse, northwest of Georgetown.

WHEN: Open year round, Tuesday to Friday, 10 a.m. to 4:30 p.m.;

Saturday, 10 a.m. to 4 p.m. (The Museum is staffed by volunteers and sometimes has to close due to a shortage of staff. If you're coming from a distance, call ahead to ensure it will be open during your visit.)

WHAT: Canada's military history is portrayed through life-size exhibits of headgear, uniforms, badges, medals, paintings, weapons, documents, aviation artifacts and military vehicles. No washrooms. Not wheelchair accessible.

CONTACT: 416-877-6522, The Canadian Military Studies Museum.

Grimsby

Grimsby Public Art Gallery

WHERE: 25 Adelaide St. Take Ontario St. Exit to Grimsby from the Queen Elizabeth Way and drive south on Ontario to Adelaide. Turn right onto Adelaide.

WHEN: Year round, daily, Friday to Monday, 1 p.m. to 5 p.m.; Tuesday to Thursday, 1 p.m. to 9 p.m. Closed on statutory holidays.

WHAT: The Gallery offers monthly exhibitions and related pro-grammes. The Gallery Shop offers Canadian crafts. Wheelchair-accessible washroom.

CONTACT: 416-945-3246, Grimsby Public Art Gallery.

Guelph

Church of Our Lady

WHERE: Downtown Guelph.

WHEN: Year round.

WHAT: The Church, which dominates the city from a hilltop, is nicknamed the Cologne Cathedral of Canada, after the church on which it was modelled. The Church is a good landmark for visitors who find themselves lost on the winding streets of this mid-size city, which was laid out for horse-and-buggy traffic in 1827 by Guelph's founder, John Galt.

Kortright Waterfowl Park

WHERE: On Kortright Rd., about 2 km (1.2 mi.) west of Hanlon Expressway on the Speed River.

WHEN: Year round.

WHAT: More than ninety species of duck, swan and other water birds have been identified in this park.

Macdonald Stewart Art Centre

WHERE: 358 Gordon St., north of the University of Guelph campus.

WHEN: Open year round, Tuesday to Sunday and holiday Mondays, noon to 5 p.m.

WHAT: Galleries feature historical and contemporary Canadian art, including displays of Inuit art and a sculpture park surrounding the building. Lectures, tours, films, art classes and demonstrations are offered. Shop sells art and art supplies. Washrooms. The first two of three floors of galleries are wheelchair accessible.

CONTACT: 519-837-0010, Macdonald Stewart Art Centre; 519-837-3808, Art Shop.

Riverside Park

WHERE: Woolwich St., on the banks of the Speed River.

WHEN: Year round. Rides and a snack concession open mid-May to late September, weekends, 12:30 p.m. to 7:30 p.m. Mid-June through August, also open weekdays, 2:30 p.m. to 7:30 p.m.

WHAT: At 13.4 m (44 ft.) in diameter, this is one of the largest mechanical floral clocks in Ontario. Its face is planted with 6,000 to 7,000 flowers. A scale model of John Galt's house and John Galt

Gardens is adjacent. There is a fee to ride on the restored carousel, train and paddle boats. Wheelchair-accessible washrooms, snack bar, picnic areas, bandshell, baseball diamonds, soccer fields and playgrounds.

CONTACT: 519-837-5618.

Schneider's Reliable Sweets

WHERE: 1007 York Rd. North off Hwy. 401 on Guelph Line to Hwy. 7, then west approximately 6.5 km (4 mi.).

WHEN: Open year round, daily, 10 a.m. to 5 p.m. Closed December 25 and January 1.

WHAT: Watch old-fashioned hand-made candies—sweets boiled in copper kettles—being poured onto marble slabs to cool. Factory outlet store open daily. Wheelchair-accessible washrooms.

CONTACT: 519-767-1080, Schneider's Reliable Sweets.

University of Guelph, Arboretum and Nature Centre

WHERE: Hwy. 6 (Old Brock Rd.) and College Ave.

WHEN: Open year round, dawn to dusk. Nature Centre open Saturday and Sunday, noon to 4 p.m. Campus open Monday to Friday, 8:30 a.m. to 4:45 p.m.

WHAT: The 165.2-ha (408-a.) Arboretum is open all year for walking tours. Guide sheets are provided. In the Gosling Wildlife Gardens in the Nature Centre, demonstrations show how to attract wildlife to your property. Some trails in the Arboretum are wheelchair accessible. Picnics permitted. Wheelchair-accessible washrooms. Visitors may also tour the 445.5-ha (1,100-a.) campus.

CONTACT: 519-824-4120, Ext. 2113, University of Guelph Arboretum.

Hamilton

Art Gallery of Hamilton

WHERE: In downtown Hamilton on King St., across from Jackson Square Shopping Mall and the Sheraton Hamilton Hotel.

WHEN: Open year round. Free admission on Thursday from 10 a.m. to 9 p.m. Admission charged on other days.

WHAT: The gallery houses one of Canada's major art collections—over 7,000 paintings, graphics, photographs and sculptures. Selections from the permanent collection are displayed throughout the year. Gift shop. Wheelchair-accessible washrooms.

CONTACT: 416-527-6610, Art Gallery of Hamilton.

Cathedral of Christ the King

WHERE: 714 King St. W.

WHEN: Open year round. Forty-minute tours available on weekdays.

WHAT: The 1933 Gothic-design cathedral features eighty-two stained glass windows and a Steinmayer organ with 4,913 pipes. The Cathedral is decorated in six types of marble whose weight totals 45.4 tonnes (50 tons).

CONTACT: 416-522-5744, Cathedral of Christ the King; 416-546-4222, Tourism and Convention Services.

Hamilton Farmers Market

WHERE: 55 York Blvd.

WHEN: Open year round, Tuesday, Thursday, Saturday, 7 a.m. to 6 p.m.; Friday 9 a.m. to 6 p.m.

WHAT: Canada's largest indoor farmers market includes 176 stalls occupying more than 1,800 m² (20,000 sq. ft.). The new market adjoins Jackson Square and the Eaton Centre. Snack bar. Wheelchair-accessible washrooms.

CONTACT: 416-546-2096 Market Manager, Hamilton Farmers Market.

Hamilton Spectator

WHERE: 44 Frid St.

WHEN: Open year round, Monday to Friday, including evenings. Tours by appointment only, arranged one month in advance.

WHAT: The guided tour covers all departments, including the press room, with its three-storey presses. Wheelchair-accessible washrooms.

CONTACT: 416-526-3333, Ext. 650, The Hamilton Spectator.

McMaster University

WHERE: 1280 Main St. W.

WHEN: By advance notice.

WHAT: The University was founded in Toronto in 1887 and moved to Hamilton in the 1930s. There are now 12,000 students on the campus, which is surrounded by parkland. Open-air guided tours last approximately ninety minutes. Washrooms. Campus wheelchair accessible.

CONTACT: 416-525-9140, Ext. 4787, Division of Student Liaison, McMaster University.

Mohawk Trail School Museum

WHERE: 360 Mohawk Rd. W.

WHEN: Open July and August, daily, 1 p.m. to 4 p.m.

WHAT: Museum-type displays of educational artifacts and children's playthings are found in the former 1882-vintage S.S. No. 5 Barton School. No washroom. Wheelchair accessible.

CONTACT: 416-383-3368, curator; 416-527-5092, Hamilton Board of Education.

Royal Botanical Gardens

WHERE: From Toronto: take the Queen Elizabeth Way, then Hwy. 403 west. Exit Hwy. 6 north, right at first light, then left onto Plains Rd. From Hamilton-Niagara: cross the Burlington Skyway, exit at Plains Rd., turn left at traffic light and follow signs. From London: exit on Hwy. 6 south from Hwy. 401, follow Hamilton signs, exit left onto Plains Rd. W. and follow signs. Signs for RBG Centre lead to main information centre.

WHEN: Open year round. Outdoor areas open daily, 9:30 a.m. to 6 p.m. Mediterranean Garden open daily, 9 a.m. to 5 p.m. Floral Art Shop open daily 10 a.m. to 5 p.m.; closed from Christmas to mid-January and Monday from Christmas to March. Nature Interpretive Centre open daily, 10 a.m. to 4 p.m. No charge for the nature trails. There is a charge for the outdoor garden areas and the Mediterranean Garden, a two-storey garden-greenhouse.

WHAT: The gardens comprise 1,100 ha (2,700 a.) of natural areas, colourful displays and plant collections. The Arboretum contains the world's largest lilac collection. You will find almost half a hectare (an acre) of iris in the Laking Garden, .8 ha (2 a.) of roses in the Rose Garden and 125,000 spring bulbs in the Rock Garden. Nearby you can visit Cootes Paradise, a wildlife sanctuary with 500 ha (1,200 a.) of marsh and wooded ravines criss-crossed by 50 km (30 mi.) of nature trails.

CONTACT: 416-527-1158 or 1-800-668-9449 from Ontario and Quebec.

Waterfalls

WHERE: Spencer Gorge Wilderness Area. Take Hwy. 5 west of Hwy. 6, drive south on Brock Rd. and east on Harvest Rd.

WHEN: Year round.

WHAT: This Y-shaped gorge is fed by two creeks, Spencer and Logie's, each of which plunges over the Niagara Escarpment in a pretty waterfall. Park your car at the Webster's Falls area. On foot, follow a section of the Bruce Trail, which will take you first to a promontory above the junction of the two creeks and then to Tews Falls, almost as high as Niagara Falls. There are two viewing platforms from which to view the cascade.

CONTACT: 416-525-2181, Hamilton Region Conservation Authority.

Jordan

Winery tour, Cave Spring Cellars

WHERE: 3836 Main St.

WHEN: Tours offered July 1 through October, Saturday, 11 a.m., 1 p.m. and 3 p.m.; Sunday, 1 p.m. and 3 p.m. Retail store open year round, Monday to Saturday, 10 a.m. to 5 p.m.; Sunday, noon to 5 p.m.

WHAT: A wine-tasting follows a tour of the production and bottling areas. Not wheelchair accessible. Washrooms.

CONTACT: 416-562-7797, Cave Spring Cellars.

Kitchener
(See also Waterloo listings)

Glockenspiel

WHERE: Speakers Corner, King St. and Benton St.

WHEN: Year round.

WHAT: Canada's first glockenspiel depicts the fairy tale of Snow White and the Seven Dwarfs. The twenty-three-bell carillon plays several times daily. (Times available from Kitchener-Waterloo Oktoberfest Inc. office at nearby 17 Benton St.)

Homer Watson House and Gallery

WHERE: Exit from Hwy. 401 on Homer Watson Blvd., turn right on Conestoga College Blvd.

WHEN: April to mid-December, open Tuesday to Sunday and holiday Mondays, noon to 4:30 p.m.; Thursday, noon to 8 p.m. Closed from mid-December to end of May. Donations accepted.

WHAT: This Scottish Gothic-style house on spacious grounds beside the Grand River was home to Canada's first internationally renowned artist from 1883 until his death in 1936. In 1894 Watson painted a frieze on the walls of his studio, and in 1906 he added the gallery space. From 1947 to 1975 the house was operated as the Doon School of Fine Arts. Now, in addition to a display of Watson artifacts, his gallery and two other rooms feature changing contemporary and traditional art exhibits. Workshops throughout the year. Wheelchair-accessible washrooms.

CONTACT: 519-748-4377, Homer Watson House and Gallery.

Kitchener Farmers Market

WHERE: 49 Frederick St., corner of Duke St.

WHEN: Saturday markets held all year, 5 a.m. to 2 p.m. Wednesday markets held from mid-May to early October, 7 a.m. to 2 p.m.

WHAT: Local produce, Mennonite baking and handcrafts are offered from about 175 indoor stalls on two levels.

CONTACT: 519-741-2287, Kitchener Farmers Market.

Kitchener-Waterloo Art Gallery

WHERE: The Centre in the Square, 101 Queen St. N.

WHEN: Open Tuesday to Saturday, 10 a.m. to 5 p.m.; Sunday, 1 p.m. to 5 p.m. and one hour before theatre performances. Closed Monday and statutory holidays. Donations accepted.

WHAT: One of Canada's top-ranked art galleries rotates its permanent collection and a variety of exhibitions that change monthly in seven galleries. Washrooms, gift shop, wheelchair accessible, fine arts library.

CONTACT: 519-579-5860, Kitchener-Waterloo Art Gallery.

Peter Etril Snyder Studio

WHERE: 75 Frederick St.

WHEN: Open Monday to Friday, 9:30 a.m. to 6 p.m.; Saturday, 9 a.m. to 5 p.m.

WHAT: This art studio-retail outlet features reproductions of Peter Etril Snyder's paintings, prints, collector plates and limited edition prints that depict Mennonite life, rural life and historical life painting. Wheelchair accessible.

CONTACT: 519-741-0890, Peter Etril Snyder Studio.

Pioneer Memorial Tower National Historic Site

WHERE: 437 Pioneer Tower Rd., well signposted from Hwy. 8.

WHEN: Open May to October, daily, dawn to dusk.

WHAT: A monument to the spirit of Waterloo County pioneers, this tower, built in 1926, affords a fine view of the Grand River and surrounding farmland. Several of the founders are buried in the cemetery. Free parking.

CONTACT: 519-742-5273, Woodside National Historic Site.

Woodside National Historic Site

WHERE: 528 Wellington St. N. From Hwy. 401 follow Hwy. 8 west. Follow beaver signs on King St. From Conestoga Expressway (Hwy. 86) take Wellington St. W. Exit.

WHEN: Open year round, 10 a.m. to 5 p.m. Closed statutory holidays in winter.

WHAT: The boyhood home of Canada's tenth prime minister, William Lyon Mackenzie King, is restored to represent a middleclass home of the early 1890s. An interpretive area includes a theatre and a display on King's life and career. Staff in period costume guide visitors and answer questions. You can also have a picnic or explore 4.7 ha (11.5 a.) of wooded parkland. Special events throughout the year. Washrooms. Not wheelchair accessible.

CONTACT: 519-742-5273, Woodside National Historic Site.

Middleport

Middleport General Store

WHERE: 13 km (8 mi.) southeast of Brantford in the Hamlet of Middleport, on Hwy. 54.

WHEN: Open April through October, daily.

WHAT: This country store, in business since 1850, sells general merchandise, ice cream cones, shakes and sundaes.

CONTACT: 416-765-2520, Middleport General Store.

Milton

Chudleigh's

WHERE: On Hwy. 25, 3 km (2 mi.) north of Hwy. 401 at Exit 320.

WHEN: Year round. November to June, open Wednesday to Sunday, 10 a.m. to 5 p.m. July to October, open daily, 9 a.m. to 7 p.m. Closed December 25 and 26 and January 1.

WHAT: Children's hay mow and wagon rides are offered through orchards during pick-your-own-apples time, August to October. There is a charge for seasonal activities, which include corn roasts, apple picking, cross-country skiing and maple syrup demonstrations. Charge for horse and wagon rides year round. Bakery, country lunches, wheelchair-accessible washrooms.

CONTACT: 416-878-2725, Chudleigh's.

Halton Region Museum

WHERE: Kelso Conservation Area. From Hwy. 401: take Exit 320B north to Regional Rd. 9, west to Tremaine Rd. (Town Line) and turn south to Regional Rd. 28. Turn west through Kelso gates. From Queen Elizabeth Way: take Hwy. 25 north to Derry Rd., west to Tremaine and north to Regional Rd. 28, west through Kelso gates.

WHEN: Open year round, Monday to Friday, noon to 4 p.m. Victoria Day weekend through Thanksgiving, also open Sunday and holidays, noon to 4 p.m. Admission to museum by voluntary donation. Admission charged to Conservation Area.

WHAT: The complex depicts the history of Halton from prehistoric times to the present with a collection of more than 35,000 artifacts. Special events and programmes are held year round. Washrooms, gift shop. Conservation Area has snack bar, beach, pool, picnic areas, boat rentals, miniature golf, horseshoes, fishing, downhill skiing. Not wheelchair accessible.

CONTACT: 416-875-2200, Halton Region Museum.

Milton Farmers Market

WHERE: In downtown Milton, from Martin St. to James St.

WHEN: Open first Saturday in June to last Saturday in October, 7 a.m. to 11:30 a.m.

WHAT: Fresh food stuffs, crafts and other items are offered in what organizers claim is Ontario's only main street market.

CONTACT: 416-878-0581, Milton Chamber of Commerce.

Nanticoke

Nanticoke Generating Station

WHERE: At Nanticoke, Nanticoke Rd. south from Hwy. 3, just east of Jarvis.

WHEN: Open year round. Day tours preferred but evening and weekend tours can be accommodated. Closed holidays. NOTE: Groups only, minimum five persons, age twelve and older. Tours by prior arrangement, minimum two weeks' notice.

WHAT: Tours of the world's largest coal-fired thermal electrical power plant consist of a video presentation and guided plant tour. Washrooms. Tour and washrooms not wheelchair accessible.

CONTACT: 519-587-2201, Ext. 3503, Ontario Hydro Thermal Power Station.

Niagara Falls

From spring through fall, the area around the Falls is often heavily congested and parking spaces are at a premium. If you plan a day trip to see the many attractions, use public transportation. The Falls Shuttle Bus operates from the Lundy's Lane area and the train and bus stations. A day pass allows free transfer to the People Mover and all city buses. The People Mover operates on a loop between the Rapidsview parking lot and the Spanish Aero Car at the Giant Whirlpool, stopping at a dozen major attraction areas. With either pass unlimited use is available.

Floral clock

WHERE: On the Niagara Parkway about 3 km (2 mi.) north (downriver) from Niagara Falls.

WHEN: Spring through fall.

WHAT: One of the world's largest floral clocks boasts a 12.2-m (40-ft.) "living" face planted in a different design each year.

CONTACT: 416-356-2241, Niagara Parks Commission.

Festival of Lights

WHERE: On both sides of the border.

WHEN: From the last week of November to early January.

WHAT: The Festival started in 1981 with massive corporate displays of Christmas lights, but the idea caught on with smaller businesses and private residents. It now stretches the 56-km (35-mi.) length of the Niagara Parkway, from Fort Erie to Niagara-on-the-Lake. The city claims a number of superlatives during this time of year: world's largest Christmas tree (the Skylon Tower); world's largest gift (Your Host Motor Inn decorated to look like a giant gift-wrapped box); world's largest candle (the Minolta Tower); and world's largest bells (the four 17-m (56-ft.) bells atop gates at the Ontario Hydro plant above the Horseshoe Falls). The free spectacle draws about two million people each year. For a price, tours are offered that range from two-and-a-half to three-and-a-half hours in length.

Niagara Falls

WHERE: South of Rainbow Bridge on the Niagara Pkwy.

WHEN: Year round. The Falls are illuminated by coloured spot-lights every night of the year. Only white lights are used for the first and last fifteen minutes of the illumination show. Following is the illumination schedule: During the Festival of Lights, from late November to early January, 5:30 p.m. to 10:30 p.m. Early January to mid-February, Sunday to Thursday, 6:30 p.m. to 9 p.m.; Friday and Saturday, 6:30 p.m. to 10:30 p.m. Middle to end of February, 7 p.m. to 9:30 p.m. March 7 to early April, 8:30 p.m. to 11 p.m. May, 9 p.m. to midnight. June, 9:15 p.m. to midnight. July, 9:15 p.m. to 12:30 a.m. August, 9 p.m. to 12:30 a.m. First week of September, 8 p.m. to 12:30 a.m. Balance of September and October, 8 p.m. to 11 p.m. November, 7 p.m. to 9:30 p.m.

WHAT: The three falls of Niagara—the American Falls, the Horse-shoe Falls and Bridal Veil Falls—are illuminated by a changing kaleidoscope of colours. There is no charge for the show, which may be seen from numerous vantage points, including the towers surrounding the Falls. There is a charge for ascending the towers.

CONTACT: 416-356-2241, Ext. 239, Niagara Falls Illumination Board.

Niagara Falls Brewing Company

WHERE: 6863 Lundy's Ln.

WHEN: Open year round, daily. Tours offered Monday to Friday, 3 p.m.; Saturday, 11 a.m., 1:30 and 3 p.m.; Sunday, noon and 1 p.m.

WHAT: This cottage brewery continues a regional tradition of hand-crafting small volumes of beers and ales. Five bottled brands are available, including what is believed to be North America's only Eisbock beer. During the brewing process this higher alcohol beer is frozen to concentrate the flavour and body, and bottled in a champagne-type bottle. Tours and free tasting take about one hour. The product and beer-related gift items are for sale in the gift shop.

CONTACT: 416-356-BREW, Niagara Falls Brewing Company.

The Niagara Parks
Greenhouse and Fragrance Garden

WHERE: 1 km (.6 mi.) south (upriver) of Horseshoe Falls on the Niagara Pkwy.

WHEN: Open year round, daily, 9:30 a.m. Closing times vary but never earlier than 6 p.m. Closed Christmas Day.

WHAT: Common and exotic plants are grown in a huge greenhouse, with special seasonal displays. In summer there's an outdoor fragrance garden for the blind. Washrooms, garden shop, wheelchairs available. Greenhouse is wheelchair accessible.

CONTACT: 416-356-4699, Niagara Parks Greenhouse.

Niagara Parks Botanical Gardens
and School of Horticulture

WHERE: About 3 km (2 mi.) north of Niagara Falls.

WHEN: Summer through fall.

WHAT: Students display their expertise with flowers and shrubbery on the 40.5-ha (100-a.) landscaped grounds of the school. Free parking. Christmas shop.

CONTACT: 416-356-8554, Niagara Parks Botanical Gardens.

Oak Hall

WHERE: 7400 Portage Rd. S., just north of Marineland.

WHEN: Open year round, Monday to Friday, 8:30 a.m. to 4:45 p.m. Closed holidays.

WHAT: The living room, reception hall and dining room of this magnificent mansion contain an art collection and furnishings that date from the 1919 visit of the Prince of Wales, later King Edward VIII. Oak Hall is the headquarters of the Niagara Parks Commission. Washrooms, wheelchair accessible.

CONTACT: 416-356-2241, Niagara Parks Commission.

Rainbow Tower Carillon

WHERE: At the Canadian end of the International Rainbow Bridge.

WHEN: Concerts on all holidays and during the Festival of Lights. Brochures with timetable available at all tourist information outlets. Call to check dates and times.

WHAT: This set of fifty-five tuned bells boasts one of the largest musical ranges in the world. The bass, which weighs 9 tonnes (10 tons) is the fifth-largest bell in the world. The smallest bell in the set, weighs 4 kg (9 lb.).

CONTACT: 416-354-5641, Niagara Falls Bridge Commission.

Table Rock House and Restaurant

WHERE: Queen Victoria Park, Niagara Pkwy., at the brink of the Horseshoe Falls.

WHEN: Year round. In summer, open daily, 9 a.m. to 11 p.m.; weekends, 9 a.m. to 5 p.m. In winter, open daily, 9 a.m. to 5 p.m.

WHAT: Table Rock was the name given to the original limestone ledge which overhung the gorge at that point. The ornate building now on Table Rock contains the entrance to the Scenic Tunnels (to which admission is charged). There is a two-storey annex providing a panoramic view of the complete Falls landscape. A new observation deck overlooking the Falls is wheelchair accessible.

CONTACT: 416-356-2241, Niagara Parks Commission.

Winery tour, Brights Wines

WHERE: 4887 Dorchester Rd. Exit the Queen Elizabeth Way at Thorold Stone Rd. E. Drive to Dorchester and turn right.

WHEN: Year round, daily. May to October, tours offered Monday to Saturday, 10:30 a.m., 2 p.m., 3:30 p.m.; Sunday, 2 p.m. and 3 p.m. November to April, tours offered Monday to Friday, 2 p.m. and 3:30 p.m.; Saturday and Sunday, 2 p.m. and 3:30 p.m.

WHAT: Brights Wines, founded in 1874, is Canada's oldest and largest winery. Following a one-hour guided tour through the modern and the century-old wine cellars, visitors can sample the product. Washrooms, wine shop. Wheelchair accessible.

CONTACT: 416-357-2400, Brights Wines.

Niagara-on-the-Lake

Niagara Apothecary Museum

WHERE: 55 Queen St. at King St.

WHEN: Open mid-May to Labour Day, daily, noon to 6 p.m.

WHAT: This apothecary, erected in 1866, is now maintained and operated as a museum. Few modern changes are evident and the walnut and butternut fixtures and crystal gasoliers have survived. There is a rare collection of apothecary glass on display.

CONTACT: 416-962-4861, Niagara Apothecary Museum.

Niagara River Recreation Trail

WHERE: Along the Niagara River between Niagara-on-the-Lake and Anger Ave. in Fort Erie.

WHEN: Year round.

WHAT: A 56-km (35-mi.) paved trail for non-motorized travel parallels the Niagara Pkwy. and the Niagara River. Ideal for bicycling, jogging, walking and bird-watching. Picnic tables and barbecues along the route.

CONTACT: 416-356-2241, Niagara Parks Commission.

Winery tour, Konzelman Winery

WHERE: Lakeshore Rd.

WHEN: Tours offered May through Labour Day, Saturday, 2 p.m. Retail store.

WHAT: A tour of the wine-making and bottling processes is followed by a tasting.

CONTACT: 416-935-2866, Konzelman Winery.

Winery tour, Stonechurch Vineyards

WHERE: 1270 Irvine Rd.

WHEN: January to March, open Friday and Saturday, 10 a.m. to 5 p.m. April through December, open Monday to Saturday, 10 a.m. to 6 p.m. Never open Sundays.

WHAT: A tour of the wine-making and bottling facilities is followed by a tasting. Retail shop, gift shop, picnic tables, wheelchair-accessible washrooms.

CONTACT: 416-935-3535, Stonechurch Vineyards.

Winery tour, Inniskillin Wines Inc.

WHERE: South on the Niagara River Parkway on Line 3, Service Rd. 66.

WHEN: Year round, May through October, open 10 a.m. to 6 p.m. November to April, open 10 a.m. to 5 p.m. June through October, tours offered daily, 10:30 a.m. and 2:30 p.m. November to May, tours offered Saturday and Sunday, 2:30 p.m.

WHAT: Displays in a restored nineteenth-century barn illustrate the wine-making process. Limited edition vintages are available at the wine boutique, where there is a tasting bar. Not wheelchair accessible.

CONTACT: 416-468-3554, Inniskillen Wines Inc.

Winery tour, Reif Winery

WHERE: 3 km (2 mi.) south of Niagara-on-the-Lake on Niagara Pkwy. between Line 2 and Line 3.

WHEN: Year round. April to October, open daily, 10 a.m. to 6 p.m. November through March, open 10 a.m. to 5 p.m. Telephone for tour times during winter.

WHAT: This is a small, traditional winery. Tours are available of the bottling process, wine cellar and oak wine casks. Tasting of estate-bottled wines. Retail store, washrooms, picnic facilities, wheelchair accessible.

CONTACT: 416-468-7738, Reif Winery.

Normandale

Normandale Fish Culture Station

WHERE: On the east side of Regional Rd. 10, just north of Turkey Point Provincial Park, near Normandale, about 12 km (7.5 mi.) south of Simcoe.

WHEN: Open year round, daily, 8:30 a.m. to 4 p.m.

WHAT: Thousands of rainbow, lake trout and brown trout and Atlantic salmon are raised each year for stocking the Great Lakes. Several areas are provided to view small fish; larger fish are kept in ponds. Picnic area. Cross-country ski and hiking trails. Wheel chair accessible. No washrooms.

CONTACT: 519-426-3412, Normandale Fish Culture Station; 519-426-7650, Ministry of Natural Resources.

Oakville

Royal Canadian Golf Association Museum and Canadian Golf Hall of Fame

WHERE: From the Queen Elizabeth Way drive north at Dorval Dr. Exit and follow the signs to Glen Abbey Golf Club.

WHEN: Hall of Fame and Museum open year round, Monday to Friday, 9 a.m. to 4:45 p.m. Library open by appointment. Golf course open mid-April to mid-November. Canadian Open Golf Championship held first weekend in September.

WHAT: The Glen Abbey course, designed by Jack Nicklaus, is also headquarters of the Royal Canadian Golf Association and the Canadian Golf Foundation. The Golf House, a former monastery, is home to the Royal Canadian Golf Association Museum and the Canadian Golf Hall of Fame. Displays include golf trophies, antique golf clubs and clothing and other golfing artifacts. A restaurant serves breakfast and lunch from May to November. Wheelchair accessible.

CONTACT: 416-844-1800, Glen Abbey Golf Club, Royal Canadian Golf Association Museum and Canadian Golf Hall of Fame.

Oakville Galleries

WHERE: Centennial Gallery, 120 Navy St., corner of Lakeshore. Exit Trafalgar Rd. S. from Hwy. 401 and the Queen Elizabeth Way. The Gairloch Gallery is at 1306 Lakeshore Rd. E.

WHEN: Centennial Gallery: open year round, Tuesday to Thursday, noon to 9 p.m.; Friday and Saturday, noon to 5 p.m.; Sunday, 1 p.m. to 5 p.m. Gairloch Gallery: January to March, open Saturday and Sunday, 1 p.m. to 5 p.m. April to December, open Tuesday to Sunday, 1 p.m. to 5 p.m. Hours change when exhibitions are being installed.

WHAT: Centennial Gallery holds ten to twelve exhibitions yearly. Gairloch Gallery, which also features changing exhibitions, occupies a 1922 lakeside mansion on 4.5 ha (11 a.). North of the main house, the Studio gift shop offers a wide selection of art works and crafts. Centennial Gallery is wheelchair accessible; assistance is required at Gairloch Gallery.

CONTACT: 416-844-4402, Oakville Galleries.

Oakville Museums

WHERE: 8 Navy St., downtown.

WHEN: Custom House and Erchelss Home: open Tuesday to Friday, 1 p.m. to 4:30 p.m.; Saturday and Sunday, noon to 5 p.m. Old Post Office: open mid-June to mid-October, same hours as other buildings. Free admission Friday, 1 p.m. to 4:30 p.m. Small admission charge at other times.

WHAT: At the 1856 Custom House you can visit a permanent exhibit, Oakville and Its People: 1827-1927. Changing exhibits are displayed at the Post Office. The 1830s-vintage Erchelss (pronounced Air-Kliss) Home contains twenty-odd rooms, five of which are restored to the 1925 era. Others are used for changing exhibitions and a display of kitchen artifacts.

CONTACT: 416-845-3541, Oakville Museums.

Ohsweken

Six Nations tours and Native craft shops

WHERE: In the Village of Ohsweken on the Six Nations Reserve, about 14 km (9 mi.) southeast of Brantford.

WHEN: Open year round. A fee is charged for guided tours and museum entry, but there's no charge for browsing the craft shops or looking around on your own.

WHAT: One of Canada's largest Native communities boasts numerous historic sites. In the village, three Native craft shops sell leather work, soapstone carvings, and jewelry. Free tourism literature and self-guided tour information is available at Six Nations Tourist Office in White Pine Village, Ohsweken.

CONTACT: 519-445-4528, Tourist Office, Six Nations Reserve.

Orangeville

Dufferin County Museum

WHERE: 53 Zina St., next to County Court House.

WHEN: Open year round, Monday to Friday, 8:30 a.m. to 4:30 p.m.

WHAT: Artifacts illustrate the history of Dufferin County. Archives are open to researchers. Washrooms, snack and lunch available at court house.

CONTACT: 519-941-2816, Dufferin County Museum.

Orton

Burdette Gallery Ltd.

WHERE: 16 km (10 mi.) southwest of Orangeville. Take Hwy. 9 west to Dufferin Rd., turn left, follow to Concession Rd. 11, turn left. Gallery is about 1 km (.6 mi.) on right.

WHEN: Open year round, daily, including holidays, 10 a.m. to 5 p.m.; except Friday, 10 a.m. to 4:30 p.m. Closed December 25, 26 and January 1.

WHAT: This art gallery and retail outlet sells original paintings, wildlife sculpture in wood, limited edition prints and carving

supplies. Washrooms, self-guided tour. Not wheelchair accessible.

CONTACT: 519-928-5547, Burdette Gallery Ltd.

Paris

Cobblestone architecture

WHEN: Year round.

WHAT: Nine cobblestone buildings in town and four in adjacent South Dumfries Township were erected by Levi Boughton between 1825 and 1865. Cobblestones 15 to 23 cm (6 to 9 in.) in length are set in horizontal rows in a bed of mortar. A free list and street-map showing eleven houses and two churches is available at most stores or the town office at 66 Grand River St. N.

CONTACT: 519-442-6324, Town of Paris municipal office.

First long-distance telephone call

WHERE: From Brantford to Robert White's Boot and Shoe Store in downtown Paris.

WHEN: Year round.

WHAT: A plaque at 91 Grand River St. marks this historic event.

Heritage buildings

WHERE: In Paris and area.

WHEN: Year round.

WHAT: In addition to its unique cobblestone buildings, Paris boasts several dozen buildings of architectural and historic merit, seven of which are designated under the *Ontario Heritage Act*. A free list of the buildings and free street map is available at most stores or the town office at 66 Grand River St. N.

CONTACT: 519-442-6324, Town of Paris municipal office.

Paris Farmers Market

WHERE: Paris Fairgrounds.

WHEN: Open spring through fall, Saturday, 7 a.m. to 2 p.m.

WHAT: Fresh produce, fish, meats, cheeses, baked goods, quilts, and handcrafts are sold.

CONTACT: 519-442-6324, Town of Paris municipal office.

Port Colborne

Farmers Market

WHERE: Market Square, Charlotte St. and Catharine St.

WHEN: Open year round, Friday, 6 a.m. to noon.

WHAT: Up to sixty vendors from the region offer baked goods, flowers, plants, imported seafood, and seasonal produce.

Port Colborne Historical and Marine Museum

WHERE: Lake Erie entrance to Welland Canal, 1.5 km (1 mi.) south of Hwy. 3 on King St.

WHEN: Open May through December, daily, noon to 5 p.m.

WHAT: This seven-building complex, in a park-like setting in downtown Port Colborne, houses displays that reflect the heritage of the area and the city's relationship to the Welland Canal. The museum complex also includes a barn, a log house, an 1850s log home, a blacksmith's shop and the wheelhouse from the tug *Yvonne Dupre Jr.* At Arabella's Tea Room, tea and homemade biscuits are served June through September, Tuesday to Sunday, 2 p.m. to 4 p.m. Picnic area. Site and buildings are wheelchair accessible.

CONTACT: 416-834-7604, Port Colborne Historical and Marine Museum.

The Shrinking Mill

WHERE: Lakeshore Rd., Port Colborne.

WHEN: Year round.

WHAT: As you look eastwards down the straight, tree-lined stretch of Lakeshore Rd., the grain elevator of Maple Leaf Mills is in full view. When you start to drive closer, the structure appears to shrink. To view this phenomenon correctly, drive west from Port Colborne on Hwy. 3 and turn left at Cement Plant Rd. Continue south to the stop sign at Lakeshore Rd. and make another left turn. Follow Lakeshore Rd. east towards Gravelly Bay.

Port Dover

Port Dover Harbour Museum

WHERE: Black Creek near the lift bridge.

WHEN: Open year round, daily, 10 a.m. to 5 p.m. Closed December 25 and 26 and January 1. Donations accepted.

WHAT: A former net shanty with modern addition contains several hundred artifacts covering the history of Lake Erie's fishing industry. Washrooms, picnic tables, self-guided tours, resource room, gift shop, all wheelchair accessible.

CONTACT: 519-583-2660, Port Dover Harbour Museum.

Queenston

Brock's Monument National Historic Site

WHERE: Just south of the Village of Queenston atop the Niagara Escarpment, about 11 km (7 mi.) south (upriver) of Niagara-on-the-Lake.

WHEN: Open Victoria Day weekend through Labour Day, daily, 10 a.m. to 6 p.m.

WHAT: In 1810, Gen. Isaac Brock was sent to assume command of Fort George at Niagara-on-the-Lake. The following year Brock was promoted to major-general and appointed provisional lieutenant-governor of Upper Canada. When the War of 1812 broke out, he was the heart and soul of the defence of the province. With brilliant audacity he attacked Detroit in August, capturing Gen. William Hull and his entire army. For this act, Brock was knighted—but news of the honour did not reach Canada before Brock died at Queenston Heights in October in the battle that defeated the American invaders. The 56.4-m (185-ft.) monument was erected in 1854. Visitors can climb interior stairs to the top for a spectacular view of the battleground and surrounding area.

CONTACT: 416-262-4759, summer; 416-468-4257, all year.

Samuel E. Weir Collection and Library of Art

WHERE: Corner of Queenston St. and the Niagara Pkwy. Exit the Queen Elizabeth Way at Hwy. 405, then follow the Niagara Pkwy. to Queenston.

WHEN: Victoria Day to Thanksgiving, open Wednesday to Saturday, 11 a.m. to 5 p.m.; Sunday, 1 p.m. to 5 p.m.; other times by appointment. Times subject to change.

WHAT: The late Samuel E. Weir, QC, built this gallery and library to house his collection of historical Canadian art, European paintings and books. Canadian artists represented include Tom Thomson and members of the Group of Seven, Cornelius Krieghoff, Marc-Aurele de Foy Suzor-Cote, J. W. Morrice and Maurice Cullen, as well as Royal Canadian Academicians and British topographical artists who worked in Canada in the early nineteenth century. The collection also includes examples of British Georgian portraiture, historical American painting and French impressionist art.

CONTACT: 416-262-4510, Samuel E. Weir Collection and Library of Art.

Rothsay

World's largest culvert

WHERE: County Rd. 10, 2 km (1.2 mi.) west of the Village of Rothsay, south of Hwy. 9, midway between Arthur and Palmerston.

WHEN: Year round.

WHAT: The world's largest soil and steel bridge spans the Mallett River on Wellington County Rd. 10. The culvert spans over 17.6 m (58 ft. 1 5/16 in.) across the river and is over 7.3 m (24 ft. 1.7 in.) high at its highest point.

CONTACT: 519-837-2600, engineering technologist, County of Wellington Engineering and Road Dept.

St. Catharines

Art Centre and Gallery (Rodman Hall)

WHERE: Rodman Hall, 109 St. Paul Ct. Exit from the Queen Elizabeth Way at Ontario St.

WHEN: Open year round, Tuesday to Friday, 9 a.m. to 5 p.m.; Saturday and Sunday, 1 p.m. to 5 p.m.

WHAT: Exhibitions include paintings, graphics, sculpture, drawings and tapestries from Canada, the U.S., and Europe. The gallery also offers lectures, concerts, children's programmes and films. Washrooms, tea room, gift shop, art rental, wheelchairs available, wheelchair accessible.

CONTACT: 416-684-2925, Art Centre and Gallery (Rodman Hall).

Happy Rolph Bird Sanctuary and Children's Farm

WHERE: Read Rd., St. Catharines. From the Queen Elizabeth Way drive north at Niagara St. Exit, then east at Lakeshore Rd. 1 km (.6 mi.) past the Welland Canal.

WHEN: Open year round, daily, 10 a.m. to dusk. Petting zoo open mid-May to Thanksgiving.

WHAT: This park on Lake Ontario, fully landscaped with trees and shrubs, is popular with children of all ages. Visitors can feed the waterfowl on three ponds. In summer there's a petting farm with goats, sheep, donkeys, a pony, cow, chickens and rabbits. Playground, nature trail, washrooms, picnic tables. Wheelchair accessible.

CONTACT: 416-937-7210, City of St. Catharines Parks and Recreation Dept.

Juice plant, Wiley Bros. Ltd.

WHERE: Corner of First St. and Eighth Ave., 1.5 km (.9 mi.) south of Hwy. 81, on the Wine Route.

WHEN: Open year round, weekdays, 8 a.m. to 5 p.m., (in summer to 6 p.m.); Saturday, 9 a.m. to 5 p.m.; Sunday, noon to 5 p.m.

WHAT: Tours of the juice plant operation take thirty to sixty minutes, including tastings. A retail shop sells juices, honey, Wiley's own home-made jams and jellies and other natural food products. Wheelchair-accessible washrooms.

CONTACT: 416-682-0877, Wiley Bros. Ltd.

Morningstar Mill and DeCew House

WHERE: Take Hwy. 406 to St. David's Rd. W., turn left on Merrittville Hwy. Take the first right on DeCew Rd.

WHEN: Open Victoria Day to Thanksgiving, daily, 1 p.m. to 5 p.m. Closed Mondays and statutory holidays.

WHAT: The ruins of DeCew House are on your right as you drive down pretty DeCew Rd. Laura Secord ran to this house from Queenston with her news of a planned American attack. The Morningstar Mill is next on your right. The present mill was rebuilt in 1895 after the original, built in 1872, was destroyed by fire. Mill tours available. Picnic facilities. No washrooms. The mill is not wheelchair accessible.

CONTACT: 416-685-9455, St. Catharines Tourism and Convention Bureau.

North America's smallest jail

WHERE: In Lakeside Park at Port Dalhousie (annexed by St. Catharines).

WHEN: Year round. Jail may be seen only from the outside.

WHAT: For years, the Town of Tweed, Ontario boasted that it had North America's smallest jail. Then Creemore announced that its jail was smaller. Now Port Dalhousie has come up with an even smaller jail, which it also claims is the oldest in Ontario. The Port's tiny lock-up, built in 1840, measures about 4.6 m (15 ft., 2.5 in.) by about 5.8 m (19 ft., 2 in.). Also of interest in Port Dalhousie Park is a reconstructed wooden lock, a walk along a pier to an octagonal lighthouse and five-cent rides on a magnificently restored antique carousel.

CONTACT: 416-685-9455, St. Catharines Tourism and Convention Bureau.

Winery tour, Henry of Pelham Winery

WHERE: 1469 Pelham Rd. Exit the Queen Elizabeth Way at Seventh St., go south 5 km. (3 mi.), then left on Old Hwy. 8 for 1 km. (.6 mi.) and turn right on Fifth St. Drive south 3 km (2 mi.) to the corner of Fifth and Pelham.

WHEN: Open year round, daily, 10 a.m. to 6 p.m. Tours offered 11 a.m., 1 p.m. and 4 p.m.

WHAT: This small family-owned winery specializes in quality wines. Thirty-minute tours demonstrate the process of wine-making, followed by tasting. Washrooms, wheelchair accessible, picnic area.

CONTACT: 416-684-8423, Henry of Pelham Winery.

Flower trial gardens, Stokes Seeds

WHERE: Martindale Rd., north of the Queen Elizabeth Way.

WHEN: Year round. Store and gardens open Monday to Friday,

8 a.m. to 4:30 p.m. Store is also open Saturday, same hours. The gardens may be seen on Saturday and Sunday but there is no attendant to answer questions. Gardens best seen mid-July through October. Harvest and vegetable de-seeding, mid-September to mid-October.

WHAT: One of the official sites of the All-America Trials, the gardens include 1.2 ha (3 a.) of beds separated by grass walkways, and mass plantings of hundreds of different varieties and colours. No washrooms, difficult for wheelchairs.

CONTACT: 416-688-4300, Stokes Seeds.

Welland Canal Viewing Complex at Lock III

WHERE: From the Queen Elizabeth Way or Hwy. 406, take Glendale Ave. Exit to Canal Rd., turn right and follow blue and white signs.

WHEN: Year round, daily. Victoria Day to Labour Day, open 9 a.m. to 9 p.m. Rest of year, open 9 a.m. to 5 p.m. Closed December 25 and 26 and January 1.

WHAT: Ships from more than thirty countries pass through the 42.5-km (26.4-mi.) canal, which lifts ships 99.5 m (326.5 ft.) from Lake Ontario to Lake Erie in about twelve hours. In an average year, 1,200 ocean-going vessels and 3,000 lake freighters pass through the canal. The new Welland Canal Viewing Centre, open year round, includes a new information centre, videos and interpretive displays, a covered viewing stand, restaurant and gift shop. Viewing stand and washrooms are wheelchair accessible. The complex also includes the St. Catharines Historical Museum, to which a small admission fee is charged.

CONTACT: 416-984-8880, St. Catharines Historical Museum.

St. Davids

Winery tour, Chateau des Charmes Wines Ltd.

WHERE: At St. Davids, 5 km (3 mi.) south of Virgil (Hwy. 55) on Creek Rd. at Line 7.

WHEN: Year round. June through Labour Day, tours offered daily at 11 a.m., 1:30 p.m. and 3 p.m. September to June, tours offered Saturday and Sunday, 11 a.m., 1:30 p.m. and 3 p.m.

WHAT: This small cottage winery offers tours and wine tasting. In summer the wine-tasting is held outside. Retail shop. Wheelchair accessible with assistance.

CONTACT: 416-262-4219, Chateau des Charmes Wines Ltd.

St. George

The Adelaide Hunter-Hoodless Homestead

WHERE: St. George, 1 km (.6 mi.) west of Hwy. 5 and Hwy. 24 on Blue Lake Rd.

WHEN: Open year round, Monday to Friday, 10 a.m. to 4 p.m.; Sunday, noon to 5 p.m., or by appointment. Closed December 24 to January 2 and month of February. Donations encouraged.

WHAT: This is the birthplace and childhood home of Adelaide Hunter-Hoodless, who established domestic science courses in the public school system and founded the Women's Institute movement, the YWCA and the Victorian Order of Nurses. The homestead contains furnishings and personal belongings of the Hunter and Hoodless families that reflect the period when Adelaide lived there (1850-1880). The two-storey rural white frame house is surrounded by 1.2 ha (3 a.) of landscaped parkland. Washrooms, picnic tables. Wheelchair access to first floor.

CONTACT: 519-448-1130, the Adelaide Hunter-Hoodless Homestead; off-season, 613-234-1090, Federated Women's Institutes of Canada, Ottawa.

St. Jacobs

Stockyard Farmers Market and Flea Market

WHERE: Weber St. and King St., north of Waterloo, 2 km (1.2 mi.) south of St. Jacobs.

WHEN: Operates year round, Thursday, 7 a.m. to 4 p.m.; Saturday, 7 a.m. to 3 p.m. June through August, also operates Tuesday, 8 a.m. to 3 p.m.

WHAT: This farmers market sells locally grown produce, fresh and smoked meats, domestic and imported cheeses, baked goods, homemade candy, and handcrafts. Flea market, picnic tables, wheelchair-accessible washrooms.

CONTACT: 519-747-1830 or 519-664-2293, Stockyard Farmers Market and Flea Market.

Maple Syrup Museum of Ontario

WHERE: 8 Spring St., in the Old Factory.

WHEN: Year round. May to December open Monday to Saturday, 10 a.m. to 6 p.m.; Sunday, 12:30 a.m. to 5:30 p.m. January to March, same hours but closed Monday. Donations welcomed.

WHAT: A collection of artifacts shows the methods used by pioneers and modern-day producers to create maple products from maple tree sap. An adjacent store sells maple products, gourmet food and kitchen equipment. The museum is wheelchair accessible, the washrooms are not.

CONTACT: 519-664-3626, Maple Syrup Museum of Ontario.

St. Williams

St. Williams Forest Station

WHERE: At St. Williams, 26 km (16 mi.) southwest of Simcoe and 10 km (6 mi.) west of Turkey Point on Hwy. 24.

WHEN: Open year round, Monday to Friday, 8 a.m. to 4:30 p.m. Grounds and picnic area open on weekends but there is no attendant. No guided tours without appointment.

WHAT: Canada's first provincial forestry station, established in 1908, covers 1600 ha (4000 a.), including 80 ha (200 a.) devoted to nursery stock production. Picnicking, fishing. Washrooms in summer.

CONTACT: 519-586-3576, St. Williams Forest Station.

Simcoe

Christmas Panorama

WHERE: Wellington Park and Clifton Park.

WHEN: Switched on December to January 6, daily, 5:30 p.m. to midnight.

WHAT: More than sixty large displays with more than 25,000 coloured lights depict fantasies and religious and Christmas scenes.

CONTACT: 519-426-5867, Simcoe Chamber of Commerce.

Lynnwood Arts Centre

WHERE: 21 Lynnwood Ave. (Hwy. 24 and Hwy. 3), in a park beside the Lynn River.

WHEN: Open year round, Tuesday to Friday, 9 a.m. to 5 p.m.; Saturday and Sunday, 1 p.m. to 5 p.m. Closed holidays.

WHAT: The former home of Duncan Campbell, built in 1851, is a fine example of Greek Revival architecture and a designated national historic site. There are monthly exhibitions of paintings, drawing and sculptures. Wheelchair-accessible washrooms.

CONTACT: 519-428-0540, Lynnwood Arts Centre.

Vineland

Winery tour, Vineland Estates

WHERE: 3620 Moyer Rd., Vineland.

WHEN: Open end of May through October, daily, 10 a.m. to 5:30 p.m. Tours offered at 11 a.m., 1 p.m. and 3 p.m.

WHAT: Visitors can tour processing and bottling operations. Tasting room, retail shop. Not wheelchair accessible. Washrooms.

CONTACT: 416-562-7088, Vineland Estates.

Virgil

Winery tour, Hillebrand Estates Winery

WHERE: Just west of Virgil on Hwy. 55.

WHEN: Open year round, 10 a.m. to 6 p.m., including most holidays. Tours offered daily, 11 a.m., 1 p.m., 3 p.m. and 4 p.m.

WHAT: A tour of the winery includes a video presentation and wine tasting. Retail store. Washrooms wheelchair accessible.

CONTACT: 416-468-7123, Hillebrand Estates Winery.

Waterloo
(See also Kitchener listings)

Brick Brewing Company Limited

WHERE: 181 King St. S.

WHEN: Year Round. Tours offered Sunday, 3 p.m.; other days by appointment only.

WHAT: Free tasting follows the tour. Gift shop with beer memorabilia. Retail store. Not wheelchair accessible.

CONTACT: 519-576-9100, Brick Brewing Company Limited.

Enook Galleries

WHERE: 29 Young St. E.

WHEN: Open Tuesday to Saturday, 10 a.m. to 5:30 p.m. Closed all statutory holidays.

WHAT: The galleries display Inuit and Indian art, Papua New Guinea art, contemporary Canadian art, original prints, sculpture, wall hangings and handcrafted gift items. Washrooms. Not wheelchair accessible. Sign language spoken.

CONTACT: 519-884-3221, Enook Galleries.

Heritage Time Teller

WHERE: King St. and William St.

WHEN: Operates year round, daily, every hour on the hour from 10 a.m. to 10 p.m.

WHAT: An animated mechanical display depicts the history of the Kitchener-Waterloo area through music. The bandshell structure features a beer stein band that introduces each musical programme with a brief historical narration. Four different songs are played throughout the day. Programmes are changed to suit the season.

CONTACT: 519-576-0571, Oktoberfest office; 519-886-2440, Kitchener-Waterloo Chamber of Commerce.

The Seagram Museum

WHERE: 57 Erb St. W.

WHEN: Year round. May through October open daily, 10 a.m. to

6 p.m. Rest of the year, same hours but closed Monday. Closed December 25, 26 and January 1.

WHAT: This museum, devoted to the wine and spirits industry, includes twelve galleries that explain the technology of distilling and wine-making. A video carries visitors from the glens of Scotland's whisky distilleries to the hillsides of California's vineyards. Part of the Museum is housed in a former century-old barrel warehouse, the rest in a soaring modern exhibition area. Tour guides are available to answer questions. Restaurant, gift shop, and specialty liquor store selling Seagram products. Wheelchair-accessible washrooms.

CONTACT: 519-885-1857, The Seagram Museum.

University of Waterloo Campus tours

WHERE: University Ave. W.

WHEN: Sixty- to ninety-minute guided tours offered September through April, Monday to Friday, 10:30 a.m. and 1:30 p.m., except holidays. Campus is open to self-guided tours the rest of the year.

WHAT: Guided tours are available of this 405-ha (1000-a.) campus. A brochure is available for self-guided tours. Snack bar. Cafeteria. Wheelchair accessible.

CONTACT: 519-885-1211, Ext. 3614, University of Waterloo.

Museum and Archive of Games, University of Waterloo

WHERE: B. C. Matthews Hall, University of Waterloo, Columbus St. entrance.

WHEN: Open all year, but days and hours vary. Call to verify. Small parking fee.

WHAT: This is the only museum of its kind in Canada, dedicated solely to the study of games. The collection includes about 5,000 artifacts, ranging from ancient Egyptian games to modern computer games on floppy disks. Visitors can play some of the games in a hands-on area. Archives are open to researchers by appointment.

CONTACT: 519-888-4424, University of Waterloo, Museum and Archive of Games.

Biology-Earth Sciences Museum, University of Waterloo

WHERE: University of Waterloo Campus, top floor of the Earth Sciences Chemistry Building.

WHEN: Open Monday to Friday, 8:30 a.m. to 4 p.m. Closed statutory holidays except Canada Day.

WHAT: Exhibits trace the history of the earth from the start of life millions of years ago to the present day. Displays feature ancient life forms such as dinosaurs, rock, mineral and gem collections and an outdoor geological garden containing samples of Ontario rocks. Wheelchair-accessible washrooms.

CONTACT: 519-885-1211, Ext. 2469, University of Waterloo, Biology-Earth Sciences Museum.

Museum of Visual Science and Optometry, University of Waterloo

WHERE: University of Waterloo, north campus, 3rd floor, Optometry Building. Access off Columbia St.

WHEN: Open Monday to Friday, 8:30 a.m. to 6 p.m. Closed statutory holidays.

WHAT: Unique in Canada and one of four on the continent, this museum contains collections of early instruments used in the examination of the eye, material on the history of optometry, early diplomas and books and a collection of early spectacles, contact lenses and similar devices. Wheelchair-accessible washrooms.

CONTACT: 519-885-1211, University of Waterloo, Museum of Visual Science and Optometry.

Waterloo County Farmers Market

WHERE: From Hwy. 401, follow Hwy. 8 through Kitchener to Hwy. 86 (Conestoga Pkwy.). Drive west on Northfield Dr., turn right at Weber St. N. and continue 1 km (.6 mi.) to the market.

WHEN: Open year round, Saturday, 6 a.m. to 2 p.m. June through Thanksgiving, also open Wednesday, 8 a.m. to 2 p.m.

WHAT: Booths offer home cooking, meats, sausage, fresh fruits and vegetables, cheeses, poultry and handcrafts. Many vendors are area Mennonites who arrive by horse and buggy.

CONTACT: 519-664-2817, Waterloo County Farmers Market.

Waterloo Park

WHERE: In Waterloo, bounded by Albert St., Yonge St. and Westmount St.

WHEN: All year, daily.

WHAT: This park includes an animal menagerie of deer and farm animals, Waterloo's first school house and a potter's workshop. In summer, the park offers a horticultural display, outdoor swimming pool and four creative play areas, one fully wheelchair-accessible.

CONTACT: 519-886-2310, Service Centre, Waterloo Park; 519-886-1550, City of Waterloo, Dept. of Recreation and Culture.

Welland

Farmers Market

WHERE: Downtown, Young St. or Division St. east of King.

WHEN: Open year round, Tuesday, Thursday and Saturday, 6 a.m. to noon.

WHAT: Niagara's oldest market, founded 1907, offers locally grown fruits, vegetables and meats, as well as cheeses, baked goods, home-

---

made clothing, art and quilts. Dairy bar. Market and washrooms are wheelchair accessible.

CONTACT: 416-735-1700, Ext. 235, Farmers Market.

Historic tour of Downtown Welland

WHERE: Throughout the city.

WHEN: Year round.

WHAT: This walking tour includes the 1856 Welland County Court House, an 1841 stone aqueduct and homes and churches built in the mid- to late-1800s. Free brochure with map available from Tourism of Welland Niagara, 32 E. Main St.

CONTACT: 416-735-8696, Tourism of Welland Niagara.

Merritt Island

WHERE: From downtown Welland, take Cross St. N.

WHEN: Year round, sunrise to sunset.

WHAT: This island in the middle of the city is about 5 km (3 mi.) long, bordered by the Old Welland Canal (now a recreational waterway) and the Welland River. Children's playground, picnic facilities, barbecues, swimming, fishing, wheelchair-accessible washrooms, hiking, biking, cross-country ski trails, landscaping along the canal banks.

CONTACT: 416-735-8696, Tourism of Welland Niagara.

Murals

WHERE: All through Welland. Free tour map available.

WHEN: Year round. Best seen during daylight hours.

WHAT: Twenty-seven giant murals on the walls of buildings around the city portray Welland's heritage and history.

CONTACT: 416-788-3000, Festival of Arts; 416-735-8696, Tourism of Welland Niagara.

New Welland Canal

WHERE: From downtown Welland drive east on Lincoln St.

WHEN: April through November.

WHAT: In 1973 a 13.25-km (8-mi.) canal was built around the east side of Welland, linked to the original Welland Canal dating from 1829. Two tunnels on E. Main St. and Townline Rd. carry car and train traffic under the new section of the canal. Driving east on Lincoln St., you can see ocean and lake ships in the bypass channel. (See *Welland Canal Viewing Complex at Lock III* in St. Catharines section.)

CONTACT: 416-735-0541 for vessel information; 416-735-4052 for navigation recorded message.

Old Welland Canal

WHERE: Through the centre of Welland.

WHEN: Year round.

WHAT: The old canal is now a recreational waterway used for boating, waterskiing, swimming and fishing. The treed, grassy banks are used for hiking and picnicking. Boat-launching facilities. Rowing, canoeing, waterskiing contests.

Rose Garden (Chippewa Park Rose Garden)

WHERE: Prince Charles Dr., east on Fitch.

WHEN: May to October.

WHAT: A rose named for the City of Welland is one of the many varieties found in the fifty rose beds of this garden, founded in 1932.

West Montrose

Kissing Bridge

WHERE: In the hamlet of West Montrose a few kilometres east of Elmira, on County Rd. 86.

WHEN: Year round.

WHAT: Ontario's last remaining covered bridge is called the Kissing Bridge—a name that dates from horse-and-buggy days when the feebly lighted structure was a popular spot for couples. The 61-m (200-ft.) bridge, which spans the Grand River, was built in 1881. The banks of the river near the bridge are privately owned, but considerate picnikers—those who leave behind only footprints—are usually welcome.

Winona

Winery tour, Andres Wines Ltd.

WHERE: 679 South Service Rd., Winona, about 16 km (10 mi.) east of Hamilton.

WHEN: Year round. Store open daily, 10 a.m. to 5 p.m.; Saturday and Sunday, noon to 5 p.m. Tours offered weekdays, 11 a.m., 1 p.m. and 3 p.m.; weekends 1 p.m. and 3 p.m.

WHAT: The tour is free but there is a $1.50 charge for tasting seven wines. Store sells wines and wine-related gift items. Wheelchair-accessible washrooms.

CONTACT: 416-643-TOUR, Andres Wines Ltd.

Georgian Lakelands

Includes: Alliston, Barrie, Bracebridge, Bradford, Collingwood, Gravenhurst, Huntsville, Kincardine, Midland, Orillia, Owen Sound, Penetanguishene, Port Elgin, Tobermory, Walkerton, Wasaga Beach, Wiarton and their environs.

This region embraces summer resorts on fine Lake Huron beaches, the rugged Bruce Peninsula, ski resorts on the Niagara Escarpment on the south shores of Georgian Bay and Lake Simcoe, the largest inland lake in Southern Ontario.

Festivals, Carnivals, Celebrations, Special Events:

JANUARY: Orillia, *Wonderland of Lights* (starts in mid-November); Owen Sound, *Festival of Northern Lights* (starts in late November); Midland, *Winterfest;* Orillia, *Old Fashioned Winter Carnival;* Port Sydney, *Winter Carnival* (bangers and mash variety night, nail driving); Wiarton, *Groundhog Festival* (Wiarton Willie Prediction, smooch races); Collingwood, *Winterfest.*

FEBRUARY: Huntsville, *Winter Wonderfest* (horse-drawn sleigh rides); Bracebridge, *Winter Carnival* (Polar Bear Dip, motorcycle ice races, log sawing); *Southampton Heritage;* Penetanguishene, *Winter Carnival and Winterama;* Wasaga Beach,

Winterfest; Baysville, *Annual Valentines Winter Carnival;* Barrie, *Winterfest;* Gravenhurst, *Muskoka Winter Carnival.*

MARCH: Honey Harbour, Georgian Bay Islands National Park, *Annual Fish Fry* (snowshoe races, winter cookout); Hawkestone, Shaw's Maple Syrup Pancake House, *Tours of Bush;* Bracebridge, *Maple Syrup Festival;* Midland, *Spring Harvest Celebration of Sap to Syrup;* Paisley, *Maple Festival* (production methods through the years); Barrie, *Spring Tonic Festival.*

APRIL: Wiarton, *Annual Purple Valley Maple Syrup Festival;* Windermere, *Sugar Bush Day;* Milford Bay, *Annual Pancake and Maple Syrup Festival.*

MAY: Bracebridge, *Muskoka Kite Festival;* Orillia, *The Great Antique Bed Race.*

JUNE: Wasaga Beach, *Junefest;* Barrie, *Pizza Pizza Salute to Summer* (rock bands, midway, beer gardens); Hanover, *Aquafest* (loonie egg race, strawberry social); Kilworthy, *Morrison Pioneer Days* (steam engine display); Huntsville, Muskoka Pioneer Village, *Strawberry Social;* Orillia, *Christmas in June* (bikini contest, night sail past); Dundalk, *Square, Step Dancing and Clogging Competition;* Kincardine, *Pipe Band Parade;* Collingwood, *Canadian Beaver Caper;* Beaverton, *Settler's Day* (strawberry tea, lawn sale).

JULY: Southampton, *Visions of Stone* (stone show); Barrie, *Pizza Pizza Canada Day Festival* (rock band acts); Midland, *Annual Huronia Open Fiddle and Step Dance Contest;* Barrie, *Annual Promenade Days;* Southampton, *Jamboree* (square and round dancing); Barrie, *Molson Canadian Hot Air Balloon Festival* (children's entertainment, agility dog tournament); Kincardine, *Highland Games;* Thornbury, *Southern Georgian Bay Chili Cookoff* (bluegrass music); Barrie, *George Forgan Memorial Games* (pipe bands, highland dancers, caber toss, hammer throw); Midland, Sainte Marie Among the Hurons, *Candlelight Tours;* Orillia, *Scottish Festival;* Walkerton, *Homecoming;* Midland, Sainte Marie Among the Hurons, *Shondecti* (canoe parade, living history highlights); Orillia, *Leacock Heritage Festival* (evening of humorous song, old fashioned children's festival, Leacock Medal of Humour for Writing readings); Meaford, *Range Tour* (bus tours of military rifle range base); Cookstown, *Hillbilly Daze* (barbecue, blue grass bands, cloggers); Owen Sound, *Spoke and Bustle* (steam traction engines, butter churning, wood stove cooking, shingle splitting); Penetanguishene, *Re-enactment Weekend* (black powder demonstrations, encampments, 19th-century lifestyle demonstrations).

AUGUST: Orillia, *Leacock Garden Party;* Orillia, *Rotary Funfest Weekend;* Alliston, *Potato Festival;* Owen Sound, *Summerfolk Music and Craft Festival;* Coldwater, *Old Tyme Day;* Gravenhurst, *1890 Victorian Social at Norman Bethune Memorial House;* Phelpston, *Annual Outhouse Drag Race* (outhouses on wheels raced around village block by teams of six pushers and one driver); Hanover, *Happy Days;* Penetanguishene, *Songs of the Sail* (songs of the sea, workshops, concerts, crafts).

SEPTEMBER: Wasaga Beach, *Oktoberfest;* Orillia, *Oktoberfest;* Flesherton, *Split Rail Festival;* Rosemont, *Cider Festival.*

OCTOBER: Port Elgin, *Pumpkinfest* (official international pumpkin contest); Orillia, *Annual Traditional Thanksgiving Pow Wow;* Owen Sound, *Pratie-Oaten* (potato harvest celebration, potato dishes served, Celtic music and dancing); Bala, *Annual Bala Cranberry Festival.*

NOVEMBER: Orillia, Huntsville, Coldwater, Gravenhurst, Midland, Port Elgin, *Santa Claus parades.*

DECEMBER: Orillia, Leacock Museum, *Stephen Leacock's Birthday Party;* Collingwood, Bracebridge, Hanover, Wasaga Beach, Wiarton, Baysville, *Santa Claus parades.*

More detailed information on the festivals, carnivals, celebrations and other attractions of Georgian Lakelands is available from: Georgian Lakelands Travel Association, 66 Coldwater St. E., Orillia, Ontario L3V 1W5, Tel. 705-325-7160.

Angus

Base Borden Military Museum

WHERE: On Hwy. 90, just west of Angus, about 16 km (10 mi.) west of Barrie.

WHEN: Open year round, Tuesday to Friday, 9 a.m. to noon and 1:15 p.m. to 3 p.m; weekends and holidays, 1:30 p.m. to 4 p.m.

Closed Christmas to New Year's. Closed Mondays, but open on holiday Mondays and then closed Tuesday. Washrooms. Wheelchair accessible. Admission is free but proof of vehicle ownership and insurance may be required for admission to Base Borden.

WHAT: Budget at least two hours for a good look at all the old military hardware and memorabilia. Tanks, half-tracks and other vehicles of war are scattered through an adjoining park.

CONTACT: 705-423-3531, Base Borden Military Museum.

Barrie

Barrie Horticultural Society Arboretum

WHERE: Sunnidale Park, corner of Cundles Rd. and Sunnidale Rd.

WHEN: Open year round. Best seen in growing season. Donations accepted.

WHAT: The Arboretum features 4.9 ha (12 a.) of trees and shrubs, including 143 varieties of deciduous trees, ninety varieties of deciduous shrubs and seventy-six varieties of evergreens. Trees and shrubs are labelled so visitors can examine them before making purchases for their own property. Washrooms and picnic area nearby. Wheelchair accessible.

CONTACT: 705-726-0134, Barrie Horticultural Society Arboretum.

MacLaren Art Centre

WHERE: 147 Toronto St., corner Wellington St., beside Royal Victoria Hospital.

WHEN: Open year round, Tuesday to Friday, 9:30 a.m. to 5 p.m.; Saturday, 10:30 a.m. to 3 p.m.; Sunday 1 p.m. to 4 p.m.

WHAT: Art exhibitions change year round. Washrooms. Not wheelchair accessible.

CONTACT: 705-721-9696, MacLaren Art Centre.

Midhurst Forest Tree Nursery

WHERE: 5 km (3 mi.) northwest of Barrie on Hwy. 26 across from the entrance to Springwater Provincial Park.

WHEN: Year round, Monday to Friday, 8 a.m. to 4:30 p.m. Closed holidays.

WHAT: Free conducted tours are available if arranged in advance. You can also take a self-guided walking or driving tour. The tours illustrate how forest tree seedlings are grown and explain why reforestation is required. Midhurst Nursery produces over seven million tree seedlings per year. Washrooms. Limited wheelchair access.

CONTACT: 705-728-2900, Midhurst Forest Tree Nursery, Ministry of Natural Resources.

Walking tours

WHERE: Around Barrie.

WHEN: Year round.

WHAT: The Local Architectural Conservation Advisory Committee has prepared four maps that outline walking tours of Barrie's downtown area. The maps are illustrated with line drawings of historic or architecturally interesting buildings. They are available free at Barrie Visitor and Convention Bureau, 80 Bradford St.

CONTACT: 705-726-6573, Barrie Visitor and Convention Bureau.

Big Chute

Big Chute Marine Railway

WHERE: At Big Chute, about 7 km (4.3 mi.) west of Hwy. 69, northwest of Orillia.

WHEN: Summer.

WHAT: Boats as long as 24.4 m (80 ft.) are carried on two railway lines between the lower and upper stretches of the Severn River, a vertical distance of 17.7 m (58 ft.).

Bracebridge

The Chapel Gallery

WHERE: 45 Muskoka Rd. S. Turn off Shier St. near the bridge over the Muskoka River. Beside Woodchester Villa and Museum.

WHEN: Year round. September to June, open Tuesday to Saturday, 10 a.m. to 5 p.m.; July and August, open daily, 10 a.m. to 5 p.m. Donations accepted.

WHAT: In a reconstruction of the first Presbyterian church in Bracebridge, mid-1800s vintage, the Muskoka Arts and Crafts Inc. mounts monthly exhibitions of local, regional and national artists and handcrafts. Lectures, films, workshops. Art works for sale.

CONTACT: 705-645-5501, The Chapel Gallery.

Woodchester Villa and Museum

WHERE: 46 Muskoka Rd. S. Turn off Shier St. near the bridge over the Muskoka River.

WHEN: Victoria Day to Thanksgiving, open weekends, 10 a.m. to 5 p.m. July 1 to Labour Day, open daily, 10 a.m. to 5 p.m. Guided tours available. Donations accepted.

WHAT: One of Ontario's few remaining three-storey octagonal houses was built in 1882 for mill owner Henry James Bird. It is now the home of the Bracebridge Museum.

CONTACT: 705-645-8111, Woodchester Villa and Museum.

Chatsworth

Chatsworth Fish Culture Station

WHERE: 6 km (4 mi.) south of Chatsworth, 1.5 km (.9 mi.) west of Hwy. 6, 19 km (12 mi.) south of Owen Sound.

WHEN: Open year round, daily, 9 a.m. to 4 p.m. Guided tours may be arranged on weekends.

WHAT: This is one of the largest fish hatcheries operated by the Ontario Ministry of Natural Resources. Self-guided tours. Wheelchair-accessible washrooms.

CONTACT: 519-794-2340, Chatsworth Fish Culture Station.

Coldwater

Coldwater Canadiana, Woodrow Homestead Heritage House

WHERE: South end of Coldwater on Woodrow Rd., between Hwy. 12 and Hwy. 400.

WHEN: Victoria Day weekend to June and Labour Day to Thanksgiving, open Saturday and Sunday, 11 a.m. to 4 p.m. July and August, open Tuesday to Sunday, 10 a.m. to 5 p.m. July and August, Devon cream tea and craft demonstrations, Wednesday 1 p.m. to 3:30 p.m. Donation box.

WHAT: Historical artifacts are displayed in this restored 1840-vintage log house, in its original location on the bank of the Coldwater River. The back room was the original house built by Scottish settler Archibald Woodrow. The two-storey front section was added in 1864. A carriage house, barn, print shop, blacksmith's shop and railway flag station have been moved onto the homestead site. Guided or self-guided tours, picnic tables, outside washrooms. Not wheelchair accessible.

CONTACT: 705-835-5032, Coldwater Canadiana, Woodrow Homestead; off-season, 705-835-2800, curator.

Collingwood

Blue Mountain Pottery 87 Inc.

WHERE: Mountain Rd., Hwy. 26, at west end of Collingwood.

WHEN: Year round. May through June, open daily, 9:30 a.m. to 6 p.m.; July through August, open daily, 9:30 a.m. to 8 p.m. Mid-May to August, tours offered Monday to Friday. September to May, open daily, 9:30 a.m. to 5 p.m.

WHAT: Visitors can tour the factory, which produces the distinctive Blue Mountain Pottery line of figurines and vases. Factory outlet store. Washrooms. Store is wheelchair accessible.

CONTACT: 705-445-3000, Blue Mountain Pottery 87 Inc.

Candy Factory

WHERE: Sixth St., 3 km (2 mi.) west of the junction of Hwy. 24 and Hwy. 26.

WHEN: Year round, daily. September to June, open Monday to Friday, 8:30 a.m. to 5 p.m.; Saturday, 10 a.m. to 5 p.m.; Sunday, noon to 5:30 p.m. July and August, open Monday to Friday, 8:30 a.m. to 8 p.m.; Saturday and Sunday, 10 a.m. to 8 p.m. Closed December 25, 26, January 1 and Easter Sunday.

WHAT: The Candy Factory was established in the early 1970s with the aim of preserving the candymakers' art through strict adherence to old-time recipes. Fresh, pure ingredients are used, without additives, and the whole operation is performed in view of visitors. Antique artifacts of the candy industry are displayed. Free samples are offered. Factory outlet store. No washroom. Wheelchair accessible.

CONTACT: 705-445-2400, The Candy Factory.

Creemore

Creemore Jail

WHERE: In the Village of Creemore, 24 km (15 mi.) south of Collingwood.

WHEN: Year round.

WHAT: This jail qualifies as one of the smallest in North America. The outside dimensions measure 6.14 m (20 ft., 2 in.) by 4.62 m (15 ft., 2 in.), which makes it smaller than the jail at Tweed but larger than one at Port Dalhousie-St. Catharines.

Creemore Springs Brewery

WHERE: Main street of Creemore.

WHEN: Year round. Tours by appointment during regular business hours.

WHAT: This small brewery, housed in an 1889-vintage former hardware store, brews beer and ale in the traditional fashion without preservatives. The brewery will take visitors on a dry tour through the brewing processes; a tasting is not provided but the product is on sale in chilled pint or quart bottles. No washroom. Wheelchair accessible with assistance.

CONTACT: 705-466-2531, Creemore Springs Brewery.

Dorset

Canada's Best Country Store

WHERE: At the junction of Hwy. 35 and Hwy. 117 in the village of Dorset, about 40 km (25 mi.) southeast of Huntsville.

WHEN: Year round. January to March, open 8:30 a.m. to 6 p.m.; Sunday, 11 a.m. to 4 p.m. July 1 through Labour Day, open daily,

8 a.m. to 9 p.m.; Sunday, 9 a.m. to 9 p.m. Rest of the year, open 8 a.m. to 6 p.m.; Friday to 9 p.m.; Sunday, 9 a.m. to 9 p.m.

WHAT: The editors of *Canadian Living* magazine awarded Robinson's General Store the sobriquet "Canada's Best Country Store." The visitor isn't likely to question this judgement. When the store opened in 1921 it offered a selection of basic goods. But as the area population grew, so did the inventory, and additions to the original building sprouted off in all directions. The store is now operated by the fifth generation of Robinsons. Since it was "discovered" by city folk during the tourism boom of the 1970s, bus tours stop so passengers can buy moose fur hats, baked goods, oil lamps, books and greeting cards—and just about anything else.

CONTACT: 705-766-2415, Robinson's General Store.

Leslie M. Frost Natural Resources Centre

WHERE: At St. Nora Lake on Hwy. 35, 11 km (7 mi.) south of Dorset.

WHEN: Open year round. July and August, free tours offered Monday to Friday, 11:30 a.m. to 12:30 p.m.

WHAT: The tours include the science rooms with exhibits relating to natural resources. Family programmes. Picnic tables, trails, wheelchair-accessible washrooms. Year round, free recreational trails on the 24,000-ha (59,000-a.) property. In winter, fee for cross-country ski trails.

CONTACT: 705-766-2451, Leslie M. Frost Natural Resources Centre.

Observation Tower

WHERE: Just north of Dorset beside Hwy. 35, about 38 km (23.6 mi.) southeast of Huntsville.

WHEN: Open year round. Road not plowed in winter, but tower is open.

WHAT: This 30.5-m (100-ft.) observation tower affords a fine view of the surrounding lakes, hills and rivers. The tower is particularly popular in autumn when the leaves are turning.

Gravenhurst

Bethune Memorial House

WHERE: 235 John St. Follow signs from Hwy. 169 or Hwy. 11.

WHEN: Open year round, daily. Labour Day through May, open 10 a.m. to 5 p.m. June through Labour Day, open 9 a.m. to 6 p.m. Closed on statutory holidays.

WHAT: This late Victorian home, the birthplace of Dr. Norman Bethune, has been restored to the 1890s, incorporating some of the family's possessions. An interpretive display describes Dr. Bethune's life and accomplishments. A visitor centre offers a video orientation, children's video, and a display of gifts from the people of China, where Bethune is a national hero. Guided tours, wheelchair-accessible washrooms. Ground floor wheelchair accessible.

CONTACT: 705-687-4261, Bethune Memorial House.

R.M.S. *Segwun*

WHERE: Gravenhurst dock.

WHEN: On view year round. Tours operate early June to early October.

WHAT: Believed to be the last operating steam-powered ship in Canada, the Royal Mail Ship *Segwun* carried mail, freight and passengers through the Muskoka lakes. Built in 1887, the boat has been lovingly restored by the non-profit Friends of the *Segwun*. There is a charge for the tours, but none to admire this historic gem. Free parking on town dock.

CONTACT: 705-687-6667, Muskoka Lakes Navigation and Hotel Company Ltd.

Huntsville

Lions Lookout Park

WHERE: Overlooking Huntsville, signposted from downtown.

WHEN: Year round.

WHAT: On a pleasant day the view from this park is lovely. Follow signs from downtown, which point you up a windy road to a rocky knoll covered in pine trees. A picnic shelter overlooks the townsite and surrounding countryside. Washrooms. Lookout is wheelchair accessible.

Madill Church

WHERE: About 6 km (3.7 mi.) south of Huntsville, just west of Hwy. 11.

WHEN: Year round.

WHAT: One of the few remaining square-timbered churches in Ontario was built in 1873 by a Wesleyan Methodist congregation. Huntsville's namesake, Capt. George Hunt, is buried in the churchyard. Hunt, who arrived in 1868, was a teetotaller who divided his land and sold lots with a "no drinking" clause written into the deeds. It is said this accounts for the development of Huntsville on the west side of the Muskoka River where there are difficult hills, rather than on the flat east side where Hunt's restrictions applied.

Midland

Castle Village and Dracula's Museum of Horrors

WHERE: Balm Beach Rd., Midland.

WHEN: Mid-March through December, open Tuesday to Saturday, 10 a.m. to 5:30 p.m.; Sunday, noon to 5 p.m. Victoria Day through Labour Day, also open Monday, 10 a.m. to 5:30 p.m. Admission to Castle Village and Dwarf Village Slides is free. There is a small admission to Dracula's Museum.

WHAT: In Castle Village you can take your pick of over 10,000 different gift items from around the world. Through the dungeon windows of Dracula's Museum you can see such characters as Jack the Ripper, Wolfman, Frankenstein and Dracula.

CONTACT: 705-526-9683, Castle Village and Dracula's Museum of Horrors.

Owen Sound

Billy Bishop Heritage Museum

WHERE: 948 3rd Ave. W.

WHEN: Open Victoria Day to Labour Day, daily, 1 p.m. to 4 p.m. Donations welcomed.

WHAT: This late Victorian brick house was the birthplace and boyhood home of Billy Bishop, Victoria Cross fighter pilot in the First World War and Canada's most decorated serviceman. The ground floor, finished circa 1905, houses displays on the Bishop family. Exhibits feature the exploits of Bishop during his active service with the Royal Flying Corps. They include the painting *Dawn Attack*, by Robert Bradford, showing Bishop's attack of the German aerodrome near Cambral in France in 1917, which gained Bishop the Victoria Cross. Washroom, guided tours, gift shop, park and picnic tables nearby. Not wheelchair accessible.

CONTACT: 519-371-0031, Billy Bishop Heritage Museum.

Marine and Rail Heritage Centre

WHERE: Former CNR railway station, 1165 1st Ave. W., on west waterfront.

WHEN: Early June through Labour Day, open Tuesday to Saturday, 10 a.m. to 4 p.m.; Sunday, 1 p.m. to 4 p.m. After Labour Day, telephone for appointment. Donations welcomed.

WHAT: Displays include marine and railway artifacts, ship models, anchors, flags and ship's wheels. A small archives is open to researchers. A one-hour audio-visual presentation on the transportation history of Georgian Bay is available for screening by appointment. A new addition is the 7.6-m (25-ft.) tugboat *Ancaster*, built in Owen Sound in 1941. The *Ancaster* worked the Ottawa River and was featured on the old Canadian one dollar bill. Washrooms, gift shop, wheelchair accessible.

CONTACT: 519-376-1815, curator, Marine and Rail Heritage Centre.

Owen Sound Mill Dam Fish Ladder

WHERE: Downtown, near 5th St. W. and 2nd Ave. W.

WHEN: April to May, for trout migrating upstream. October to November, for salmon migrating upstream.

WHAT: The fish ladder was installed to allow salmon and trout to migrate further up the Sydenham River to spawn. Viewing only.

CONTACT: 519-376-3860, Ministry of Natural Resources.

Tom Thomson Memorial Art Gallery

WHERE: 840 First Ave. W., on west bank of Sydenham River beside the library.

WHEN: September through June, open Tuesday to Saturday, 10 a.m. to 5 p.m.; Sunday, noon to 5 p.m.; Wednesday, 7 p.m. to 9 p.m. July through August, also open Monday, 10 a.m. to 5 p.m., but closed Wednesday evening. Admission by voluntary donation.

WHAT: The Gallery is located a few kilometres from the boyhood home of Tom Thomson, one of Canada's best-known landscape painters. A small display of Thomson's work and memorabilia is changed periodically throughout the year. In summer, work by Thomson and the Group of Seven is mounted, together with other selections from the permanent collection. From September to June, exhibitions change monthly. Washrooms, gallery shop, wheelchair accessible.

CONTACT: 519-376-1932, Tom Thomson Memorial Art Gallery.

Waterfalls

WHERE: Around Owen Sound.

WHEN: Year round. Best seen in spring or fall.

WHAT: Three beautiful waterfalls on three different rivers tumble down near Owen Sound, each preserved in a small park. At **Inglis Falls**, on the Sydenham River, you can dine on picnic tables around a small lake formed by the dam above the falls. Just below the falls, 40.5-ha (100-a.) Harrison Park includes tennis courts, wading and swimming pools, playgrounds, campground, picnic areas, mini-golf, paddle boats, nature trails and a restaurant. **Indian Falls**, on the Indian River, is located in the 12.2-ha (30-a.) Indian Falls Conservation Area. The horseshoe-shaped falls, which are reached by a 1-km (.6-mi.) hike from the parking area, plummet off a limestone ledge into a steep-walled canyon. **Jones Falls** is a 11.9-m (39-ft.) cataract on the Pottawatomi River reached on a short trail from the parking area of the Grey-Bruce Tourist Association Office and Information Centre, just north of the intersection of Hwy. 8, Hwy. 21 and Hwy. 70 at the Village of Springmount, 5 km (3 mi.) west of Owen Sound.

CONTACT: 1-800-265-3127 or 519-371-2071, Grey-Bruce Tourist Association Office and Information Centre.

Penetanguishene

St. James On-the-Lines Anglican Church

WHERE: 223 Church St.

WHEN: Open April through October, weekdays 10 a.m. to 4 p.m. Services held year round, Sunday, at 9:30 a.m.

WHAT: This little church, built in 1836, is believed to have been named for the line, or communications road, from Toronto to Penetanguishene. The church has a very wide aisle to permit soldiers to march in four abreast, and the pews are of individual construction. It is believed that different men of the garrison were

---

detailed to make pews, each in his own way. Not wheelchair accessible. CONTACT: 705-549-2223, St. James On-the-Lines Church.

Point Clark

Point Clark Lightkeeper's Museum

WHERE: Point Clark, 18 km (11 mi.) south of Kincardine off Hwy. 21 at Amberley.

WHEN: Open mid-June to Labour Day, daily, 11 a.m. to 5 p.m. Admission to the museum by donation. Token charge to climb the lighthouse.

WHAT: The two-storey home, built in 1857, housed the keepers of the Point Clark lighthouse. It is now a museum containing marine artifacts. Washrooms, picnic area, beach.

CONTACT: 519-395-2494, June through Labour Day; 519-395-3735, Township of Huron, clerk's office, year round.

Southampton

Bruce County Museum and Archives

WHERE: 33 Victoria St. N.

WHEN: Year round. May through Labour Day, open Monday to Saturday, 9 a.m. to 5 p.m.; Sunday, 1 p.m. to 5 p.m. After Labour Day, same hours but closed Saturday.

WHAT: Nine galleries on various themes show the history and cultural heritage of Bruce County. The Museum includes two fully furnished period buildings and archives. Summer children's programmes, special activity events and exhibitions, washrooms, gift shop. Washrooms and half of the museum wheelchair accessible.

CONTACT: 519-797-2080, Bruce County Museum.

Thornbury

Thornbury Fish Lock

WHERE: On Hwy. 26, 22 km (14 mi.) west of Collingwood.

WHEN: Visit April and May for trout going upstream, October and November for trout going downstream.

WHAT: This is the only lock of its kind in Ontario, installed to allow rainbow trout to migrate over the Thornbury Dam and further up the Beaver River to spawn.

CONTACT: 519-376-3860, Ministry of Natural Resources.

Tiverton

Bruce Nuclear Power Development

WHERE: West off Hwy. 21, just north of Tiverton.

WHEN: Year round. Mid-April through mid-October, open daily, 9 a.m. to 4 p.m. Rest of the year, closed weekends.

WHAT: Canada's largest nuclear development boasts two nuclear generating stations and a heavy water plant. In the information centre, sound films and animated displays explain nuclear power. There is also a large-scale working model of a CANDU nuclear generating station. The bus tour around the development plus a fifteen-minute film takes a total of one hour. Washrooms, picnic tables, cafeteria, first aid, all wheelchair accessible.

CONTACT: 519-368-TOUR, Bruce Nuclear Power Development.

Tobermory

The Bruce Trail

WHERE: Tobermory.

WHEN: Spring through early winter.

WHAT: Tobermory is the northern terminus of a hiking trail along the Niagara Escarpment which starts at Queenston in the Niagara Peninsula. The Escarpment, a rugged wall of limestone up to 100 m (328 ft.) high, crosses Southern Ontario, forms the eastern side of the Bruce Peninsula, submerges off Tobermory, then reappears as islands in Fathom Five Marine Park, and reappears again as Manitoulin Island. The Bruce Trail is 700 km (435 mi.) long. Its most spectacular sections are found in the Bruce Peninsula, a long finger of limestone that separates Georgian Bay from the main basin of Lake Huron. A free map of the trail is available at Tobermory and District Chamber of Commerce office.

CONTACT: 519-596-2452, Tobermory and District Chamber of Commerce.

Walkerton

Farmers Market

WHERE: Walkerton Fairgrounds.

WHEN: Open May through mid-December, Friday, 3 p.m. to 7 p.m.

WHAT: Vendors offer fresh produce, seafoods, baking and sweets, country crafts and flowers. Wheelchair-accessible washrooms, snack bar.

CONTACT: 519-881-3912 or 519-881-0037.

Wasaga Beach

Nancy Island Historic Site

WHERE: Wasaga Beach Provincial Park, Mosley St. and 3rd St. off Hwy. 92.

WHEN: Victoria Day through third weekend in June, open weekends only. Last week of June through Labour Day, open daily, 10 a.m. to 6 p.m., including weekends. A fee is charged for bringing vehicles into the park, but visitors may walk in without charge.

WHAT: This is a memorial to the supply schooner *Nancy*, sole surviving vessel on the Upper Lakes near the end of the War of 1812. She was attacked and destroyed here in 1814. Her charred hull has been recovered and now rests inside an enclosure beside the Museum, which houses displays and artifacts dealing with water travel in the early 1800s and the War of 1812. A video show in a theatre portrays the destruction of the *Nancy* and the subsequent capture of two American attacking vessels. Washrooms, picnic tables, first aid, guided and self-guided tours, all wheelchair accessible.

CONTACT: 705-429-2516, Nancy Island Historic Site; 705-429-2728, Nancy Island during operating season.

Wiarton

Cape Croker Indian Reserve

WHERE: 19 km (11.8 mi.) north of Wiarton, off County Rd. 9.

WHEN: Year round.

WHAT: A large Ojibwa settlement offers visitors craft shops, picnic areas, swimming, boating, fishing and hiking.

Metropolitan Toronto

Includes: Alton, Bolton, Bramalea, Brampton, Malton, Mississauga, Port Credit, Streetsville and their environs.

(NOTE: You can get just about anywhere within Metro Toronto on the subway cars, buses and street cars of the Toronto Transit Commission. The fare is $1.30 a trip or you can get a day pass with unlimited use for $5. That's cheaper than parking your car for one hour at many downtown lots.)

Metropolitan Toronto consists of five cities and one borough: Toronto, North York, York, Etobicoke, Scarborough and the Borough of East York. Together they cover a total of 400 square kilometres (144 square miles). Approximately two-thirds of Toronto's three million residents were born and raised somewhere else. Half a million Italians make Metro the largest Italian community outside Italy. Metro is also home to the largest Chinese community in Canada and the biggest Portuguese community in North America. The ethnic mix makes for diversified dining experiences and cultural celebrations with a multitude of races and cultures represented.

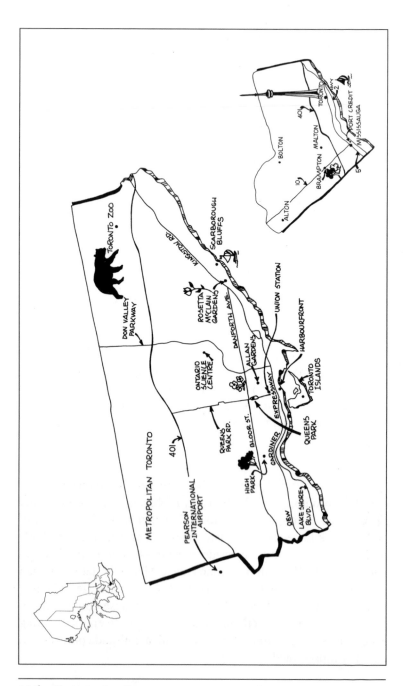

Festivals, Carnivals, Celebrations, Special Events:

JANUARY: Toronto, *Tropicanada*: Toronto, Harbourfront, *A Winter Heatwave* (celebrates the "cold" aspects of Canadian winter and focuses on warm inviting countries).

FEBRUARY: Brampton, Peel Heritage Complex, *Heritage Day* (horse and wagon rides, children's activities); North York, North York Central Library, *Annual Toronto Festival of Storytelling;* Toronto, Harbourfront, *Salute to Black History Month.*

APRIL: Toronto, *Annual Beaches Easter Parade.*

MAY: Toronto, Ontario Place, *Children's Festival;* Toronto, Harbourfront, *Annual Early Music Festival;* Rexdale, Woodbine Centre, *Kids Sense;* Mississauga, Bradley Museum, *Wonders of Wool* (sheep shearing, spinning, petting zoo); Scarborough, Scarborough Historical Museum, *Victoria's Visit* (Queen Victoria visits and receives her subjects); Toronto, *Queen Victoria's Birthday Parade;* North York, The Gibson House Museum, *The Queen's Birthday;* Etobicoke, Sherway Gardens Shopping Centre, *Simply For Kids* (hands-on arts and crafts exhibits); Streetsville, *Bread and Honey Festival* (beer tent, dog trials, petting zoo).

JUNE: Weston, Weston Farmers Market, *Opening Day Celebrations* (fiddlers, highland dancing, cloggers); Toronto, MacMillan Theatre, *The Glory of Mozart Festival;* Toronto, *Metro International Caravan;* Toronto, *Strawberry Tea at Spadina;* Port Credit, *Riverfest* (children's village, Bavarian garden, food emporium, petting zoo); Toronto, Ontario Place, *Benson and Hedges Symphony of Fire* (musical firework competition); Toronto, along Bloor St. between Bathurst and Spadina, *The Fringe of Toronto Festival* (celebration of theatre and the performing arts); Toronto, Exhibition Grounds, *CHIN International Picnic* (folk dance and singing groups, bikini pageant, kick boxing, boat and bicycle races).

JULY: Brampton, *Carabram* (ethnic groups display their cultures through song, dance, food and displays); Toronto, Metro Toronto

Convention Centre, *All-Star Fanfest* (tribute to the Toronto Blue Jays baseball team members, past and present); Toronto, *Caribana*.

AUGUST: North York, Mel Lastman Square, *Back to the Sixties* (afternoon of fun and music); Toronto, Black Creek Pioneer Village, *Corn on the Cob Days;* Mississauga, Bradley Museum, *Corn Fest.*

SEPTEMBER: North York, Mel Lastman Square, *Circus in the Square;* Thornhill, *Village Festival and Parade* (Bavarian gardens, nineteenth-century costume contest); Toronto, *Arts Week* (festival of dance, music, theatre, writing and publishing); Etobicoke, *Applewood Fall Fair.*

OCTOBER: Weston, *Fall Fair* (pumpkin carving competitions); Toronto, *Harvest Festival;* Rexdale, Woodbine Centre, *Ride and Treat* (children visit dressed up rides and receive a treat from each).

NOVEMBER: Toronto, Historic Fort York, *Remembrance Day Service;* Toronto, Black Creek Pioneer Village, *An Early Canadian Christmas;* Toronto and Brampton, *Santa Claus parades.*

DECEMBER: Toronto, Harbourfront, *Festival of Festive Breads* (breads made around the world especially for holidays); North York, *Hogmanay* (nineteenth-century style Scottish New Year celebration).

More detailed information on the festivals, carnivals, celebrations and other attractions of Metropolitan Toronto is available from: Metropolitan Toronto Travel Association, 207 Queen's Quay W., Suite 509, P.O. Box 126, Toronto, Ontario M5J 1A7, 800-363-9821 from Ontario, Greater Montreal and Continental U.S.A., or 416-368-9821.

Brampton

Chinguacousy Park

WHERE: Northeast corner of Brampton, Bramalea Rd. and Hwy. 7.

WHEN: Year round, daily. May 1 to September 15, open noon to 7:45 p.m. September 16 to April 30, open noon to 3:45 p.m. Closed Christmas and New Year's Day.

WHAT: The 40.5-ha (100-a.) park and animal farm features a variety of domestic farm animals, two greenhouses and 4.1 ha (10 a.) of formal gardens. In season, concerts are held in a bandshell. Various festivals and special events are held year round. Mini-golf, concessions, picnic areas, wheelchair-accessible washrooms.

CONTACT: 416-874-2937, Chinguacousy Park Office.

Mississauga

Dr. Flea's Flea Market

WHERE: 1590 Dundas St. E.

WHEN: Open year round, Saturday and Sunday, 10 a.m. to 5 p.m.

WHAT: More than 200 vendors are on-site. Free parking and hourly giveaways.

CONTACT: 416-848-4663, Dr. Flea's Mississauga Flea Market.

Lakeview Generating Station

WHERE: From the Queen Elizabeth Way, drive south on Dixie Rd. to Lakeshore Rd. and west to Hydro Rd.

WHEN: Open year round by appointment only, Monday to Friday (except Tuesday), 9 a.m. to 4 p.m. Tours may be arranged for Monday, Wednesday and Thursday evenings and weekends with two weeks' notice. No children under eight. Flat walking shoes recommended—no sandals.

WHAT: This coal-fired generating station has a capacity of 2400 megawatts. The ninety-minute tour includes a lecture and film followed by a walking tour of the plant. Wheelchair-accessible washrooms.

CONTACT: 416-274-3461, Lakeview Generating Station.

Mississauga Civic Centre

WHERE: 300 City Centre Dr. From Hwy. 401 to Hwy. 403, exit south at Hurontario St. (Hwy. 10) to Burnhamthorpe Rd. W. and drive 1 km (.6 mi.). Civic Centre is one block north of Burnhamthorpe Rd. on City Centre Dr., immediately west of Square One Shopping Centre.

WHEN: Year round. One-hour guided tour available Monday to Friday, 10 a.m. and 2 p.m. Evening tours available by request Monday to Friday, 6:30 p.m. and 8 p.m., with booking two weeks in advance. Closed Easter and all statutory holidays except January 1, when special community events take place.

WHAT: The Centre is a multi-purpose facility for municipal government and community use. A reflecting pool is used as a skating rink in winter. A 300-person amphitheatre is available for musical and theatrical performances. Inside the Civic Centre you will find a conservatory, main floor art gallery, public cafeteria, washrooms, and clock tower that affords a good view of the city. Guided tours are available and there's a fifteen-minute multi-image slide show. Wheelchair accessible, wheelchairs available, emergency first aid.

CONTACT: 416-896-5056, Mississauga Civic Centre.

Allan Gardens

WHERE: Bounded by Sherbourne, Jarvis, Gerrard and Carlton streets.

WHEN: Open year round, daily, 10 a.m. to 5 p.m.

WHAT: A lush all-season garden of tropical plants and trees grows under this domed greenhouse. Washrooms. Not wheelchair accessible.

CONTACT: 416-392-7291, Department of Parks and Recreation.

Archaeological Resource Centre

WHERE: Danforth Collegiate and Technical Institute, 840 Greenwood Ave. 1992 dig site, northeast corner of Trinity-Bellwoods Park, east off Gore Vale Ave.

WHEN: Open mid-May through October, Monday to Friday, 9 a.m. to 4:30 p.m.

WHAT: The Archaeological Resource Centre is an experiment in urban archaeology in the heart of the city. You can tour the dig or, if you are over the age of nine, you can participate. Make arrangements in advance by telephoning the Centre. Washrooms, wheelchair ramp at the site.

CONTACT: 416-393-0665, Archaeological Resource Centre, Toronto Board of Education.

Art at 80 Spadina

WHERE: 80 Spadina Ave.

WHEN: Year round. Nineteen of the galleries are open Tuesday to Saturday, 11 a.m. to 6 p.m. The Albert White Gallery is open same days, but its hours are 10 a.m. to 5 p.m.

WHAT: Twenty galleries of contemporary fine art in solo and group shows feature Canadian and international artists. All styles in all media are represented—from avant garde to traditional.

CONTACT: 416-366-3690, Art at 80 Spadina.

Art Gallery of Ontario and The Grange

WHERE: 317 Dundas St. W., just east of the Eaton Centre.

WHEN: Open year round. Free admission to the Art Gallery and The Grange for all on Wednesday, 5:30 p.m. to 9 p.m., and for seniors (65 and over) Friday, 11 a.m. to 5:30 p.m. Admission charge at other times.

WHAT: The AGO includes twenty large galleries highlighting Western art, Renaissance art, impressionist, post-impressionist and modernist works. The Henry Moore Sculpture Centre displays 893 pieces by the English sculptor. The Canadian Wing is devoted to Canadian art from the past three centuries. The Grange, located behind the AGO, is a Georgian manor that was the Gallery's first home and is Toronto's oldest remaining brick building. The Grange is furnished to the 1830s era. Both wheelchair accessible.

CONTACT: 416-977-0414, Art Gallery of Ontario.

Canada's Sports Hall of Fame

WHERE: Exhibition Place (beside the Hockey Hall of Fame, to which there is a small admission charge).

WHEN: Open year round, daily, 10 a.m. to 4:30 p.m. Open to 10 p.m. daily during the Canadian National Exhibition. Closed Christmas and Good Friday.

WHAT: On three floors, thousands of sports artifacts and memorabilia are displayed, some relating to sports you may have never known existed. The Hall of Fame honours outstanding achievements by Canadian athletes. Entrance ramp for wheelchairs and elevators to all three exhibit galleries. Washrooms.

CONTACT: 416-595-1046, Canada's Sports Hall of Fame.

Casa Loma

WHERE: 1 Austin Terr.

WHEN: Daily, year round.

WHAT: There is a charge to take the tour of Casa Loma, its grounds and the palatial stables. However, there is no charge to admire this ostentatious extension of Sir Henry Pellatt's ego from the outside. He built the ninety-eight-room castle between 1911 and 1914 and lived in it until the 1920s. When his fortunes reversed, he had to dismiss the forty servants and move out.

CONTACT: 416-923-1171, Casa Loma.

Centreville, Centre Island *(See also Toronto Islands)*

WHERE: Toronto Islands Park in Lake Ontario. Catch the ferry at the foot of Bay St. and stop at any of the three islands.

WHEN: Late April to mid-May and September, ferry runs on weekends, 10:30 a.m. to 6 p.m. Victoria Day through Labour Day, ferry runs daily 10:30 a.m. to 8 p.m. The park is free but there is a charge for the ferry and for the amusement rides. All-day passes are available.

WHAT: Centreville features rides and amusements for the whole family, including miniature golf. Picnic area, food concessions, steak house.

CONTACT: 416-363-1112, Beasley Amusements, Etobicoke.

City Hall

WHERE: Northwest corner of Queen St. and Bay St.

WHEN: Open year round, daily, 8:30 a.m. to 4:30 p.m.

WHAT: This futuristic building, built in 1965, features a clam-shaped council chambers flanked by two semi-circular office towers. The towers, 20 and 27 storeys tall, were impressive when built but are now dwarfed by surrounding skyscrapers. They look down on the dome of the council chambers and a large public square with a reflecting pool that is used in the winter as a skating rink. Sculptures, cafeteria, restaurant. Completely wheelchair accessible. Free concerts and other events are frequently held in Nathan Philips Square.

CONTACT: 416-392-7341, City Clerk's Department, Information and Communication Services Division.

CN Tower

WHERE: 301 Front St. W., but may be seen from almost anywhere in Metro where you get an unobstructed view.

WHEN: Daily, year round.

WHAT: There is a charge to go to the top of the world's tallest free-standing structure which is 553 m (1,815 ft. 5 in.) high. Up top there's a night club, revolving restaurant and observation deck. At the base of the tower there's a family-style restaurant and pool lounge, Canada's Business Hall of Fame, shops and Tour of the

Universe, a flight simulator which gives paying customers a realistic flight to Jupiter and back.

CONTACT: 416-360-8500, CN Tower.

David Dunlap Observatory

WHERE: 123 Hillsview Dr., Richmond Hill, 5 km (3 mi.) north of Hwy. 7, west of Bayview Ave. (GO buses will stop at Hillsview Dr. on request.)

WHEN: Tours offered all year, Tuesday, 10 a.m. (no viewing). April through October, Saturday evenings except holiday weekends, tours and viewings available by reservations only. During inclement weather, Saturday evening tours but no star-gazing. No children under seven.

WHAT: The observatory, which is part of the University of Toronto, is a centre for education and research in astronomy and astrophysics. The dome houses the main telescope, the largest in Canada, with a 188-cm (74-in.) mirror. Washrooms. Not wheelchair accessible. No pets.

CONTACT: 416-884-2112, David Dunlap Observatory.

Dr. Flea's Flea Market—Rexdale

WHERE: 4 Westmore Dr., Rexdale.

WHEN: Open year round, Saturday and Sunday, 10 a.m. to 5 p.m.

WHAT: The Rexdale flea market includes more than 250 vendors, both indoors and outdoors. Free parking. Hourly give-aways.

CONTACT: 416-745-3532, Dr. Flea's Highway 27 and Albion Flea Market.

Eaton Centre

WHERE: On Yonge St., between Dundas St. and Queen St.

WHEN: Open year round. Store hours: Monday to Friday, 10 a.m. to 9 p.m.; Saturday, 9:30 a.m. to 6 p.m.; Sunday, noon to 5 p.m.

Extended hours for Christmas season from late October. Some restaurants and services have extended hours.

WHAT: This greenery-filled, glass-roofed shrine to retail merchandising comprises 330 shops and services, restaurants, pubs and a seventeen-screen movie theatre complex, all wheelchair accessible and visited by more than one million people each week. If that's not enough to fray your credit cards, The Bay's flagship department store is linked to the Centre by an enclosed walkway above Queen St.

CONTACT: 416-979-3300, Marketing Coordinator, The Eaton Centre.

Edwards Garden

WHERE: Southwest corner of Leslie St. and Lawrence Ave. E., on Wilket Creek, approximately 3 km (2 mi.) south of Hwy. 401 on Leslie St.

WHEN: Open year round. Tours provided early May through early September, Tuesday and Thursday, 11 a.m. and 2 p.m.

WHAT: This garden park features floral displays, rock gardens, shade trees and winding streams. Snack bar open daily in summer. Washrooms wheelchair accessible.

CONTACT: 416-392-8140 or 416-392-2526, Edwards Gardens, Toronto Department of Parks and Property.

Enoch Turner Schoolhouse

WHERE: 106 Trinity St., near King St. and Parliament St.

WHEN: Open year round, Monday to Friday, 9:30 a.m. to 4:30 p.m. Closed holidays. (It's wise to call ahead in case there's a school group on tour.)

WHAT: This restored 1848 schoolhouse provides a fascinating link to Ontario's educational heritage, including a nineteenth-century school-day programme for visiting school children. Washrooms, wheelchair accessible, picnic tables in nearby park.

CONTACT: 416-863-0010, Enoch Turner Schoolhouse.

George Scott Railton
Salvation Army Heritage Centre

WHERE: 2130 Bayview Ave. (Take the Davisville 28B bus from Lawrence Station to Dawlish.)

WHEN: Open year round, Monday to Friday, 9 a.m. to 4:30 p.m.

WHAT: The Centre houses a collection of artifacts and documents relating to the work of the Salvation Army in Canada and Bermuda. Washrooms, wheelchair accessible.

CONTACT: 416-481-4441, Salvation Army George Scott Railton Heritage Centre.

Gooderham Building

WHERE: At Front St. and Wellington St., where they meet at Church St.

WHEN: Year round.

WHAT: Known as the flatiron building, this unique structure makes a signature photograph of a visit to Toronto. Morning is the best time to visit the east-facing building, but for afternoons there's also a colourful mural on the back of the building, which faces west. The architectural oddity was built for Gooderham's Distilling Company in 1892 to fit into the deep V shape of the lot.

Harbourfront
(See also The Power Plant at Harbourfront)

WHERE: Queen's Quay W., between York St. and Bathurst St. The main activity centre is located at 235 Queen's Quay W., just west of York St. (Take York St. exit from the Gardiner Expressway or Lakeshore Blvd.)

WHEN: Open daily, year round. Antique Market and Power Plant Art Gallery closed Mondays. Most shops, including Queen's Quay Terminal, open seven days a week, 10 a.m. to 9 p.m. Entire site closed December 25 and January 1. Admission free to the site and many special events.

WHAT: Harbourfront is a 37-ha (92-a.) site which stretches from Bathurst St. to York St. along 4 km (2.5 mi.) of Lake Ontario's shoreline. More than 4,000 special events are offered each year, including dance, theatre, music, art shows, seniors' programmes, films, literary readings, an antique market, sailing courses, visiting ships, multicultural festivals and community events. Free activities for all ages include crafts, art and a children's drop-in centre. Many shops, boutiques and restaurants are open daily, including Sunday and holidays. There are marinas, children's playgrounds, picnic areas and an ice-skating rink with skate rentals. In Harbourfront proper, at the foot of York St., you will find a two-level courtyard and arcade with ninety-nine boutiques and cafes. Each of the tiny shops carries a unique line of Canadian-made merchandise. All buildings, and washrooms in York Quay Centre, are wheelchair accessible.

CONTACT: 416-973-3000, Harbourfront Corporation.

High Park and Menagerie

WHERE: In High Park between Queen St. and Bloor St. W., west side of Parkside Dr. Main gate on Bloor St. W. Other entrances off Parkside Dr. and Lake Shore Blvd. at Colborne Lodge Dr. By public transportation, exit at High Park Subway Station or take the College St. streetcar east.

WHEN: Open year round, daily.

WHAT: This large, hilly park contains gardens and Grenadier Pond, so named because British soldiers used to drill on its frozen surface in the 1850s. The menagerie includes birds, bison, buffalo, deer, yaks, llamas and swans. The park also contains Colborne Lodge, home of architect John Howard, who bequeathed the land and home to the city. The home is touted as one of the first in Upper Canada to have an indoor toilet. It is also said to be haunted by Howard's wife, who died of a lingering illness in the upstairs bedroom. Restaurant, concessions, swimming pool and wading pool (May to September), tennis courts, playgrounds, nature trail, pond, wheelchair-accessible washrooms.

CONTACT: 416-392-7251, High Park, Dept. of Parks and Recreation.

Holocaust Education and Memorial Centre

WHERE: 4600 Bathurst St., Lipa Green Community Building, 4th Floor.

WHEN: Open year round, Tuesday and Thursday, 1 p.m. to 4:30 p.m.; Sunday, 11 a.m. to 4:30 p.m. Donations welcome.

WHAT: The Centre presents a panorama of Jewish life in pre-Nazi Europe and a continuous slide presentation, *Images of the Holocaust.* A half-hour audio-visual documentary, *From Out of the Depths,* portrays the experiences of European Jews before, during and after the Second World War. Cafeteria in the Jewish Community Centre in the building. Holocaust resource book available for sale. Wheelchair accessible.

CONTACT: 416-635-2883, Ext. 144, Holocaust Remembrance Committee, Jewish Federation of Greater Toronto.

James Gardens

WHERE: On the west bank of the Humber River at Edenbridge Dr. and Edgehill Rd., just east of Royal York Rd.

WHEN: Open year round.

WHAT: Terraced gardens and spring-fed pools, graceful bridges and a quiet gazebo are nestled amidst towering trees and a wide variety of plantings.

CONTACT: 416-392-8186, Metropolitan Toronto Parks and Property Dept.

Joseph D. Carrier Art Gallery

WHERE: 901 Lawrence Ave. W.

WHEN: Open Monday and Friday, 9:30 a.m. to 5 p.m.; Tuesday to Thursday, 9:30 a.m. to 8:30 p.m.; Saturday and Sunday, 10 a.m. to 5 p.m.

WHAT: The changing multi-media exhibits emphasize Canadian sculpture and other works. Sculpture patio. Gift shop. Wheelchair access to both floors. Free parking. Cafe and restaurant.

CONTACT: 416-789-7011, Joseph D. Carrier Art Gallery.

Kensington Market

WHERE: West of Spadina Ave., below College St. on Baldwin St., Augusta Ave. and Kensington Ave.

WHEN: Open year round, Monday to Saturday, from the very early morning.

WHAT: This open-air European-style market offers all manner of foodstuffs, used clothing, used records, baked goods and antiques. There are some stalls where the visitor may haggle over prices. Great cafés, bistros and restaurants.

Maple Leaf Gardens

WHERE: 60 Carlton St.

WHEN: Open year round, Monday to Friday, 9 a.m. to 6 p.m. Sometimes open on weekends.

WHAT: This 16,000-seat arena is home to the Toronto Maple Leafs hockey team. In the lobby, you'll find an interesting collection of photos chronicling the Leafs' history, including every Stanley Cup team.

CONTACT: 416-977-1641, Maple Leaf Gardens.

Market Gallery

WHERE: 95 Front St. E. at Jarvis, 2nd Floor.

WHEN: Open year round, Wednesday to Friday, 10 a.m. to 4 p.m.; Saturday, 9 a.m. to 4 p.m.; Sunday, noon to 4 p.m. Closed holidays.

WHAT: This gallery, operated by the City of Toronto, is located in the renovated section of the South St. Lawrence Market, which housed Toronto's second city hall from 1845 to 1899. The historical and contemporary exhibitions showcase the extensive archival and artistic collections owned by the city. Refreshments available in the market. Catalogues, postcards and posters for sale. Washrooms. Wheelchair accessible.

CONTACT: 416-392-7604, Market Gallery.

Metro Toronto Library

WHERE: On the east side of Yonge St., just north of Asquith Ave. (one block north of Bloor St.).

WHEN: Open year round, Monday to Thursday, 9 a.m. to 9 p.m.; Friday, 9 a.m. to 6 p.m.; Saturday, 9 a.m. to 5 p.m.; Sunday, 1:30 p.m. to 5 p.m. July and August, closed at 8 p.m. weekdays. Closed Sunday, May through Thanksgiving.

WHAT: Four tiers of balconies overlook the main floor foyer, a central fountain, lots of indoor greenery and a glass-walled elevator. Books and materials housed in the central branch are for reference only and cannot be removed from the premises. There is a periodical room on the main floor where visitors may catch up on out-of-town magazines and newspapers. Full facilities for disabled people.

CONTACT: 416-393-7000, Metro Toronto Library.

Metropolitan Toronto Police Museum

WHERE: Police Headquarters, 40 College St.

WHEN: Never closed.

WHAT: Exhibits depict the history of the Metropolitan Toronto Police Force, including artifacts relating to crimes committed in Toronto. Exhibits explain how the force is meeting contemporary challenges. A gift shop with souvenirs and police-related kitsch is open Monday to Friday, 11 a.m. to 3 p.m.

CONTACT: 416-324-6201, Metropolitan Toronto Police Museum.

North York City Hall

WHERE: 5100 Yonge St.

WHEN: Open 9 a.m. to 3:30 p.m., by appointment only.

WHAT: Forty-five-minute guided tours of municipal offices highlight the architecture and civic role of the hall.

CONTACT: 416-224-6411, North York City Hall.

Old City Hall

WHERE: 60 Queen St. E. facing down Bay St.

WHEN: Open year round during business hours.

WHAT: This lovely Romanesque Revival-style building caused as much of a stir when it opened in 1899 as Toronto's new City Hall caused when it opened in 1965. As you enter there's a great stained glass window and marble columns. The wooden floors are from Georgia and the City's coat of arms is stamped into many of the door knobs. The building is constructed of sandstone from the Credit River valley, grey stone from the Orangeville area and brown stone from New Brunswick. Outside, under the eaves, you will find carvings and gargoyles. The latter are said to be caricatures of city councillors of the day and architect James Lennox.

Ontario Legislative Buildings

WHERE: Queen's Park, one block north of College St. and University Ave.

WHEN: Labour Day to mid-May, open Monday to Friday, 9 a.m. to 5:30 p.m. Mid-May to Labour Day, open daily, 9 a.m. to 5:30 p.m. Chamber open to 4:30 p.m. The Legislature is generally in session mid-February to June and October to December.

WHAT: The Provincial Parliament Buildings of Ontario were built of pink sandstone between 1886 and 1893, combining at least four distinct architectural styles. Special features include a grand staircase in the lobby and beautiful wood carvings. Hallways are lined with paintings of serious-looking politicians and Canadian scenes and there's a display of minerals. Free tickets are needed for admission to the visitors' gallery to watch the Legislative Assembly in session. Ramps and washrooms wheelchair accessible.

CONTACT: 416-325-7500, Parliamentary Public Relations Office.

Osgoode Hall and Museum

WHERE: 130 Queen St. W., just west of City Hall.

WHEN: Museum open all year, Monday to Friday, 10 a.m. to 3:30 p.m. Closed holidays. Tours of Osgoode Hall offered July and August, Monday to Friday, 1 p.m. and 1:20 p.m.

WHAT: This Regency-style building, which became the home of the Law Society in 1832, was modified into a Palladian-style structure in 1844. It is named after the province's first chief justice, William Osgoode. Since 1874 the Supreme Court of Ontario has owned the west part of the building while the east section and the space occupied by the Great Library are still owned by the Law Society. A small museum features changing exhibits and permanent displays describing the history of the legal profession in Ontario.

CONTACT: 416-947-3300, The Law Society of Upper Canada.

The Power Plant at Harbourfront

WHERE: 231 Queen's Quay W.

WHEN: Open year round, Tuesday to Saturday, noon to 8 p.m.; Sunday, noon to 6 p.m. Closed Monday, open holiday Mondays. Admission by donation.

WHAT: Built as a power station in 1927 for the ice-making plant that supplied the nearby warehouse—now Queen's Quay Terminal— the Power Plant is now an ever-changing showcase for the best in contemporary art from across Canada and around the world. Gift shop sells art catalogues. Wheelchair accessible.

CONTACT: 416-973-4949, The Power Plant at Harbourfront.

Redpath Sugar Museum

WHERE: 95 Queen's Quay E. between Yonge St. and Jarvis St.

WHEN: Open year round, Monday to Friday, 10 a.m. to noon and 1 p.m. to 3:30 p.m. Closed December 25 and January 1.

WHAT: The museum, located inside the Redpath Refinery, depicts the history of sugar and the Ontario sugar beet industry, modern refining methods, nutritional issues, and the place of the Redpath family and company in Canadian industrial history. Wheelchair accessible.

CONTACT: 416-366-3561, Redpath Sugar Museum.

Riverdale Farm

WHERE: Riverdale Park, 201 Winchester St., three blocks east of Parliament St., north of Gerrard.

WHEN: Year round, daily. Summer, open 9 a.m. to 6 p.m. Spring and fall, open 9 a.m. to 5 p.m. Winter, open 9 a.m. to 4 p.m.

WHAT: This turn-of-the-century family farm is set on a hillside overlooking the Don River in central Toronto. Period farm implements are displayed. Livestock include horses, cattle, mules, poultry, duck, sheep, chickens and pigs. Handcraft workshops. No dogs. Don't feed the animals. Picnic area and washrooms wheelchair accessible.

CONTACT: 416-392-6794, recording with opening times, Department of Parks and Recreation, New City Hall, or 416-392-0843.

Rosetta McClain Gardens

WHERE: On the Scarborough Bluffs, south of Kingston Rd., just east of Birchmount Rd.

WHEN: Year round.

WHAT: This garden park on Metro Toronto's waterfront is perched high above Lake Ontario on the Scarborough Bluffs. The park features raised planter beds, paved pathways and adjustable benches for use by disabled visitors. Enter through a trellised gateway and follow a path to an amphitheatre-like space containing a granite boulder fountain, raised planters and a trellised pergola. From the formal garden, paths radiate to other parts of the park, including a rose garden with gazebo and a scent garden.

CONTACT: 416-392-8186, Metropolitan Toronto Parks and Property Dept.

St. Lawrence Hall and Market

WHERE: St. Lawrence Hall, 157 King St. E., 3rd Floor. North St. Lawrence Market, 92 Front St. E., corner of Jarvis. South St. Lawrence Market, 91 Front St. E.

WHEN: Year round. North Market Building open Monday to Friday, 8 a.m. to 4 p.m. Farmers Market in North Building open Saturday from 5 a.m. South Building open Tuesday to Thursday, 8 a.m. to 6 p.m.; Friday, 8 a.m. to 7 p.m.; Saturday 5 a.m. to 5 p.m. Closed Sunday and Monday.

WHAT: The complex, established in 1850, combined a hall for public gatherings and a covered market at the rear. Toronto's first City Hall was built in the South Market in 1850-51 and restored in 1967. The Great Hall, with its ornamental plaster ceiling and gas-lighted chandelier, is a faithful reproduction of the original, in which P. T. Barnum first introduced Tom Thumb.

CONTACT: 416-392-7170, St. Lawrence Hall and Market.

St. Paul's Anglican Church

WHERE: 227 Bloor St. E.

WHEN: Open year round. Tours, Saturday and Sunday, noon to 2 p.m.

WHAT: The first parish church, first consecrated in 1842, has twice been enlarged. The early English Gothic-style church can seat 2,600 people.

CONTACT: 416-961-8116, St. Paul's Anglican Church.

Scadding Cabin

WHERE: Exhibition Place, south of Dufferin St. entrance.

WHEN: Open daily during the Canadian National Exhibition, noon to 8 p.m. and on July 1 weekend, noon to 8 p.m., or by appointment. (The CNE is usually held from mid-August through Labour Day weekend.) Admission by donation.

WHAT: This 1794 log cabin is the oldest remaining house in Toronto. It was moved to its present location by the York Pioneer and Historical Society and is preserved as an example of a late eighteenth-century pioneer residence.

CONTACT: 416-766-5964, Scadding Cabin.

Scarborough Bluffs

WHERE: Take Guildwood Pkwy. off Kingston Rd. E. Best views from Scarborough Bluffs Park at the foot of Midland Ave. or from the formal gardens of the Guild Inn on Guildwood Pkwy.

WHEN: Year round.

WHAT: Clay cliffs rise almost 90 m (300 ft.) from Lake Ontario. Visitors can see evidence of five glacial ages, demarcated by layers of sand and clay that once formed the floor of prehistoric lakes.

Scarborough Civic Centre

WHERE: 150 Borough Dr., northwest corner of McCowan Rd. and Ellesmere Rd., just south of Hwy. 401.

WHEN: Open year round, Monday to Friday, 9:30 a.m. to 4:30 p.m.; Saturday and Sunday, 11:30 a.m. to 4 p.m.

WHAT: The Civic Centre, in the heart of the Scarborough city centre, bas been home to Scarborough's municipal government since its opening in 1973. Monthly art exhibitions, weekly Sunday afternoon concerts, skating on the Square in winter.

CONTACT: 416-396-7212, Scarborough Civic Centre.

Second City "improvs"

WHERE: Second City dinner theatre, 110 Lombard St.

WHEN: Monday to Thursday, 10:15 p.m. to 11 p.m.

WHAT: Following their regular shows, the actors offer impromptu sketches inspired by audience suggestions. There is no admission charge for this portion of the show.

CONTACT: 416-863-1111, Second City.

Sigmund Samuel Building

WHERE: 14 Queen's Park Ct. W., opposite the Ontario Parliament Buildings.

WHEN: Victoria Day through Labour Day, open Monday to Saturday, 10 a.m. to 5 p.m.; Sunday, 1 p.m. to 5 p.m. Rest of the year, open same hours but closed Monday. Closed December 25 and January 1.

WHAT: This building contains a museum of antique Canadian room settings, furnishings, ceramics, silver and glassware with regularly changing exhibitions from the extensive collection of Canadian fine and decorative arts. One gallery is a wood-panelled room from 1820 Quebec. Wheelchair accessible with assistance.

CONTACT: 416-586-5524, Sigmund Samuel Building, Royal Ontario Museum.

Toronto's First Post Office

WHERE: 260 Adelaide St. E., one block east of Jarvis St. Parking off George St.

WHEN: Open year round, weekdays, 9 a.m. to 4 p.m.; weekends, 10 a.m. to 4 p.m. Closed holidays.

WHAT: Toronto's first post office and the Bank of Upper Canada building in the same block have been designated national historic sites. They are the only two surviving buildings on their original site in the Town of York. The post office is also the oldest building representing the British postal period (prior to 1851) in Canada. A postmaster in period costume provides contemporary postal service. For a small fee you can write a letter with a quill pen, seal it with sealing wax and mail it with the post office's distinctive cancellation. Wheelchair access from the parking lot.

CONTACT: 416-865-1833, Curator, Toronto's First Post Office.

Toronto Islands

WHERE: Immediately south of the city in Lake Ontario.

WHEN: Year round.

WHAT: The three connected islands are reached by ferries departing the foot of Bay St., every 15 minutes in summer, and less frequently the rest of the year. **Centre Island**, where the action is, includes Centreville (listed elsewhere), an amusement park for children. **Hanlan's Point Island** and **Ward's Island** are pleasant places to get away from the city's hectic pace. You can walk for miles amid huge old trees and along boardwalks. Hanlan's Point Island has free tennis courts. The Royal Canadian Yacht Club and Queen City Yacht Club are located in the islands and commuter flights land and take off from Island Airport. On Ward's Island, there's a small community of island residents living in winterized summer cottages.

CONTACT: 416-392-8193, Metropolitan Toronto Parks, recorded information about ferry schedules and fares.

Toronto Sculpture Garden

WHERE: 115 King St. E.

WHEN: Open year round, daily, from dawn to dusk.

WHAT: The art works featured are contemporary and many are large.

Toronto Stock Exchange

WHERE: 2 First Canadian Pl., King St. and York St. (St. Andrew subway station).

WHEN: Open year round, Monday to Friday, 9 a.m. to 4:30 p.m. Presentation and one-hour tour, Tuesday to Friday, 2 p.m.

WHAT: One of the world's major stock exchanges moved to its stunning new quarters in the Exchange Tower in 1983. The trading floor is one of the most technologically advanced in the world. Facilities include a visitors centre with display panels explaining the role and history of the market, a large public observation gallery and an auditorium for presentations. The Exchange is Canada's largest public marketplace for trading stocks and options. Wheelchair accessible.

CONTACT: 416-947-4670, Toronto Stock Exchange.

Ukrainian Museum of Canada, Ontario Branch

WHERE: St. Vladimir Institute, 620 Spadina Ave.

WHEN: Open year round, Tuesday to Friday, 11 a.m. to 4 p.m.; Saturday and Sunday, 1 p.m. to 4 p.m. Closed Mondays. Donations welcome.

WHAT: Exhibits depict Ukrainian cultural heritage and its contribution to the Canadian mosaic. A collection of regional costumes from the Ukraine is included. Archives, gift boutique. Wheelchair-accessible washrooms.

CONTACT: 416-923-3318, Ukrainian Museum of Canada.

Union Station

WHERE: On Front St. across from the Royal York Hotel.

WHEN: Never closed.

WHAT: This vast, cavernous monument to railroading opened in 1927. The palace-like facade is ornamented with twenty-two pillars of Bedford limestone, 11.5 m (38 ft.) tall, each weighing 68.5 tonnes (75.5 tons). The Italian tiled ceiling of the main lobby soars to 26 m (86 ft.).

University of Toronto Campus tour—and ghosts

WHERE: From the Map Room, Hart House, University of Toronto Campus, Queen's Park Ct. W. at Wellesley.

WHEN: One-hour walking tours offered June through August, Monday to Friday, 10:30 a.m., 1 p.m. and 2:30 p.m. Other times by appointment.

WHAT: The University of Toronto was established in 1827 when King George IV signed the charter for "a King's College in the Town of York, Capital of Upper Canada." With its tree-lined pathways and Gothic-style buildings covered in vines, the campus is redolent with history—and several ghosts. There are more than 200 university buildings in the area south of Bloor St. between Spadina Ave. and Bay St., two of which are haunted.

CONTACT: 416-978-4111, September to June; 416-978-5000, June to September, Alumni and Community Relations, University of Toronto.

Upper Canada Brewing Company

WHERE: 2 Atlantic Ave., south of King St., four blocks east of Dufferin.

WHEN: Year round. Tours Tuesday to Friday, 2 p.m.; Saturday, 1:30 p.m., 3 p.m. and 4:30 p.m. Retail store open Monday to Saturday, 10 a.m. to 8 p.m.

WHAT: Only 100 per cent natural ingredients are used by this cottage brewery in making its beer and ales. Free tastes are available at the sample bar. A gift shop sells beer-phernalia ranging from mugs to clothing. Wheelchair-accessible washroom.

CONTACT: 416-534-9281, Upper Canada Brewing Company.

Water Filtration Plant public tours

WHERE: Tour assembles at south entrance of the R. C. Harris Filtration Plant, 2701 Queen St. E. at Victoria Park.

WHEN: Forty-five-minute tours available year round, Saturday and Sunday, 10 a.m., 11:30 a.m., 1:30 p.m. and 3 p.m. Additional summer tours on Thursdays, same times. Children under ten must be accompanied by an adult. Not wheelchair accessible.

WHAT: This water filtration plant is distinguished by its palatial architecture.

CONTACT: 416-392-8209, Head Office, Metro Toronto Works Dept.

William Ashley Crystal Museum

WHERE: William Ashley Store, 50 Bloor St. W.

WHEN: Open year round, Monday to Wednesday, 10 a.m. to 6 p.m.; Thursday and Friday, 10 a.m. to 7:30 p.m.; Saturday, 9:30 a.m. to 5:30 p.m.

WHAT: The Art Of Glass exhibit features a small collection of works by international artisans. Wheelchair accessible through Holt-Renfrew store next door.

CONTACT: 416-964-2900, William Ashley Crystal Museum.

Ontario Science Centre

WHERE: Don Mills Rd. south of Eglinton Ave. E.

WHEN: Open year round, daily, 10 a.m. to 6 p.m., Friday to 9 p.m. Free admission and parking on Friday, 5 p.m. to 9 p.m. Admission and parking fee charged at all other times. Seniors free at any time.

WHAT: This hands-on fun place doesn't offer guided tours because the object is discovery. There are fifteen mini-theatres with short film or slide shows and it's hard to get past any of the 800-plus exhibits without learning something painlessly.

CONTACT: 416-429-4100, Ontario Science Centre.

Royal Ontario Museum

WHERE: 100 Queen's Park Ct.

WHEN: Open year round. Free admission Tuesdays, 4:30 p.m. to 8 p.m. Seniors free daily, 10 a.m. to 8 p.m. Admission charge at all other times.

WHAT: The continent's second-largest museum (after New York's Metropolitan) has collected more than six million items since 1912. There's a great dinosaur exhibit, a complete Ming tomb and a Jamaican limestone bat cave, to name but a few of the exhibits, which would take a week to cover in full. Snack bar, three gift shops, wheelchair accessible.

CONTACT: 416-586-5549, Royal Ontario Museum.

Spencer Clark Collection of Historic Architecture

WHERE: At the Guild Inn, 201 Guildwood Pkwy.

WHEN: Year round.

WHAT: The Guild Inn is an elegant hostelry, distinguished by its unique collection of architectural bits and pieces, which are scattered around the grounds. The collection was rescued from the remains of fifty Toronto-area buildings that were torn down or renovated. It includes the white marble facade of the old Imperial

---

Bank of Canada building, a fireplace from the home of Sir Frederick Banting, co-discoverer of insulin, and a 5-m (17-ft.) sign from Toronto's second firehall that reads "Engine House No. 2." The collection is owned by Metro Toronto.

Weather forecasts

WHERE: The Canada Life Building, Queen St. W and University Ave.

WHEN: Year round.

WHAT: A beacon tower atop the building signals weather forecasts: lights running up, temperature is rising; lights running down, temperature is falling; lights unchanging, temperature steady; steady red light on top, overcast; flashing red, rain; flashing white, snow; green, clear and sunny.

Getaway Country

Includes: Aurora, Bancroft, Beaverton, Belleville, Bobcaygeon, Cobourg, Haliburton, Lindsay, Markham, Newmarket, Oshawa, Peterborough, Picton, Trenton, Tweed, Whitby.

This region runs from the outskirts of Toronto through sparsely-settled farm country laced with lakes, north to the southern boundaries of Algonquin Park and east to the white sand beaches of historic Prince Edward County.

Festivals, Carnivals, Celebrations, Special Events:

JANUARY: Peterborough, Hutchison House, *Hogmanay* (Scottish festival); Bobcaygeon-Fenelon Falls, *North Victoria Frost Fest* (candlelight parades, sled dog race, polar plunge); Stanhope, *Snowfrolics;* Peterborough, *Snowfest;* Whitby, Lynde Shores Conservation Area, *Winter Bird Feeder Tour;* Minden, *Kinsmen Winter Carnival* (car racing on ice, fishing derby); Richmond Hill, *Winter Carnival* (bed races, sky diving, hot air balloons).

FEBRUARY: Wilberforce, *Loop Winter Carnival* (costumed ice skating party, toboggan run, hymn sing); Grafton, *From the Heart* (Valentine masterpieces); Bancroft, *Frosty Frolics;* Haliburton,

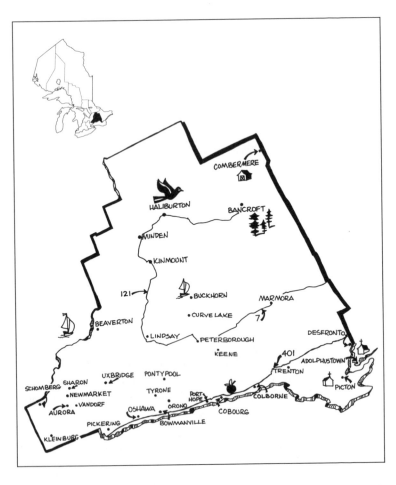

Winter Carnival; Vaughan, *Winterfest;* Peterborough, Lift Lock Visitor Centre, *Heritage Canoe Festival.*

MARCH: Peterborough, *Annual Trident Ice Floe Races;* Oshawa, Purple Woods Conservation Area, *Tours and Pancake Weekend;* Brighton, Presqu'ile Provincial Park, *Waterfowl Viewing Weekends;* Warkworth, *Maple Syrup Festival;* Stouffville, *Maple Syrup Festival.*

APRIL: Port Hope, *Float Your Fanny Down the Ganny* (canoe, kayak and crazy craft race the Ganaraska River); Whitby, *Spring*

Wings and Splash Downs (four look-outs to see migrating birds).

MAY: Maple, Canada's Wonderland, *Special Events* (start and run through September); Peterborough, Lang Pioneer Village, *Pioneer Mother's Day;* Belleville, Hastings County Museum, *Queen Victoria's Birthday;* Peterborough, Hutchison House Museum, *Lace Tea and Embroidery Demonstration;* Bobcaygeon, *Kids Karnival;* Colborne, *Apple Blossom Time;* Peterborough, *Netherlands Day;* Peterborough, Lang Pioneer Village, *Pioneer Sheep and Wool Craft Day;* Mount Albert, *Sports Day and Spring Fair.*

JUNE: Sharon, *June Day at Sharon Temple;* Markham, *Village Festival* (country hoedown dance, beer tent with band); Consecon, *Great Consecon Canoe Race and Fun Day;* Markham, *Founder's Day at Markham Museum;* Port Perry, Scugog Shores Historical Museum, *Pioneer Days;* Newmarket, *Summer Festival* (Fenian Raid re-enactment, wreck-a-rama, duck race); Haliburton, *County Highland Games;* Peterborough, *Summer Festival of Lights* (outdoor entertainment, performing boats, continues through July and August); Greenwood, *Teddy Bear's Picnic;* Cobourg, *Annual Cobourg Highland Games;* Stouffville, *Strawberry Festival* (car rally, variety show, fireworks); Cobourg, *Waterfront Festival* (folk music).

JULY: Bowmanville, *Kids at the Mill Summer Camp* (arts, crafts, plays by camp members); Belleville, *Waterfront Festival and Folklorama;* Pickering, *Uncle Rodney's Amazing Bargain Emporium* (petting zoo, clowns, Dixieland music); Carrying Place, *Kente Portage Festival* (military re-creation, black powder canoe races, native events); Wilberforce, *Country Good Times* (amateur contests, parade, flea market); Cobourg, *Family Fun Day* (Tugboat Annie race, Jolly Roger pirate ship); Trenton, *Bathtub Days and Summer Festival* (bathtub race, Bavarian garden); Bobcaygeon, *Kawartha Lakes Ontario Open Fiddle and Step Dance Contests;* Ennismore, *Shamrock Festival* (marathon bingo, horse pulls, bed races); Minden, *Rotary Summer Carnival.*

AUGUST: Gooderham, *Horseshoe Days Festival* (talent contest, horseshoes, demolition derby); Haliburton, *Rotary Summer Carnival;* Madoc, *Arts and Crafts Festival;* Bobcaygeon, *Square Dance Weekend;* Brighton, *History Weekend* (box lunch social, 'calathumpian' parade, boat building bee); Maynooth, *Annual Maynooth Madness* (arts and crafts, open air trunk sale, children's activities); Pickering, Pickering Museum Village, *Special Displays.*

SEPTEMBER: Kleinberg, *Binder Twine Festival* (old tyme events); King City, *Septemberfest;* Uxbridge, *Celebration of the Arts* (photography competition, author readings, film festival); Brighton, *Applefest* (hay rides, tractor pulls, pet show); Newmarket, *Intercultural Exhibit.*

OCTOBER: Bobcaygeon, *Oktoberfest;* Bowmanville, *Apple Festival and Craft Sale;* Blackstock, *Fiddle Contest;* Grafton, *All Hallow's Eve* (Victorian parlor games, costumes, nineteenth-century Hallowe'en foods).

NOVEMBER: Warkworth, *Perfect Pie Contest;* Peterborough, *Festival of Trees;* Kleinburg, Kortright Centre for Conservation, *World Naturalist and Animal Preparations for Winter;* Peterborough, Hutchison House, *Heritage Cooking Demonstration;* Trenton, Belleville, Bowmanville, Aurora, Lakefield, Consecon, Port Perry, *Santa Claus parades.*

DECEMBER: Peterborough, Lang Pioneer Village, *Victorian Christmas Festival;* Peterborough and Port Hope, *Santa Claus parades.*

More detailed information on the festivals, carnivals, celebrations and other attractions of Getaway Country is available from: Central Ontario Travel Association, 1135 Lansdowne St. W., Box 1566, Peterborough, Ontario K9J 7M2, 705-745-1321.

Adolphustown

Old Hay Bay Church

WHERE: North of Adolphustown on Hay Bay.

WHEN: Open to visitors in summer.

WHAT: The first Methodist Church in Upper Canada was built in 1792. After 1860 it was used for crop storage until the Methodists regained possession and restored the building in 1910. It is now maintained by the United Church of Canada.

Aurora

Aurora Museum

WHERE: 22 Church St., one block east of Yonge St., south of Wellington.

WHEN: Open year round, Wednesday to Saturday, 10 a.m. to noon and 1 p.m. to 5 p.m.; Sunday 1 p.m. to 5 p.m. Closed Christmas holidays.

WHAT: This local history museum is housed in a nineteenth-century eight-room schoolhouse. Changing exhibits, gift counter. Not wheelchair accessible.

CONTACT: 416-727-8991, Aurora Museum.

Bancroft

Bancroft Art Gallery

WHERE: The Old Station, Station St.

WHEN: Open year round, Wednesday to Saturday, noon to 5 p.m. Closed December 25, 26 and January 1.

WHAT: This gallery, in a renovated railway station, exhibits paintings, sculptures, prints and photography of artists from across Ontario. Exhibits change monthly. Washrooms. Wheelchair accessible.

CONTACT: 613-332-1542, Algonquin Arts Council.

Bancroft Mineral Museum

WHERE: The Old Station, Station St.

WHEN: Year round. February to April and September to October, open Monday to Saturday, 9 a.m. to 4 p.m. May to August, open Monday to Saturday, 9 a.m. to 6 p.m. July through Labour Day, open Sunday, 10 a.m. to 4 p.m.

WHAT: The Museum, constructed to look like the inside of a mine, houses minerals from around the world as well as indigenous specimens. Souvenir counter. Washrooms. Wheelchair accessible.

CONTACT: 613-332-1513, Bancroft Mineral Museum.

Eagle's Nest Lookout

WHERE: 2 km (1.2 mi.) north of Bancroft on Hwy. 62.

WHEN: Road closed in winter.

WHAT: The Eagle's Nest overlooks a vista of forests, rivers and open fields. In winter the view is from the base of the look-out and ice sculptures—formed by frozen rivulets—are illuminated at night.

CONTACT: 613-332-1513, Bancroft Chamber of Commerce.

Beaverton

Beaver River Museum

WHERE: Simcoe St. W. at Centennial Park. Beaverton is on Hwy. 23 on the east shore of Lake Simcoe.

WHEN: July and August, open Tuesday to Sunday, 1:30 p.m. to 4 p.m. May, June and September, open weekends only, 1:30 p.m.

to 4 p.m. Open House and Christmas Bazaar on first Saturday in November, 11 a.m. to 2 p.m. Washrooms wheelchair accessible, but museum buildings are not. Admission by donation.

WHAT: An 1850s log cabin and brick-clad house have been furnished to the turn-of-the-century.

CONTACT: 705-426-9641, Beaver River Museum.

Bowmanville

Darlington Nuclear Generating Station

WHERE: Westbound on Hwy. 401, take Exit 431 (Waverley Rd.). Eastbound on Hwy. 401, take Exit 425 (Courtice Rd.) and follow signs on South Service Rd. to the Centre.

WHEN: Year round. Victoria Day weekend to Thanksgiving, open daily, 9 a.m. to 4 p.m. Rest of the year, open Monday to Friday, 9 a.m. to 4 p.m. Closed statutory holidays.

WHAT: Displays and a film presentation are on view in the Information Centre. Tour takes one and a half hours by bus or three hours on foot. Washrooms, picnic tables. Wheelchair accessible.

CONTACT: 416-623-7122, or 416-623-6670, Darlington Nuclear Generating Station.

Buckhorn

The Gallery on the Lake

WHERE: 20 km (12.4 mi.) north of Peterborough. Buckhorn is at the junction of Hwy. 507 and Hwy. 36. Drive 3 km (2 mi.) east of Buckhorn on Hwy. 36 and turn on Gallery Rd.

WHEN: Open year round, daily, 9 a.m. to 5 p.m. Closed December 25 and 26 and January 1.

WHAT: The Gallery, which features original works by prominent Canadian artists, displays more than 600 paintings in a three-storey octagonal building. Boutique sells gift items, paintings, sculptures, art supplies. The Gallery is also home to the Buckhorn School of Fine Art. Washrooms, ramp for wheelchairs.

CONTACT: 705-657-3296 or 705-657-1835, The Gallery on the Lake.

Cobourg

Art Gallery of Northumberland

WHERE: Victoria Hall, 55 King St. W., 3rd Floor, West Wing.

WHEN: Year round. September to June, open Tuesday to Friday, 9 a.m. to 5 p.m.; Saturday and Sunday, 1 p.m. to 5 p.m. July and August, open Tuesday to Friday, 11 a.m. to 5 p.m.; Saturday and Sunday, 1 p.m. to 5 p.m. Closed Mondays. Donations accepted.

WHAT: A collection of Canadian, European and American paintings, Inuit artifacts, ceramics and sculptures are on view during July and August. From September through June exhibits change monthly. Washrooms, elevator, wheelchair accessible.

CONTACT: 416-372-0333, Art Gallery of Northumberland.

Cobourg Farmers Market

WHERE: Market Building, 201 Second St., near Victoria Hall.

WHEN: Operates May through October, Saturday, 7 a.m. to noon.

WHAT: About twenty vendors offer fresh farm produce, honey, flowers and handcrafts.

CONTACT: 416-372-5831, Cobourg Farmers Market.

Floral Clock

WHERE: In Victoria Park one block south of Hwy. 2 on Church St.

WHEN: Summer.

WHAT: The clock was donated to the town of Cobourg in 1981 by the Rotary Club to commemorate the club's sixtieth anniversary. The clock is 9.1 m (30 ft.) in diameter. Each year, a new design is created with 3,000 to 4,000 plants. The date is changed daily with fresh flowers.

CONTACT: 416-372-8641, Parks Supt., Town of Cobourg.

Marie Dressler House

WHERE: 212 King St. W.

WHEN: Year round. September to June, open Monday to Friday, 9 a.m. to 5 p.m.; Saturday, 9 a.m. to 2 p.m. July and August, open daily, 9 a.m. to 5 p.m. Donations accepted.

WHAT: Marie Dressler, born in this house, became Canada's first Oscar-winning actress in 1930. Born Leila Marie Koerber, she was a character actress probably best remembered for her feisty portrayal of Tugboat Annie. A room is filled with Dressler memorabilia, including life-sized figurines of Dressler and frequent co-star Wallace Beery as Min and Bill. Visitor information centre, souvenir counter, wheelchair accessible.

CONTACT: 416-372-5831, Marie Dressler House.

Victoria Hall

WHERE: 55 King St. W.

WHEN: Open year round, Monday to Friday, 9 a.m. to 5 p.m. Tours in July and August, Tuesday, Wednesday, Friday, Sunday, 2 p.m. Closed holidays.

WHAT: The citizens of Cobourg, who believed their community would become the capital of Upper Canada, began building this magnificent structure to house the government. Officially opened in 1860 by the Prince of Wales, later King Edward VII, the Hall was fully refurbished in 1983. Today you can tour some of the forty-one rooms, including a courtroom modelled after London's Old Bailey. The Palladian-style building also houses the Art Gallery of Northumberland (see separate listing above), a concert hall, council chamber, the James Cockburn Room and the Ryerson-Guillet Room. The Cockburn room represents a law office such as James Cockburn rented in the 1860s before going to Ottawa as a member of Parliament to become the first Speaker of the House of Commons. The Ryerson-Guillet Room holds display cases of community artifacts.

CONTACT: 416-372-5831, Chamber of Commerce.

Colborne

The Big Apple

WHERE: At the Colborne interchange (Exit 497) south of Hwy. 401, 22 km (14 mi.) east of Cobourg.

WHEN: Year round, daily. May to October, open 8 a.m. to 9 p.m. November to April, open 8 a.m. to 7 p.m. Closed Christmas Day.

WHAT: This 9.3-ha (23-a.) theme park features a three-storey apple containing displays and audio visual presentations on the McIntosh apple. Visitors can watch apple pies being made through the windows of a small pie factory. A fast-food restaurant and gift shop maintain the apple theme. Children's playground, mini-golf, pond with geese and ducks, petting zoo with llama, deer, goats and rabbits.

CONTACT: 416-355-3155, The Big Apple.

Combermere

Madonna House Pioneer Museum and Gift Shops

WHERE: In Combermere, 61 km (32 mi.) north of Bancroft on Hwy. 62, turn right on Hwy 517.

WHEN: Open year round. Museum and gift shop open Victoria Day weekend to Labour Day, Tuesday to Saturday, 10 a.m. to 5 p.m.

Gift shop open Labour Day to Victoria Day, Thursday to Saturday, 2 p.m. to 5 p.m. Donations accepted.

WHAT: A hundred-year-old barn houses the Pioneer Museum of Local History, which includes a workshop, farm implements, household furnishings, clothing and crafts of the early settlers. The adjacent gift shop area includes a number of buildings that house antiques, collectibles, antique fabrics, jewelry, carvings, crafts and book collection. Gift shop items have been donated, with proceeds to the world's poor. The Museum is run by Madonna House, a non-profit missionary group. Wheelchair access to museum, gift shop and outside washrooms.

CONTACT: 613-756-0103, Madonna House Pioneer Museum and Gift Shop.

Curve Lake

Whetung Craft Centre and Art Gallery

WHERE: On Curve Lake Reserve between Buckhorn and Chemong Lakes, on the Trent-Severn Waterway. North of Lakefield, 8 km (5 mi.) west of Hwy. 507 on Curve Lake Rd.

WHEN: Year round, daily. Labour Day through June, open 9 a.m. to 5 p.m. July through Labour Day, open 9 a.m. to 9 p.m. Closed Christmas through New Year's.

WHAT: The Centre is owned and operated by Ojibwa Indians. The log and stone structure is guarded at the entrance by huge totems. Inside there are displays of native crafts and fine art from First Nation and Inuit communities across Canada. Washrooms, ramps and wheelchair-accessible washrooms, picnic area, summer tea room serving native foods May through Labour Day and sometimes through Thanksgiving.

CONTACT: 705-657-3661, Whetung Craft Centre and Art Gallery.

Deseronto

Native Renaissance II

WHERE: On Hwy. 49 just north of Hwy. 2, 20 km (12.4 mi.) east of Belleville.

WHEN: Year round, daily. Mid-May to Labour Day, open 9 a.m. to 9 p.m. Mid-September to mid-May, open 9 a.m. to 7 p.m.

WHAT: This large retail complex holds an extensive selection of Native arts and crafts, a manufacturing division where crafts are created and displays, including a nineteenth-century Huron canoe. The exterior of the building is decorated with a 46-km² (5,000-sq.-ft.) mural depicting an ancient Indian village.

CONTACT: 613-396-3520, Native Renaissance II.

Haliburton

Haliburton Highlands Museum

WHERE: Bayshore Acres Rd. just outside the Village of Haliburton, intersection of Hwy. 118 and Hwy. 121.

WHEN: Year round. Winter, open Tuesday to Saturday, 10 a.m. to 5 p.m. Mid-June to Labour Day, open daily, 10 a.m. to 5 p.m.

WHAT: A modern building, open year round, houses community artifacts and a superb collection of a hundred stuffed birds, including the extinct passenger pigeon. Other facilities are open spring through fall, including an 1867 barn displaying early agricultural instruments, a settler's square-timbered house of the same era, a blacksmith's forge building and a turn-of-the-century frame home. Book counter. Washrooms. Not wheelchair accessible.

CONTACT: 705-457-2760, Haliburton Highlands Museum.

Heritage Walk

WHERE: Haliburton Village. Walk starts at Government Dock beside Head Lake across from the Anglican Church.

WHEN: Tours offered July through Labour Day, Wednesday, 10 a.m. to noon, rain date Thursday.

WHAT: Guided walking tours of the Village of Haliburton feature an historical skit, "Dr. Peake," with actors in period costume. A free illustrated brochure of historic homes is distributed after the walk.

CONTACT: 705-457-1251, Village of Haliburton.

Rail's End Gallery

WHERE: On York St. in the Village of Haliburton, adjacent to Head Lake Park.

WHEN: Open year round, Tuesday to Saturday, 10 a.m. to 5 p.m. July 1 through Labour Day, also open Sunday, noon to 5 p.m.

WHAT: This nineteenth-century railroad station, restored as a gallery, displays changing exhibits of arts and crafts, both local and international. In-house programmes include films, lectures and demonstrations. Playground, picnic and swimming facilities.

CONTACT: 705-457-2330, Rail's End Gallery.

Keene

Hope Sawmill

WHERE: Beside Hope Mill Conservation Area about 7 km (4.3 mi.) north of Keene. From Peterborough, follow Hwy. 7 east 8 km (5 mi.), take County Rd. 34 south 5 km (3 mi.) to Otonabee Region Conservation Authority signs and go east 1 km (.6 mi.).

WHEN: Mid-June to Labour Day. Please call for days and times.

WHAT: There is an admission charge to the Conservation area, but not to Hope Sawmill, a nineteenth-century sawmill still in operation.

Antique tool collection. No washrooms. Not wheelchair accessible.

CONTACT: 705-745-5791, Otonabee Region Conservation Authority.

Serpent Mounds

WHERE: 3 km (2 mi.) south of Keene.

WHEN: Open year round. Regular provincial park admission charged mid-May through Thanksgiving. Free admission rest of year.

WHAT: The Point Peninsula Native people lived here about 2,000 years ago on a hillside overlooking Rice Lake. They buried their generations of dead beneath nine prominent burial mounds, one of which is unique to Canada. It is serpentine in shape, 61 m (200 ft.) long, 7.6 m (25 ft.) wide and 1.8 m (6 ft.) high. In summer (when there is an admission charge) there is swimming, picnicking, fishing, boating, a self-guided interpretive trail, interpretive centre, film programme, guided tours, camping, showers and laundromats.

CONTACT: 705-295-6879, Serpent Mounds Provincial Park.

Kinmount

Highlands Cinema Film Museum

WHERE: North of Main St. in Kinmount, junction of Hwy. 503 and Hwy. 121, 35 km (22 mi.) north of Fenelon Falls.

WHEN: Mid-May to Thanksgiving, open Friday to Sunday, from 6:45 p.m. Mid-June through August, open daily, from 6:45 p.m.

WHAT: There is a charge for the film screenings, but no admission fee to visit this unique small museum of old movie theatre equipment and projectors, posters and books, dating from 1899. The collection is displayed in the large common lobby of three small cinemas, which are decorated in the style of the 1920s with authentic furnishings rescued from movie theatres torn down across North America.

CONTACT: 705-488-2107, Highlands Cinema Film Museum.

Kleinburg

Kleinburg Doll Museum

WHERE: 10489 Islington Ave. N. (Main St. of Kleinburg).

WHEN: Open year round, noon to 5 p.m.; weekends, noon to 6 p.m. Closed Monday.

WHAT: Eaton's beauties, bisque babies and a Charlie McCarthy ventriloquist's doll are included in this private collection of about 170 antique and character dolls. Antique shop. Not wheelchair accessible.

CONTACT: 416-893-1358, proprietor-curator, Kleinburg Doll Museum.

Lindsay

The Lindsay Gallery

WHERE: 8 Victoria Ave. N.

WHEN: Open year round, Tuesday to Friday, 10 a.m. to 5 p.m.; Saturday, 1 p.m. to 5 p.m. Closed on national holidays.

WHAT: The gallery houses a permanent collection which focuses on historical and contemporary Canadian art, with special emphasis on the drawings of Ernest Thompson Seton. Washrooms. Not wheelchair accessible.

CONTACT: 705-324-1780, The Lindsay Gallery.

Marmora

Open pit iron mine

WHERE: Just south of Hwy. 7, about 500 m (550 yd.) east of Marmora.

WHEN: Year round.

WHAT: Marmora is named for its marble quarries (from the Latin *marmor*), but the big mining operation in these parts was iron. In the mid-1950s Bethlehem Steel Corp. stripped 18 million tonnes (20 million tons) of limestone off magnetite beds to allow open pit mining. A mill reduced the raw material to concentrate for shipping to the company's plant in Lackawanna, N.Y. Docks were opened in Picton to handle the 1,350 tonnes (1,500 tons) shipped daily. The mine ceased operation some years ago and water has seeped into the pit, but the enormous excavation still draws sightseers. It can be seen from a fenced viewing area.

Minden

Agnes Jamieson Gallery

WHERE: In Minden, Library and Cultural Centre, Bobcaygeon Rd. N. (Main St.).

WHEN: Year round. January to May, open Monday to Friday, 10 a.m. to 4 p.m. Victoria Day weekend to December, open Monday to Saturday, 10 a.m. to 5 p.m. Admission by donation.

WHAT: The Gallery features rotating displays of works by Ontario artists, including Dr. Jamieson, after whom the gallery is named. There is a major display of work by Andre Lapine. Gift shop. Wheelchair-accessible washrooms.

CONTACT: 705-286-3763, Agnes Jamieson Gallery.

County Town Museum

WHERE: Main St. of Minden beside Minden Library and Cultural Centre.

WHEN: Mid-May through Thanksgiving, open Saturday, 10 a.m. to 4:30 p.m. July through August, open Tuesday to Saturday, 10 a.m. to 4:30 p.m. Admission by donation.

WHAT: Exhibits on early life in Haliburton County include a

furnished heritage home and drive shed. Wheelchair accessible.
CONTACT: 705-286-3969 or 705-286-1674, County Town Museum.

Newmarket

Elman Campbell Museum

WHERE: 543 Timothy St.

WHEN: Open year round, Tuesday to Saturday, 10 a.m. to noon and
1 p.m. to 4 p.m. Closed all statutory holidays. Donations accepted.

WHAT: In addition to a small collection of community artifacts,
the museum features a working model railroad diorama of the Canadian National and the Radial Railway. Guided tours. Parking. Gift
shop. Wheelchair-accessible washrooms.

CONTACT: 416-895-4679, Elman Campbell Museum.

Ontario Humane Society Headquarters

WHERE: 620 Yonge St. in Newmarket. (Finch subway station stop
is opposite the farm.)

WHEN: Open year round, daily, 9 a.m. to 4:30 p.m. Donations
accepted.

WHAT: This 20-ha (50-a.) farm combines an equine rescue and
rehabilitation centre, a wildlife rescue centre, an animal shelter
and a home for retired horses. Visitors can view rare breeds of
cattle and other animals at close quarters. Cross-country skiing,
washrooms, picnic tables, pets on leash welcome.

CONTACT: 416-898-7122, Ontario Humane Society.

Orono

Clarke Museum and Archives

WHERE: Northeast corner of the intersection of Hwy. 35 and Hwy. 115, about 5 km (3 mi.) north of Orono, about five minutes north of Hwy. 401 from the Lindsay-Peterborough exit.

WHEN: Open April through December, Tuesday to Friday, 10 a.m. to 4 p.m.; Saturday, Sunday and holiday Mondays, 11 a.m. to 4 p.m. Donations accepted.

WHAT: The Museum, in the former Kirby schoolhouse, focuses on area history and community development. Changing exhibits explore a variety of themes. Special events and lectures are held throughout the season. Washrooms, shady picnic grounds, gift shop, fast food restaurant next door. Museum is wheelchair accessible.

CONTACT: 416-983-9243, Clarke Museum and Archives.

Oshawa

The Robert McLaughlin Gallery

WHERE: Civic Centre, foot of Bagot St. at Centre St.

WHEN: Open year round, Tuesday to Friday, 10 a.m. to 6 p.m.; Thursday, to 9 p.m.; Saturday and Sunday, noon to 5 p.m. Donations welcome.

WHAT: This gallery of contemporary Canadian art collects the work of Painters Eleven, the first abstract painting group in Ontario, founded in the Oshawa-Whitby area in 1953. The Gallery offers Canadian art lectures and film programmes. Gallery shop, art reference library, wheelchair-accessible washrooms.

CONTACT: 416-576-3000, The Robert McLaughlin Gallery.

Peterborough

Centennial Fountain

WHERE: Little Lake, just south of city centre.

WHEN: May through October.

WHAT: The highest jet fountain in Canada shoots water 76 m (250 ft.) in the air.

Art Gallery of Peterborough

WHERE: 2 Crescent St., by Little Lake.

WHEN: Year round. Thanksgiving to Victoria Day, open Tuesday to Friday, noon to 4 p.m.; Saturday and Sunday, 1 p.m. to 5 p.m. Victoria Day to Thanksgiving, open Tuesday to Sunday, 1 p.m. to 5 p.m.; Wednesday to 9 p.m.

WHAT: The Gallery mounts changing exhibitions of contemporary and traditional art and selections from permanent collections. Art rental service. Gallery shop, reference library, wheelchair accessible.

CONTACT: 705-743-9179, Art Gallery of Peterborough.

Peterborough and District Farmers Market

WHERE: Morrow Park, Lansdowne St. and George St.

WHEN: Open year round, Saturday, 7 a.m. to 1 p.m.

WHAT: Area produce and crafts are offered at the market, which is held outdoors May through October, and indoors the rest of the year.

Peterborough Lift Lock Visitor Centre

WHERE: Hunter St. E. at Ashburnham Dr., adjacent to Peterborough Museum and Archives. Five minutes from downtown and well signposted with Canadian Parks Service beaver symbol.

WHEN: Year round. Late June to Labour Day, open daily, 9 a.m.

to 6 p.m. Rest of the year, open Wednesday to Sunday, 10 a.m. to 5 p.m. Closed December 25 and 26, January 1 and Good Friday. Winter skating 10 a.m. to 10 p.m. daily, ice conditions permitting.

WHAT: See the world's highest hydraulic lift lock, then view slides, films and displays that depict the construction of the Lift Locks and the Trent-Severn Waterway at the turn of the century. A working model of the Lift Lock explains the mysteries of this marvellous device. In winter, weather (and ice) permitting, there is public skating on the canal. Parking, washrooms, theatre, exhibition hall, skate changing and warm-up room, picnic area, gift shop, wheelchair-accessible washrooms.

CONTACT: 705-745-8389, Canadian Parks Service, Trent-Severn Waterway.

Riverview Park and Zoo

WHERE: Water St. N. (Hwy. 28).

WHEN: Open year round from dawn to dusk. Railway operates from Victoria Day to Labour Day, daily, and on weekends until Thanksgiving.

WHAT: This 20-ha (50-a.) park on the Otonabee River includes a miniature railway and a small zoo with yaks, llamas, camels, monkeys, wolves, cougars, waterfowl and pheasant. Picnic tables, barbecues, playground and spray pool.

CONTACT: 705-748-4125, Zoo Supervisor, Peterborough Utilities Commission.

Pickering

Pickering Nuclear Generating Station and Energy Information Centre

WHERE: South on Brock Dr. from Hwy. 401 at Exit 399.

WHEN: Open year round, daily, 9 a.m. to 4 p.m. Closed weekends in December and Christmas week.

WHAT: This station has produced more electricity than any other nuclear station in the world. When they are all operating, the combined capacity of eight 540 Mw reactors produce about 20 per cent of the total electrical energy demands of Ontario. Visitors receive a full range of information on nuclear power and energy. There are models, displays, films and computer games and guides available to answer questions. Picnic grounds. Washrooms not wheelchair accessible.

CONTACT: 416-839-0465, Pickering Energy Information Centre.

Picton

Glenora-Adolphustown Ferry

WHERE: Connects Hwy. 33, the Loyalist Pkwy., between Quinte's Isle and Adolphustown.

WHEN: Ferry operates twenty-four hours a day, year round. From mid-October to mid-May, departures every half hour on the hour and half-hour. From mid-May to mid-October, departures every fifteen minutes from 7 a.m. to 10:45 p.m., and every half-hour overnight.

WHAT: Two ferry boats each have a capacity for fifteen vehicles and seventy passengers. There is no charge for passengers or vehicles.

CONTACT: 613-544-2220, Ontario Ministry of Transportation.

Lake on the Mountain

WHERE: From Picton, take County Rd. 7 to Lake-on-the-Mountain Provincial Park, which is signposted just before you reach the Glenora Ferry dock. (This is the only Provincial Park in Eastern Ontario for which there is no admission fee.)

WHEN: Year round.

WHAT: The lake really shouldn't be there, perched 61 m (200 ft.) above Lake Ontario, so there have been many theories about how it was formed—including the conjecture that it is fed by the Niagara

River. The lake provides 227 1 (60 gal.) a minute of clear, cold water for the fish tanks of Glenora Fisheries Research Station, but the source of that water remains a mystery because there's no visible inlet. There are picnic tables around the lake. Across the road there's a look-out over Picton Bay.

Macaulay Heritage Park and Prince Edward County Court House

WHERE: Church St. and Union St., one block south of Hwy. 33.

WHEN: Open May through Labour Day, Monday, Wednesday and Friday, 10 a.m. to 4:30 p.m.; Saturday and Sunday, 1 p.m. to 4:30 p.m. After Labour Day, please telephone for times. Tours of court house and jail by appointment only. Admission by donation.

WHAT: The former St. Mary Magdalene Church, built in 1825, houses the Prince Edward County Museum. The adjacent rectory, Macaulay House, has been restored to *circa* 1853. Both structures were built by the Rev. William Macaulay, who also donated the land for the court house and jail, built 1832-34. John A. Macdonald, Canada's first prime minister, practised law in the court room, one of the oldest judicial structures in the province still in use. A double oak gallows, built in 1884, remains in the building. The jail now houses the county archives. At the museum there are baking and craft demonstrations in the summer, a gift shop and picnic area. Wheelchair access to some buildings and washrooms.

CONTACT: 613-476-3833, Macaulay Heritage Park.

The White Chapel

WHERE: Just off Hwy. 49, 3 km (2 mi.) north of Picton.

WHEN: Year round. Usually open Sundays in July and August. At other times, telephone for appointment.

WHAT: Also known as the Conger Chapel, or the Old Chapel, this square, wooden Methodist meeting house was built on land donated by Stephen Conger in 1809. It was the first Methodist Church in Prince Edward County and has been maintained as a place of worship longer than any other Methodist church in Ontario. Wheelchair accessible.

CONTACT: 613-476-6050, Picton United Church.

Pontypool

Fleetwood Creek Natural Area and Twenty-Mile Look-out

WHERE: About 5 km (3 mi.) north of Pontypool on Hwy. 35, just north of the junction of Hwy. 35 and Hwy. 115, 25 km (15.5 mi.) south of Lindsay.

WHEN: Open year round. No vehicular traffic allowed.

WHAT: The area comprises 365 ha (900 a.) of natural valley land in the headwaters of Fleetwood Creek. A viewing stand overlooking the valley is nicknamed Twenty-Mile Look-out. Picnic tables. Privies.

CONTACT: 705-887-3112, Kawartha Region Conservation Authority; 416-325-5000, Ontario Heritage Foundation.

Port Hope

Dorothy's Historic House

WHERE: Village of Garden Hill, County Rd. 9, 9 km (5.6 mi.) northwest of Port Hope.

WHEN: Open Victoria Day through September, weekends, 1:30 p.m. to 4 p.m. Donations accepted.

WHAT: This picturesque Ontario frame structure was built in the 1860s and restored to to resemble a working man's cottage of that period. Washrooms. Guided tours. Wheelchair accessible.

CONTACT: 416-786-2602, Dorothy's Historic House.

Ganaraska River, fish-watching

WHERE: Flows through Port Hope.

WHEN: In spring and fall.

WHAT: Visitors can watch the trout run in one of Canada's best trout streams. Trout are lifted over waterfalls by fish ladder in mid- to late-April. Trout may also be seen from several pedestrian bridges which cross the lower reaches of the river.

Schomberg

Puck's Farm

WHERE: West side of the 11th Concession of King Twp., 2 km (1.2 mi.) south of Hwy. 9, 3 km (2 mi.) west of Hwy. 27

WHEN: May to October, open Sunday and holidays, noon to 5 p.m. Rest of the year, open to groups by appointment. Call ahead for times.

WHAT: This 69-ha (170-a.) farm offers strawberries, raspberries, sweet corn and pumpkins for sale and free viewing of a variety of farmyard animals. There is a charge for pony, hay and sleigh rides. Washrooms, picnic tables, wool store, refreshments. Wheel-chair accessible.

CONTACT: 416-939-7036, Puck's Farm.

Sharon

Sharon Temple

WHERE: 18974 Leslie St. (formerly Sutton Rd.), in the village of Sharon.

WHEN: Open May through October, daily, 10 a.m. to 5 p.m. There is an admission charge to the temple, some museum buildings and the temple grounds, but the unique temple building may be viewed for free from the parking lot year round.

WHAT: This unique three-storey frame temple was built between 1825 and 1832 by a pioneer religious sect, the Children of Peace, also known as the Davidites. The building embodies many interesting features symbolic of the sect's beliefs. Other museum buildings house community artifacts. Picnic area, washrooms, gift shop, partial wheelchair access.

CONTACT: 416-478-2389, Sharon Temple.

Trenton

RCAF Memorial Museum

WHERE: Canadian Forces Base Trenton.

WHEN: Year round, including holidays. Mid-September to May, open Monday to Friday, noon to 5 p.m. June to mid-September, open Monday to Thursday, noon to 5 p.m. and 6 p.m. to 8 p.m.; Saturday and Sunday, 10 a.m. to 5 p.m.

WHAT: The Museum was founded in 1984 to commemorate the sixtieth anniversary of the Royal Canadian Air Force. Displays include RCAF artifacts, memorabilia, photographs and documents. Wheelchair-accessible washrooms.

CONTACT: 613-965-2208, RCAF Memorial Museum.

Tyrone

Tyrone Mill

WHERE: In the Village of Tyrone, 13 km (8 mi.) north of Hwy. 401 at Liberty St. Exit (Bowmanville).

WHEN: Open year round, Monday to Saturday, 9 a.m. to 6 p.m.; Sunday 1 p.m. to 5 p.m. Open House middle Saturday of September, with demonstrations and tours marking the start of apple cider pressing.

WHAT: This water-driven mill, built in 1846 for the production of flour and feed, has been converted to a sawmill which is still in operation. Visitors are welcome to browse on their own and staff is available to answer questions. Apple pressing is featured from late September through May on Wednesdays and Saturdays and other days in fall. A woodworking shop on the second floor features old woodworking equipment. Gift shop with jams, jellies, mustards, candies. Snack bar on weekends. Wheelchair access to ground floor.

CONTACT: 416-263-8871, Tyrone Mills Ltd.

Uxbridge

The Uxbridge Quaker Meeting House

WHERE: Concession Rd. 6, just west of Uxbridge.

WHEN: Year round.

WHAT: The simple board-and-batten meeting house was built by a Quaker community established in 1805 by twelve families from Pennsylvania.

Vandorf

Whitchurch-Stouffville Museum

WHERE: At Vandorf on Woodbine Ave.

WHEN: Year round. Late May to October, open Monday, Thursday and Friday, 10 a.m. to 5 p.m.; Saturday, Sunday and holidays, 1 p.m. to 5 p.m. Rest of year, open Monday to Friday, 10 a.m. to 5 p.m. Special events through the year. Donations welcomed.

WHAT: The Museum comprises two schoolhouses, an 1880 farm home, log cabin and barn. The exhibit buildings feature life from the community's past. In summer there are demonstrations of baking and pioneer handcrafts. Gift shop. Wheelchair access to one gallery.

CONTACT: 416-727-8954, Whitchurch-Stouffville Museum.

Ontario East

Includes: Arnprior, Barry's Bay, Brockville, Carleton Place, Chalk River, Cornwall, Gananoque, Kanata, Kingston, Morrisburg, Napanee, Ottawa, Pembroke, Perth, Petawawa, Renfrew, Vanier and their environs.

This region of lakes and scattered farms was the first part of Ontario to be settled and is generously dotted with stone buildings, some of which were built as long as 300 years ago. Ontario East contains the nation's capital, Ottawa, and the historic city of Kingston, which probably has more museums per capita than any other place in the province.

Festivals, Carnivals, Celebrations, Special Events:

JANUARY: Petawawa, *Sno Frolic;* Chalk River and area, *Lions Winter Carnival* (lumberjack show, pet contest, log chopping contests).

FEBRUARY: Stonecliffe, *Winter Carnival* (log sawing, nail driving); Kanata, *Rendezvous Kanata* (fishing derby, skating show); Ottawa-Hull, *Winterlude* (snow and ice sculpture competitions, cultural and artistic performances); Prescott, *Frost Festival* (hay rides, lumberjack contests, giant bonfire); Almonte, *Chilli Days Winter Festival* (chili cookoff, curling, sleigh rides, outdoor volleyball).

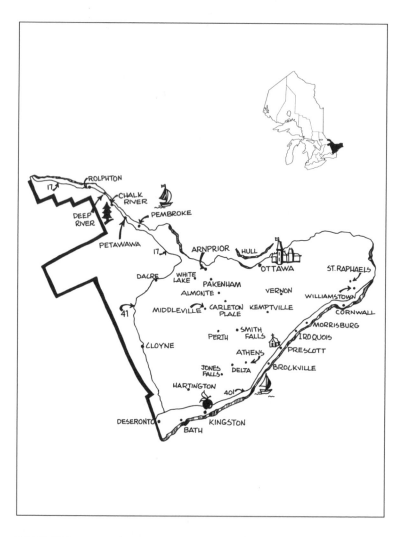

MARCH: Pakenham, *First Taste of Spring* (old and new methods of maple syrup production, mule and horse-drawn sleigh rides); Nepean, *Log Farm Sugarbush* (taffy on the snow).

APRIL: Ottawa, *Wildlife Festival* (films, exhibits, workshops, field trips); Pakenham, *The Great Canadian Maple Cook Off and Auction* (maple desserts judged and auctioned, fiddle music); Perth,

Festival of Maples (all-day stage entertainment, petting zoo, maple syrup contest).

MAY: Ottawa, *The Canadian Tulip Festival* (community picnic in Major's Hill Park); Cornwall, *Health Escapade Santé* (children's games, exhibits by health and social agencies); Nepean, *Log Farm Housewarming;* Brockville, *Symphony of Lights;* Deseronto, *Landing of the Mohawks* (re-enactment of historic landing at Tyendinaga Mohawk Territory); Ottawa, Dow's Lake, *Boat Show;* Kingston, Old Fort Henry, *Victoria Day Celebrations;* Morrisburg, Upper Canada Village, *Heirloom Garden Weekend* (activities showing how the garden contributed to the lifestyle of the 1860s); Nepean, *Odawa Pow Wow* (tribute to aboriginal peoples of North America, dancing, drumming, craft market); Kingston, *Copper Sunday* (Royal Military College cadets parade); Brockville and District, *Multicultural Festival;* Ottawa, *The Toshiba National Capital Marathon;* Kanata, *Mayfair* (radio-controlled airplanes, karate, rides, games); Carp, *Farmers Market.*

JUNE: Carp, *Strawberry Festival;* Kingston, *Folklore;* Cornwall, *La Semaine Français* (concerts, plays, dances celebrating the culture and heritage of the French community); Morrisburg, Upper Canada Village, *Sheep Shearing Weekend;* Petawawa, *Civic Centre Days* (dances, bingo, parade, smash up derby); Ottawa, *Franco-Ontarien Festival* (outdoor concerts, international food, entertainment); Brockville, *The Great Balloon Rodeo* (balloon festival exclusively for specially shaped balloons); Brockville, *Riverfest* (entertainment, high diving, Bavarian gardens, fireworks, bow fishing competition); Kingston, *Kingfest* (arts and crafts); Cornwall, *Multicultural Festival.*

JULY: Carp, *Pioneer Day;* Cornwall, *Worldfest* (groups from foreign countries perform cabaret style performances); Kingston, Old Fort Henry, *Sunset Ceremony* (re-creation of infantry drill, military tactics and military music of the British Army 150 years ago); Prescott, Fort Wellington, *Loyalist Military Pageant* (three re-enacted battles featuring the demonstrations of nineteenth-century military tactics); Ottawa, Canadian Museum of Civilization and National Gallery of Canada, *Cultures Canada* (celebration of multiculturalism); Kingston, *Buskers Rendezvous* (street performers from across North America, jugglers, comedians); Carleton Place, *Orange Day Parade and Celebrations* (speeches, parade); Arnprior, *Salute the Ottawa Valley* (parade, boat races, shanty breakfasts, lumberjack contests); Ottawa, *International Jazz Festival;* Prescott, *Loyalist Days* (beach party, beer gardens, amateur night); Perth, *Come on Home Anniversary* (horse-drawn parade, military re-enactment, International World Cup Equestrian Event); Wendover, *Western Festival* (bingo, casino, amateur night, fiddler dance); Almonte, *Ice Cream Festival* (bathtub races, wool flotilla, tethered balloon rides); Kanata, Pinhey's Point, *Heritage Festival* (heritage and antique exhibits, corn roast).

AUGUST: Deep River, *Summer Fest* (street dance, pottery display, beer tent); Carleton Place, *Mississippi River Daze* (fair, sidewalk sale, circus); Ottawa, *Central Canada Exhibition* (agricultural shows, midway, concerts); Cornwall, Inverarden Regency Cottage Museum, *Teddy Bear Picnic;* Almonte, *North Lanark Highland Games* (piping and pipe band competitions, heavy weight athletics, Scottish foods); Athens, *Corn Fest* (bake sales, games, children's parade); Pembroke, *Old Time Fiddling and Step Dance Contest;* Maxville, *Glengarry Highland Games* (Pipe bands competition, heavy weight sports); Beachburg, *Molson Whitewater Challenge* (survival game, rafting, scavenger hunt, air band contest).

SEPTEMBER: Carp, *Maple Syrup Festival.*

OCTOBER: Manotick, Watson's Mill, *The Fall Flour Festival.*

NOVEMBER: Brockville, *Symphony of Lights;* Carleton Place, Ottawa, Brockville, Almonte, *Santa Claus parades.*

DECEMBER: Napanee, The Allen MacPherson House, *Christmas at the Laird's;* Brockville, Brockville Museum, *Dickens Readings* (costumed readers, Christmas sweets and wassail); Perth, Lancaster, *Santa Claus parades.*

More detailed information on the festivals, carnivals, celebrations and other attractions of Ontario East is available from: Eastern Ontario Travel Association, 209 Ontario St., Kingston, Ontario K7L 2Z1, 613-549-3682.

Almonte

Mill of Kintail Gift Shop and Exhibits

WHERE: Off Hwy. 15, 7 km (4.5 mi.) north of Almonte.

WHEN: Year round. Mid-May to mid-October, open Wednesday to Sunday, 10:30 a.m. to 4:30 p.m. Mid-October to mid-May, open noon to 4 p.m.

WHAT: There is a small admission charge to tour the mill, but no charge to visit the changing exhibits in the gift shop, formerly the Gate House. Visitors may use free cross-country ski trails in winter or a picnic area on this lovely site in summer. The mill was built in 1830 and restored in 1930 as a studio and home by surgeon-sculptor Robert Tait McKenzie.

CONTACT: 613-256-3610, Mill of Kintail Museum and Gift Shop.

Mississippi Valley Textile Museum

WHERE: 3 Rosamond St. E., Almonte.

WHEN: July and August, open Monday to Saturday, 10 a.m. to 5 p.m.; Sunday, 1 p.m. to 5 p.m. April through October, open Monday to Saturday, 10 a.m. to 5 p.m. Donations accepted.

WHAT: Displays and artifacts provide information about the early mills and the origins of the Canadian textile industry. Washrooms, free parking. Gift shop displays the work of local artisans. Not wheelchair accessible.

CONTACT: 613-256-3754, Mississippi Valley Textile Museum.

North Lanark Regional Museum

WHERE: Follow signs off Hwy. 44 just north of Almonte, about 66 km (42 mi.) west of Ottawa.

WHEN: Museum open Victoria Day through Thanksgiving weekend, Wednesday, Saturday, Sunday, and holiday Mondays, 1 p.m. to 5 p.m.

Tea room open Sunday in June and Wednesday and Sunday in July and August, 2 p.m. to 4 p.m.

WHAT: Information and artifacts relate to the area's early settlers. In the basement a permanent display depicts an old general store. There is also a pioneer log building display. Parking, picnic area, washroom. Wheelchairs accessible with assistance.

CONTACT: 613-256-1805, North Lanark Regional Museum.

Arnprior

Arnprior and District Museum

WHERE: 35 Madawaska St., corner of John St.

WHEN: Open mid-June to mid-September, Tuesday to Friday, noon to 5 p.m.; Saturday and Sunday, 1 p.m. to 4 p.m. Closed Mondays and statutory holidays. Donations welcome.

WHAT: The Museum, in a handsome stone building which was formerly the post office, displays community artifacts, including those associated with the area's lumbering heritage. Washrooms, parking, souvenir desk, picnic area in adjacent Simpson Park. Not wheelchair accessible.

CONTACT: 613-623-4902, Arnprior and District Museum.

Athens

Outdoor murals

WHERE: On the walls of buildings in this pretty town on Hwy. 42, about 25 km (15.5 mi.) west of Brockville.

WHEN: Year round.

WHAT: Since 1986 artists have been invited to paint eleven murals on buildings around the town as a tourist attraction.

CONTACT: 613-924-2044, Athens Municipal Office.

Bath

Bath Museum

WHERE: In the Village of Bath, 20 km (12.4 mi.) west of Kingston, one and a half blocks north of Loyalist Pkwy.

WHEN: Open Victoria Day through Labour Day, Saturday, Sunday and holidays, 1 p.m. to 4 p.m.; weekdays by appointment. Donations welcomed.

WHAT: Bath, one of Ontario's oldest communities, was settled in 1784 by soldiers discharged by Jessup's Rangers. This collection of community artifacts is housed in Layer Cake Hall, an 1859 board-and-batten structure with Gothic features. Local books for sale at gift counter. Not wheelchair accessible.

CONTACT: 613-352-7473 or 613-352-3361, Village of Bath office.

Brockville

Brockville Railway Tunnel

WHERE: Armagh S. Price Park.

WHEN: Open mid-June through Labour Day. Caboose with tourist information and museum, open Tuesday to Sunday, 10 a.m. to 5 p.m.

WHAT: Canada's oldest railway tunnel, built between 1854 and 1860, stretches over 500 m (1,600 ft.) under the city. The tunnel, closed to rail traffic in 1954, is now open to visitors. The nearby 1954 caboose displays contain city and railroad artifacts.

County Courthouse and Jail

WHERE: Courthouse Square.

WHEN: Open year round, Monday to Friday. Tours available 8 a.m. to 4 p.m.

WHAT: The courthouse and jail, built in 1842, is one of the oldest remaining structures of this type in Ontario.

CONTACT: 613-342-3840, administrative clerk-treasurer.

Carleton Place

Canadian Co-operative Wool Growers Ltd.

WHERE: 142 Franktown Rd., beside CN rail line.

WHEN: Year round, by appointment. Guided tour must be pre-arranged. Open Monday to Friday, 9 a.m. to noon and 1 p.m. to 4 p.m., except statutory holidays. Closed January.

WHAT: Half-hour tours of this depot, in an old CN roundhouse, include a demonstration of the grading of raw Canadian wool. The Real Wool Shop sells blankets, clothing and other wool-related items. Farm supply store, Lambsdown Park mini-golf. Washrooms. Not wheelchair accessible.

CONTACT: 613-257-2714, Canadian Co-operative Wool Growers Ltd.

Victoria School Museum

WHERE: 267 Edmund St., off Hwy. 15.

WHEN: Open mid-June through September, Tuesday to Sunday, 10 a.m. to 4 p.m. Other times by appointment. Donations welcome.

WHAT: This stone school and community museum was the original 1872 town hall of Carleton Place and a school from 1879 to 1969. An outreach programme, Museum in a Trunk, visits area schools. Changing displays. Washrooms, gift counter. Wheelchair access to museum but not washrooms.

CONTACT: 613-253-1395, Victoria School Museum.

Chalk River

Petawawa National Forestry Institute

WHERE: Hwy. 17, 14 km (8.7 mi.) west of Petawawa, 15 km (9.3 mi.) east of Deep River.

WHEN: Open year round. Visitor centre open June through Labour Day, daily, 9 a.m. to dusk (9 p.m.).

WHAT: The Institute was the birthplace of forest research in Canada in 1918. It covers almost 100 km² (38.6 sq. mi.) of forested landscape. At the visitor centre, fun and learning are combined in a unique outdoor experience for all ages. Visitors may stroll through the pine woods on a winding trail, view experimental forest areas on a self-guided auto tour or examine a variety of indoor and outdoor exhibits. There is bass and muskellunge fishing in Corry and Cartier Lakes, boat-launching facilities on both lakes, a sandy beach on Corry Lake, and 60 km (37 mi.) of cross-country ski trails, some groomed. Washrooms. Not wheelchair accessible.

CONTACT: 613-589-2880, Petawawa National Forestry Institute.

Chalk River Research Laboratories
—Atomic Energy of Canada Limited

WHERE: Off Hwy. 17, 8 km (5 mi.) east of Deep River. Turn left in Chalk River, drive 1 km (0.6 mi.) to the gate. From the gate, it's another 7 km (4.3 mi.) to the visitor centre and laboratories.

WHEN: Open year round. All visitors must have valid identification, preferably with photograph (driver's licence, birth certificate or passport is satisfactory). Children do not require ID. Children below Grade Six are not allowed on laboratory tours, but a supervised children's programme is available. Tours available mid-June through Labour Day, Monday to Friday, 10:30 a.m., 1 p.m., and 2:30 p.m. Tours last from seventy-five to ninety minutes.

WHAT: The birthplace of Canada's nuclear programme, AECL's Chalk River facilities include public information centre that features models, exhibits and films. Tours may include nuclear research reactors, an accelerator-cyclotron facility, ZEEP (Zero Energy Experimental Pile), NRX, the world's oldest operating nuclear reactor, built in 1947 and the NRU, one of the world's largest research reactors and waste management areas. Wheelchair accessible washrooms. By prior arrangement a lift van is available for disabled people. Picnic tables, snack food.

CONTACT: 613-584-3311, Ext. 4429, Public Information Centre, AECL Research Chalk River Laboratories.

Cloyne

Cloyne Pioneer Museum

WHERE: In the Village of Cloyne beside the Municipal Office on Hwy. 41, 65 km (40 mi.) north of Napanee.

WHEN: July through Labour Day, open Monday to Saturday, 10 a.m. to 4 p.m. Rest of the year, open by appointment. Donations welcomed.

WHAT: This replica of an early pioneer log cabin features many early artifacts, including tools, clothes, dishes and farm implements. Washrooms, picnic tables. Not wheelchair accessible.

CONTACT: 613-336-8185, curator, Cloyne Pioneer Museum; 613-336-8712, president, Cloyne Pioneer Museum.

Cornwall

Cornwall Regional Art Gallery

WHERE: 164 Pitt St. off Second St.

WHEN: Open year round, Tuesday to Friday, 10:30 a.m. to 5:30 p.m.; Saturday, 9:30 a.m. to 4:30 p.m. Closed statutory holidays.

WHAT: Shows of regional artists change monthly. Works of local artisans are sold in the Gallery Shoppe. Art classes are offered.

Washrooms. Wheelchair accessible.

CONTACT: 613-938-7387, Cornwall Regional Art Gallery.

Historic Walking Tour

WHERE: Downtown Cornwall.

WHEN: Year round.

WHAT: This one- or two-hour walk takes you past fifteen buildings of interest, including the 1833 district courthouse and jail, an 1820 inn, 1881 industrial row housing for cotton mill workers and the 18-km (11.2-mi.) Cornwall Canal built between 1834 and 1842 to bypass the Long Sault Rapids. A copy of the walking tour map is available from Cornwall Tourism and Convention Office at 340 Pitt St.

CONTACT: 613-933-0074, Cornwall Tourism and Convention Office.

Inverarden Regency Cottage Museum

WHERE: Hwy. 2 just west of Boundary Rd., Exit 796 from Hwy. 401.

WHEN: Open April to November, Monday to Saturday, 11 a.m. to 5 p.m.; Sunday, 2 p.m. to 5 p.m. Open other times by appointment, weather permitting. Tea Room open mid-June to Labour Day, Sunday, 2 p.m. to 4 p.m.

WHAT: The finest example of Regency Cottage architecture in Ontario was built in 1816 for North West Company fur trader John McDonald of Garth. The fourteen-room cottage is situated on 1 ha (2.5 a.) of grounds overlooking the St. Lawrence Seaway. Artifacts on display include fine Canadian and English Georgian furnishings. Travelling arts and crafts exhibits. Local photographic and historic archives. Slide show on the restoration. Washroom, gift counter. Not wheelchair accessible.

CONTACT: 613-938-9585, Curator, Inverarden Regency Cottage Museum.

Rossi Artistic Glass

WHERE: 450 Seventh St. W., behind Holiday Inn.

WHEN: Year round. Tours offered Monday to Friday, 8:30 a.m. to 4:30 p.m.; Saturday, 9 a.m. to 1 p.m. Showroom open to 5 p.m. Closed all holidays.

WHAT: See demonstrations of free-form glass blowing. Washrooms, retail outlet. Wheelchair accessible.

CONTACT: 613-938-7760, Rossi Artistic Glass.

R. H. Saunders
Energy Information Centre, Ontario Hydro

WHERE: West Cornwall. Second St. off Hwy 2. Centre located in R. H. Saunders generating station, 6th Floor. Exit 786 from Hwy. 401 eastbound. Exit 789 from Hwy. 401 westbound.

WHEN: June, open Monday to Friday, 10 a.m. to 4 p.m. July through August, open daily, 10 a.m. to 5 p.m. Rest of the year, open by appointment only.

WHAT: A series of audio-visual and descriptive displays explain the generation and transmission of electrical energy in Ontario. A working scale model shows the workings of the Saunders hydro-electric generating station. Films, slide shows, literature, self-guided tour and panoramic view of the St. Lawrence River, power dam and seaway. Washrooms, picnic tables, refreshment machines, wheelchair accessible.

CONTACT: 613-938-1518, R. H. Saunders Energy Information Centre, Ontario Hydro.

The United Counties Museum

WHERE: 731 2nd St. W. across from Domtar Paper Mills.

WHEN: Open May to October, Monday to Saturday, 10 a.m. to noon and 1 p.m. to 5 p.m.; Sunday, 2 p.m. to 5 p.m. Donations accepted.

WHAT: The stone house, built in 1840 by United Empire Loyalist William Wood, was occupied until 1953 by Wood's descendants. In 1957 it was converted to a museum and houses a collection of regional pioneer and Victorian artifacts. Washrooms. Wheelchair accessible with assistance.

CONTACT: 613-932-2381, The United Counties Museum.

Dacre

Magnetic Hill

WHERE: 2 km (1.2 mi.) south of the junction of Hwy. 132 and Hwy. 41, south of the Village of Dacre, about 30 km (18.6 mi.) southwest of Renfrew.

WHEN: Spring through fall.

WHAT: On a former section of Hwy. 41 your car will appear to roll uphill with the engine turned off—but it's only an optical illusion. If the sign has been vandalized or stolen, look for a white line painted across the paved road. Stop there, turn off your engine, release the brakes—and defy gravity.

Deep River

Ferguson's Stopping Place

WHERE: Deep River, on Hwy. 17.

WHEN: Information centre open June through Labour Day, daily, 9 a.m. to 7 p.m.

WHAT: Twelve heritage buildings are preserved on this site, which was a stopping place on the Pembroke-Mattawa Road. Visitors may not enter the mid-1800s buildings, including barns and an hotel, all of which require structural repairs. The local tourist information centre is situated on the property. Washrooms, picnic tables, guided tours. Not wheelchair accessible.

CONTACT: 613-584-2000, Deep River Economic Development Office.

Delta

Old Stone Mill

WHERE: In Village of Delta, 37 km (23 mi.) west of Brockville on Hwy. 42.

WHEN: Open Victoria Day weekend to Labour Day, daily, 10 a.m. to 5 p.m. Open weekends to Thanksgiving, otherwise by appointment.

WHAT: The Delta stone gristmill was built in 1810 on the site of an earlier wooden mill. The mill, which continued operation in various hands until 1949, is now a national historic site that contains displays of the local industrial heritage. Wheelchair accessible. No washrooms.

CONTACT: 613-928-2658, Old Stone Mill; 613-924-2444, curator.

Hartington

The Holleford Crater

WHERE: 5 km. (3 mi.) northwest of Hartington off Hwy. 38, about 30 km (18.6 mi.) north of Kingston.

WHEN: Year round.

WHAT: In 1955, geologists studying aerial photographs of the Canadian Shield discovered a crater 2.5 km (1.6 mi.) in diameter and almost 244 m (800 ft.) deep. The crater, believed to be the result of a meteorite that landed 500 million years ago, is marked by a provincial plaque on the Babcock farm on Holleford Rd. The crater is surrounded by privately owned land and is accessible only with permission of the owner.

CONTACT: 613-372-2736 or 613-372-2786, Irwin Babcock.

Iroquois

Iroquois Seaway Locks

WHERE: Town of Iroquois, on Hwy. 2, 13 km (8 mi.) southwest of Morrisburg.

WHEN: Year round. Best seen during navigation season, spring through early winter.

WHAT: Iroquois, population 1,200, was the largest town to be entirely relocated when the St. Lawrence Seaway flooded the area. From a look-out visitors can watch ships from around the world locking through the only shipping lock in eastern Ontario.

Jones Falls

Jones Falls Lock Station on the Rideau Canal

WHERE: At Jones Falls, 3 km (2 mi.) west of Hwy. 15 on County Rd. 11, about 48 km (30 mi.) south of Smiths Falls.

WHEN: Open Victoria Day weekend to mid-October, daily. The Blacksmith Shop and Sweeney House are open during lock operating hours from Victoria Day to Labour Day.

WHAT: This major lock station on the Rideau Canal offers historical highlights of the area, including a 19-m- (62.3-ft.-) high stone arch dam, restored blacksmith shop and defensible lockmaster's house. Four locks raise boats 18 m (59 ft.). Washrooms, trails, picnic area, interpretive programme and period costumed staff. Not wheelchair accessible.

CONTACT: 613-359-3577, Southern Area Office, Rideau Canal, Canadian Parks Service.

Kemptville

Kemptville College of Agriculture

WHERE: Just south of Kemptville on County Rd. 44 (old Hwy. 16.).

WHEN: Open year round. Best seen mid-May through August. Tours must be pre-arranged.

WHAT: Tours are available of the dairy, maple syrup, and extensive horticultural research operations. The College operates an equestrian programme September through March. Washrooms, picnic area, some wheelchair access.

CONTACT: 613-258-8246, Kemptville College of Agriculture.

G. Howard Ferguson Forest Station

WHERE: 2 km (1.2 mi.) north of Kemptville on Hwy. 16.

WHEN: Open year round, Monday to Friday, 7:30 a.m. to 4:30 p.m. Closed statutory holidays.

WHAT: Self-guided tours are available through 8 km (5 mi.) of nature trails. This 40.5-ha (100-a.) tree nursery includes pine, spruce, poplar, oak and other varieties. Twenty-minute slide show. Wheelchair-accessible washrooms, picnic tables, cross-country skiing and several kilometres of sandy forest roads suitable for cycling.

CONTACT: 613-258-8355, G. Howard Ferguson Forest Station, Ministry of Natural Resources.

Kingston

Agnes Etherington Art Centre

WHERE: University Ave. and Queen's Ct.

WHEN: Open year round. Free admission Thursday, 5 p.m. to 9 p.m. July and August, free admission Thursday, noon to 5 p.m.

Small admission charge at other times.

WHAT: The permanent collection of over 7,500 works includes paintings, sculptures, graphics, European Old Masters, Inuit art, heritage quilts, antique silver and an excellent collection of African art. Art catalogues, posters, tote bags and cards are sold. Wheelchair ramps.

CONTACT: 613-545-2190, Agnes Etherington Art Centre.

Bellevue House National Historic Site

WHERE: Division St. Exit 617 from Hwy. 401, south 4.5 km (2.8 mi.) to Union St., then west to Centre St., and south one and a half blocks.

WHEN: Year round, daily. Labour Day to May, open 10 a.m. to 5 p.m. June through Labour Day, open 9 a.m. to 6 p.m. Closed on holidays from Remembrance Day (November 11) to Easter Monday inclusive.

WHAT: Bellevue House, an Italian-style villa built between 1838 and 1840, was an early home of Sir John A. Macdonald, who later became Canada's first prime minister. The house, orchard and gardens are maintained in the style of the 1840s, when Macdonald lived there. The site also includes a visitor centre with films and an extensive display introducing his life and career. Washrooms, wheelchair accessible.

CONTACT: 613-545-8666, Bellevue House, Parks Canada.

Canadian Forces Communications and Electronics Museum

WHERE: Vimy Barracks, Hwy. 2, Canadian Forces Base Kingston, just east of town.

WHEN: Open year round, Monday to Friday, 8 a.m. to 4 p.m., except holidays. Victoria Day weekend to Labour Day, also open Saturday and Sunday, 10 a.m. to 4 p.m.

WHAT: This museum features Canadian military communications equipment. Snack bar, gift shop, washrooms, wheelchair accessible.

CONTACT: 613-541-5395, Canadian Forces Communications and Electronics Museum.

Kingston Archaeological Centre

WHERE: 370 King St. W.

WHEN: Open year round, Monday to Friday, 9 a.m. to 4 p.m. Admission by donation.

WHAT: The Centre documents the 8,000-year history of human habitation in the area with a collection of one million artifacts, most of which are in storage. Not wheelchair accessible.

CONTACT: 613-542-3483, Kingston Archaeological Centre.

Kingston City Hall

WHERE: 216 Ontario St., across from Confederation Park.

WHEN: Year round. Tours available, June through August, Monday to Friday, every half-hour, 8:30 a.m. to 4:30 p.m.

WHAT: This building is a magnificent example of British Renaissance Tuscan Revival-style architecture and nineteenth-century craftsmanship in limestone. It was erected between 1843 and 1844 when Kingston was capital of the United Provinces. Wheelchair-accessible washrooms.

CONTACT: 613-546-4291, Kingston City Hall.

Kingston Farmers Market

WHERE: Behind City Hall.

WHEN: Open year round, weather permitting, Tuesday, Thursday, and Saturday, 6 a.m. to 6 p.m. Craft market open mid-May through October, Sunday, 6 a.m. to 6 p.m. When the weather is pleasant, craft vendors often bring their goods to weekday markets.

WHAT: One of Canada's oldest farmers markets was created by the Crown in 1801 and continues on the same open-air site today. The craft market on Sundays offers handcrafts, clothing, jewelry, and art work. No wheelchair access on Saturdays.

CONTACT: 613-548-4415, Kingston Area Visitor and Convention Bureau.

Kingston Mills Blockhouse and Anglin Visitor Centre

WHERE: 4 km (2.5 mi.) north of Kingston, 1 km (0.6 mi.) north of Hwy. 401, 2 km (1.2 mi.) west of Hwy. 15.

WHEN: Visitor centre open mid-May to mid-June, Monday to Thursday, 8:30 a.m. to 4:30 p.m.; Friday to Sunday, 8:30 a.m. to 7:30 p.m. Blockhouse open mid-May to mid-June, 9 a.m. to 4 p.m. Mid-June to early September, open 10 a.m. to 5 p.m.

WHAT: This lock station, at the southern entrance to the Rideau Canal system, features four locks that raise boats 14 m (46 ft.). A military blockhouse is restored to the 1839 era, when it was garrisoned by the Fourth Batallion of Incorporated Militia of Upper Canada following the Upper Canada Rebellion of 1837-38. The visitor centre screens a film about the Loyalists and the lock station, which was completed in 1832. Not wheelchair accessible. Picnic grounds. Washrooms.

CONTACT: 613-359-5377 or 613-283-5170.

Kingston Penitentiary Museum

WHERE: 555 King St. W. Exit Division St. from Hwy. 401 and proceed south for 250 m (300 yds.). Turn right on Counter St. to Sir John A. Macdonald Blvd., then left. Proceed through four stop lights past walled-in women's prison. Take right turn just past prison.

WHEN: Open mid-May through August, Monday to Friday, 8:30 a.m. to noon and 1 p.m. to 4:30 p.m.

WHAT: The Museum displays artifacts and documents related to the early history of Kingston Penetentiary, early industry and medical practices. Exhibits include punishment devices from earlier times and a variety of contraband items ranging from weapons and pot pipes to escape devices. Not wheelchair accessible.

CONTACT: 613-545-8460, Kingston Penitentiary Museum.

Lake Ontario Park

WHERE: King St. W., just west of Portsmouth Ave.

WHEN: Open mid-May to mid-September, daily.

WHAT: There is a charge for the rides, but no admission fee to this 15.4-ha (38-a.) park with supervised swimming, picnic area and wheelchair-accessible washrooms.

CONTACT: 613-542-6574, Lake Ontario Park; 613-546-4291, Kingston Dept. of Parks and Recreation.

Miller Museum of Geology and Mineralogy

WHERE: Miller Hall, Queen's University. From Hwy 401, south on Division St. Exit approx. 5 km. (3 mi.).

WHEN: Open year round, Monday to Friday, 8:30 a.m. to 4:30 p.m., except holidays.

WHAT: The Museum houses a collection of rocks, minerals and fossils. Displays depict geological processes, including a detailed explanation of the geology of the Kingston area. A new exhibit focuses on the dinosaurs of Alberta. Wheelchair accessible.

CONTACT: 613-545-6767, Curator, Miller Museum of Geology and Mineralogy.

Royal Military College of Canada Museum

WHERE: Fort Frederick, Royal Military College, east of Kingston on Hwy. 2.

WHEN: Open end of June through Labour Day, daily, 10 a.m. to 5 p.m. College grounds open to the public year round. Donations accepted.

WHAT: The Museum, located in Canada's largest Martello Tower, tells the story of the Royal Military College, its graduates and the history of the Royal Dockyard, which was located at the site from 1789 to 1853. The Museum also displays the outstanding small arms collection of General Porfirio Diaz, President of Mexico from 1886 to 1912. Washrooms, picnic tables, souvenir counter. Group visits may be made out of season by appointment. Not wheelchair accessible.

CONTACT: 613-541-6664 during Museum hours; 613-541-6663, Office; or 613-541-6652, Royal Military College of Canada.

Walking Tour of Kingston

WHERE: Downtown Kingston. Walk starts at the Visitor and Convention Bureau, 209 Ontario St.

WHEN: Year round.

WHAT: Many of Kingston's historically and architecturally interesting buildings are among the twenty-five included in this tour. The Kingston and Area Visitor and Convention Bureau provides a free copy of a the map and descriptions of the buildings.

CONTACT: 613-548-4415, Kingston and Area Visitor and Convention Bureau.

Guided Walking Tour of Queen's University Campus

WHERE: Tours start from 131 Union St. on the campus.

WHEN: Year round, by appointment. No tours in May.

WHAT: The sixty- to ninety-minute tour of the campus covers the equivalent of five city blocks and includes approximately seventy buildings. Wheelchair accessible washrooms.

CONTACT: 613-545-2217, Queen's University.

Wolfe Island ferry

WHERE: Kingston terminal is at the intersection of Ontario St. and Barrack St.; the Wolfe Island terminal is at Village Dock in Marysville.

WHEN: Ferry operates year round, weather permitting. There are frequent sailings from 5:45 a.m. to 2 a.m. Free to passengers and vehicles.

WHAT: The ferry has a capacity of fifty vehicles and 330 passengers. A one-way trip takes about twenty minutes and provides a fine view of downtown Kingston, Old Fort Henry and the Martello towers at Royal Military College. From Wolfe Island a ferry connects to Cape Vincent, N.Y., May through October.

CONTACT: 613-544-2220, Ontario Ministry of Transportation.

Middleville

Middleville Museum

WHERE: In Middleville, about 25 km (15.5 mi.) north of Perth on County Rd. 16, which runs northeast from Hwy. 511 at Hopetown.

WHEN: Open late May through Thanksgiving, Saturday, Sunday, Monday and Wednesday, 1 p.m. to 4 p.m. Closed Thursday to Sunday except by appointment. Donations accepted.

WHAT: This small museum displays community artifacts, including household utensils, quilts, bonnets, bustles, bottles, jars, toys, dolls and dishes. Parking, picnic area, washrooms. Wheelchair access to first floor only.

CONTACT: 613-259-2785, Middleville Museum.

Morrisburg

Upper Canada Migratory Bird Sanctuary

WHERE: 14 km (8.7 mi.) east of Morrisburg off Hwy. 2.

WHEN: Open April through November. Fall feeding mid-September to mid-November, daily, 2:30 p.m.

WHAT: The Sanctuary consists of 1,400 ha (3,500 a.) of land and water, with an interpretive centre and viewing stand. It is a shelter for migrating Canada Geese and ducks. Spring and fall are the best times to view the migratory birds, but summer visitors can see many wild birds that remain at the Sanctuary.

CONTACT: 613-534-2847, St. Lawrence Parks Commission.

Ottawa

See Ottawa section.

Pakenham

Stone bridge

WHERE: In the Village of Pakenham on Hwy. 15 about 12 km (7.5 mi.) south of Arnprior.

WHEN: Year round.

WHAT: This limestone bridge across the Mississippi River, built at the turn of the century, is touted as the only five-span stone bridge in North America. Picnic tables are located adjacent to the bridge, which spans a series of rapids.

CONTACT: 613-624-5430, Pakenham Municipal Office.

Pembroke

Swallow roost

WHERE: Pembroke Marina.

WHEN: Swallows roost from early June through August. Best seen during first two weeks of August.

WHAT: A small stand of willows is home to a colony of swallows that roosts in early June and reaches peak numbers during the first two weeks of August. From then on the flock diminishes as each cold front inspires more birds to head for South America. In 1983 an estimated 115,000 swallows summered in the roost, but most years the flock numbers between 25,000 and 100,000. The six species of swallow attract the elusive merlin, a small falcon which is one of the few birds capable of preying on them in mid-air. Serious bird watchers are on the site a half-hour before sunrise to watch the birds perform their spectacular aerobatics as they set out for a day of fly-catching. The same displays can be seen a half-hour before sunset, when the swallows return.

Perth

Garden for the Blind

WHERE: From downtown, follow Christie Lake Rd. off Wilson St. and turn at the Lanark County Administration Building.

WHEN: Open daily in growing season, early summer to early fall.

WHAT: The Garden was designed for people who are blind, elderly and physically disabled. It's a hands-on place where visitors can wander among waist-high plant boxes and examine leaf and flower textures and shapes. A self-guiding system leads the visitor from one plant box to the next, but a guide is usually on hand if needed to answer questions. Herbs and geraniums give way to other flavours and fragrances, and there are shaded benches and a splashing fountain to provide respite from the summer heat. During business hours, drinking water and washrooms are available at the adjacent Lanark County Administration Building.

CONTACT: 613-267-3865 or 613-267-3200, The Round Garden Inc., A Garden for the Blind.

Inge-Va

WHERE: 66 Craig St. (Hwy. 43) in Perth.

WHEN: Year round. The house is included in Perth's self-guided walking tour. Visitors may tour the grounds and examine the exterior of the Regency cottage. The inside may be seen by appointment only.

WHAT: This home was built in 1823 by the Maj. Rev. Michael Harris, Perth's first Episcopalian minister in the district, who arrived in 1819. Inge-Va means "come here" in the Tamil language of Sri Lanka. The Reverend Mr. Harris landscaped the grounds with a series of precisely laid-out gardens and paths, including parts of the present-day rose garden. The property now belongs to the Ontario Heritage Foundation. Parking, washrooms, wheelchair access to ground floor.

CONTACT: 416-325-5000, Ontario Heritage Foundation; 613-267-3200, Perth Chamber of Commerce.

Last Duel Park
....

WHERE: Downtown, on the banks of the River Tay.

WHEN: Year round.

WHAT: The historic plaque that tells the story of the last fatal duel in Canada is not located at the site of the duel in this park. Instead, it is found at 66 Craig St., in front of the superb 1824 colonial Georgian-style home of the loser, nineteen-year-old law student Robert Lyon.

CONTACT: 613-267-3200, Perth Chamber of Commerce.

Mammoth Cheese
....

WHERE: Canadian Pacific Railway station.

WHEN: Year round.

WHAT: As a marketing gimmick to promote Canadian cheese, authorities in Ottawa decided Canada would exhibit a monster cheese at the World's Fair in Chicago in 1893. The cheese was 1.8 m (6 ft.) high and 8.5 m (28 ft.) in circumference, and weighed 9,979 kg (22,000 lb.). This is vastly larger than Ingersoll's much-touted cheese of 1866, which weighed only 3,311 kg (7,300 lb.). A cement replica of the Perth cheese is on view at the railway station.

McMartin House
....

WHERE: 125 Gore St.

WHEN: Open year round, Monday to Friday, 2 p.m. to 4:30 p.m.

WHAT: This house was built in 1830 for Daniel McMartin, the first lawyer in Perth. The American Federal style building is unusual to Ontario and shows the degree to which cultural influences transcended national boundaries.

CONTACT: 613-267-5531, Perth and District Senior Craft Fellowship; 613-267-3200, Perth Chamber of Commerce; 416-325-5000, Ontario Heritage Foundation.

Perth Walking Tour

WHERE: Downtown Perth.

WHEN: Year round.

WHAT: The Perth Local Architectural Conservation Advisory Committee and the Chamber of Commerce have prepared two walking tours, each of which takes thirty minutes if you saunter. One route follows the Tay Canal past the site of the Last Duel and the old Burying Ground. The other passes fifteen historically interesting buildings or sites in only two square blocks. A free map of the walking tours is available from Perth Chamber of Commerce, 80 Gore St. E.

CONTACT: 613-267-3200, Perth Chamber of Commerce.

Silversides Tool Museum

WHERE: Perth Wildlife Reserve, 3 km (2 mi.) south of Perth off County Rd. 1.

WHEN: Open by appointment, May through October.

WHAT: The Museum, housed in a log house, contains more than 2,000 nineteenth-century tools from Lanark County. Six exhibits display implements used in blacksmithing, agriculture, forestry, coopering, carpentry and leathercraft. Washrooms, nature trails, interpretive centre, wheelchair access to main floor.

CONTACT: 613-267-5721, Rideau Valley Conservation Authority.

Petawawa

Canadian Airborne Forces Museum and CFB Petawawa Military Museum

WHERE: CFB Petawawa, 20 km (12.4 mi.) north of Pembroke on the Ottawa River.

WHEN: Year round, Labour Day to June, open Sunday to Wednesday, 1 p.m. to 4 p.m. July to Labour Day, open daily, 9 a.m. to 4 p.m.

WHAT: Two military museums depict the histories of Base Petawawa and the Canadian Airborne Forces with exhibits and audio-visual presentations. There is an extensive outdoor aircraft and military vehicle display. Guided tours last approximately ninety minutes. Wheelchair-accessible washrooms.

CONTACT: 613-588-6238, Curator of Museums, CFB Petawawa.

Prescott

The Blue Church

WHERE: About 3 km (2 mi.) west of Prescott on Hwy. 2.

WHEN: Year round.

WHAT: This small wooden chapel, painted pale blue, was built in 1845 to replace an earlier structure damaged by fire. It is the burial place of Irish-born Barbara Heck, who emigrated to New York with her husband Paul and founded the first Methodist Society and the first Wesleyan Church in America. After the American Revolution she and her husband moved to Canada, settling near the church in 1785 and forming a pioneer Methodist Society. She died in 1804.

Fort Wellington National Historic Site

WHERE: Hwy. 2, 5 km (3 mi.) west of International Bridge.

WHEN: Year round. Victoria Day through Labour Day, open daily, 10 a.m. to 6 p.m. September to mid-October, open daily, 10 a.m. to 5 p.m. Mid-October to May, open by reservation, Monday to Friday, 8 a.m. to 4:30 p.m., except major holidays.

WHAT: This fort, constructed during the War of 1812, originally included a blockhouse, artillery barracks and officers' quarters. During the Rebellion of 1837-38 the ruins of the earlier structures were removed and the present blockhouse and officers quarters were built. The buildings are furnished to the 1846 period and there are costumed guides. Visitor centre, picnic area. Wheelchair-accessible washrooms.

CONTACT: 613-925-2896, Fort Wellington, Canadian Parks Service.

The Forwarders' Museum

WHERE: Centre St. and Water St. From Hwy. 401 take Exit 716.

WHEN: Open mid-May through Labour Day, Tuesday to Saturday, 10 a.m. to 4 p.m.; Sunday, noon to 4 p.m. Donations accepted.

WHAT: Built early in the nineteenth century and used as a warehouse, this small stucco-over-stone building on the St. Lawrence River played a major part in Prescott's history. The Museum commemorates the forwarding trade between 1800 and 1850 when Prescott, located at the head of the rapids between it and Montreal, was a major transshipment point. The museum explains forwarding (a means of getting goods around the river rapids) and displays artifacts from the first half of the nineteenth century. Free parking. Picnic area. Gift shop. Washrooms. Not wheelchair accessible.

CONTACT: 613-925-5788, The Forwarders' Museum.

Rolphton

Peter A. Nichol Driftwood Museum and Craft Centre

WHERE: At Rolphton, Moore Lake Rd., just off Hwy. 17, 15 km (9.3 mi.) west of Deep River.

WHEN: Open year round, daily, 10 a.m. to 8 p.m.

WHAT: The Museum displays driftwood sculptures by forty local artists. There are birds, animals and abstract shapes formed by the action of nature on wood. Washrooms, wheelchair accessible.

CONTACT: 613-586-2247, Peter A. Nichol Driftwood Museum and Craft Centre.

St. Raphael

St. Raphael Ruins

WHERE: In hamlet of St. Raphael, north of Williamstown on County Rd. 18 between Martintown and Brown House Corner.

WHEN: Year round.

WHAT: In 1786, 500 Scottish Highlanders led by Father Alexander Macdonnell emigrated to this area from Knoydart, Scotland, and built a church known as the Blue Chapel. In 1815 the settlers began building a larger stone structure to replace the original church. The interior was built without pillars, using hardwood pegs instead of nails. The church was completed in 1821 and remained in use until it was gutted by fire in 1970. The stonework and design of the exterior walls is so massive and intricate that the Ontario Heritage Foundation has had them stabilized so they will not deteriorate further, and the grounds have been landscaped. During summer, church services and plays are performed in the roofless ruins.

Smith Falls

Hershey Canada Inc.

WHERE: Hershey Dr. off Hwy. 43E.

WHEN: Open year round, Monday to Saturday, 9 a.m. to 5 p.m. Self-guided tours. (On Saturday you may not see any production work.) The plant has a shut-down period each summer. Call ahead before planning a visit.

WHAT: On a self-guided tour through this chocolate-factory you can view the different stages of production and packing. Signs posted along the elevated viewing galleries explain each process. Free samples, washrooms, picnic tables, store with Hershey products and some deals on damaged or mislabelled goods. Theatre with video. Not wheelchair accessible.

CONTACT: 613-283-3300, Hershey Canada Inc., Visitors Dept.

The Smiths Falls Railway Museum

WHERE: 90 William St. W. near Hwy. 15, Hwy. 43 and Hwy. 29

WHEN: Open May to October, daily, 10 a.m. to 4 p.m. Train rides on Sundays. Donations welcomed.

WHAT: The Museum is housed in the former Canadian Northern Ontario-Canadian National Railway station, built in 1914 and declared a site of national historic importance. Railroading artifacts are displayed, and the last of four Wickham inspection cars in Canada is used to take visitors on short rail trips. Owned and operated by the Rideau Valley Division of the Canadian Railroad Historical Association. Gift shop. Washrooms. Wheelchair accessible.

CONTACT: 613-283-5696, Smith Falls Railway Museum.

Vernon

Osgoode Township Museum

WHERE: Hwy. 31 in Vernon, about 40 km (25 mi.) southeast of Ottawa.

WHEN: May 24 to Labour Day, open Tuesday to Saturday, 11 a.m. to 5 p.m. Labour Day to May 24, open Saturday, 11 a.m. to 5 p.m. or by appointment.

WHAT: The Museum, in a former schoolhouse, features both

---

artifacts and records rooms, with an emphasis on agricultural life in the township. A new building houses an agricultural collection. Washroom, parking, children's playground. With assistance, wheelchair access to the first floor.

CONTACT: 613-821-4062, Osgoode Township Museum, June through October.

White Lake

Waba Cottage Museum

WHERE: In White Lake, facing White Lake.

WHEN: Victoria Day to end of June and Labour Day to Thanksgiving, open weekends only, 1 p.m. to 4:30 p.m. July through Labour Day, open daily, 1 p.m. to 4:30 p.m. Donations accepted.

WHAT: This was the original home of Laird Archibald McNab, the thirteenth Chief of the McNab clan. McNab founded the settlement in this area in 1825 and tried to establish a feudal feifdom, the only one in Canada's history. The Museum is located in McNab's home, which he built in 1830. In 1936, the home was dynamited by its owner at the time, who was disgruntled with negotiations with a branch of the Ontario government. Reconstructed in 1937, it now contains exhibits highlighting local history and the settlers. Also located on the grounds is an 1878 log school house and an 1868 log "temple" penny reading house originally built by a temperance society. (People would pay a penny to listen to readings, usually chronicling the evils of the Demon Rum.) Books on local history are sold at the Museum. Large picnic area, washrooms, wheelchair accessible.

CONTACT: 613-623-8853, Waba Cottage Museum; 613-623-7820, curator.

Williamstown

Bethune-Thompson House

WHERE: 19730 John St. (County Rd. 17) in Williamstown, 25 km (15.5 mi.) northeast of Cornwall.

WHEN: Open year round, Sunday, 1 p.m. to 5 p.m.

WHAT: Early settler Peter Ferguson built this vertical beam residence of squared timbers in 1784. It later served as the manse of the Rev. John Bethune, the first Presbyterian minister in Upper Canada and great-great-grandfather of Dr. Norman Bethune. The home was then used by cartographer and explorer David Thompson, who mapped major travel routes in Canada and the United States.

CONTACT: 613-347-7192, curator; 416-325-5000, Ontario Heritage Foundation.

Ottawa

O ttawa has a wealth of delights, from museums and beautiful natural scenery to lovely historic buildings and the best in dining and entertainment. It's a city that impresses foreign visitors and instills a large dose of national pride in Canadians who visit.

Queen Victoria chose Ottawa as the country's capital for five reasons, all of which were valid at the time: the site was politically acceptable to both Canada East and Canada West; it was centrally located; it was remote from the hostile United States; it was industrially prosperous; and it had a naturally beautiful setting at the confluence of the Ottawa and Rideau rivers.

Ottawa's festivals and special events are included at the start of the Ontario East chapter. More detailed information on the festivals, carnivals, celebrations and other attractions of Ottawa is available from: Ottawa Tourism and Convention Authority, Ottawa-Carleton Centre, 2nd Floor, 111 Lisgar St., Ottawa, Ontario K2P 2L7, 613-237-5150.

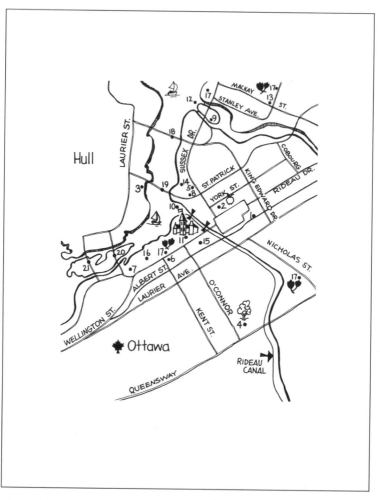

1 Arts Court	12 Rideau Falls
2 Byward Market	13 Rideau Hall
3 Canadian Museum of Civilization	14 Royal Canadian Mint
4 Canadian Museum of Nature	15 Sparks St. Mall
5 Canadian War Museum	16 Supreme Court of Canada
6 Currency Museum	17 Tulips
7 National Library of Canada	18 Pont Macdonald Cartier
8 National Gallery	Bridge
9 Ottawa City Hall	19 Pont Alexandria Bridge
10 Ottawa Locks	20 Pont Du Portage Bridge
11 Parliament Buildings	21 Pont Chaudière Bridge

Agricultural Museum, Central Experimental Farm

(Also see listing for Central Experimental Farm.)

WHERE: Follow Queen Elizabeth Driveway southwest past Dows Lake and turn right at the traffic circle. The Museum is at the Dairy Barn, in the Central Experimental Farm, off Prince of Wales Dr.

WHEN: Museum open daily, 9:30 a.m. to 5 p.m., except Christmas and New Year's Day. Donations welcome.

WHAT: The Museum features two permanent exhibits, "Haying in Canada" and "A Barn in the 1920s," both illustrating early farm machinery. Picnic areas on lawns. Wheelchair access to washrooms, barns and museum.

CONTACT: 613-993-4802, Central Experimental Farm Agricultural Museum.

Arts Court

WHERE: 2 Daly Ave., just behind the Rideau Centre.

WHEN: Open year round. Gallery hours, Tuesday to Sunday, 10 a.m. to 5 p.m.; Thursday, to 9 p.m. Admission free to gallery; varying prices for special presentations.

WHAT: Ottawa's municipal arts centre, located in the historic former Carleton County Courthouse, includes an art gallery, a multi-purpose theatre, and workshop and office space for artists and arts organizations from the Ottawa region. A programme of art exhibitions and performances, seminars and lectures is held year round. Wheelchair accessible.

CONTACT: 613-233-3449, Arts Court.

Basilica of Notre Dame Cathedral

WHERE: Sussex Dr., between Guigues St. and St. Patrick St.

WHEN: Year round. Open for prayer from 7 a.m. to 5:30 p.m. Services Monday to Friday, 7:30 a.m. and 5 p.m.; Saturday, 7:30 a.m.

to 4:30 p.m.; Sunday, 9 a.m., 10:30 a.m., noon and 5 p.m.

WHAT: Colonel By gave the land to the Catholics of Bytown in 1832 and construction began on the present building (which replaced a small wooden chapel) around 1840. Since 1858 the church has been an architectural landmark in the capital. Many of the stone and wood carvers who came here to work on the Parliament Buildings also worked on Notre-Dame. An Italian sculptor who had unsuccessfully competed for a commission on Parliament Hill earned his fare home by carving the Madonna and Child which now stand between the Basilica's two tall spires. The church's elaborately decorated interior, completed around 1890, is mostly wood. Some of the wood, like the large columns supporting the roof, is decorated with a false marble finish. More than a hundred carved wooden statues stand around the main altar. Wheelchair accessible.

CONTACT: 613-236-7496, Parish office, Basilica of Notre Dame Cathedral.

Billings Estate Museum

WHERE: 2100 Cabot St. Go south on Bank St., cross the Rideau River at Billings Bridge and take Riverside east. Turn right on Pleasant Park and right on Cabot.

WHEN: Open mid-May through October, Sunday to Thursday, noon to 5 p.m. Admission by donation.

WHAT: Here's a way to experience history as it was witnessed by four generations of one of Ottawa's earliest settled families. This neoclassical house was built overlooking the Rideau River in 1828. Together with its spacious grounds, outbuildings and historic cemetery, the Museum tells the story of Ottawa's evolution from wilderness settlement to national capital. A guided tour of the house takes thirty to forty-five minutes; grounds tours are self-guided. Picnic area, parking, gift shop, afternoon teas, washrooms. Full facilities for disabled people.

CONTACT: 613-564-1363, Billings Estate Museum.

Byward Market

WHERE: East of Chateau Laurier and one block north of Rideau St. between York St. and George St.

WHEN: Outdoor market, year round, daily. Mid-March to mid-November, open 6 a.m. to 6 p.m. Mid-November to mid-March, open 8 a.m. to 5 p.m. Indoor market open year round, daily, 9:30 a.m. to 5:30 a.m., except January through March, closed Sunday and Monday. Closed December 25, 26, and January 1.

WHAT: Farmers from surrounding districts bring their produce to this market, which has operated since the 1830s. There are 129 shops selling everything from fresh veggies to crafts and plants. Restaurants and outdoor cafés serve shoppers in summer. No wheelchair access to second floor of Market Building.

CONTACT: 613-564-1521, Byward Market.

Canada Council Art Bank

WHERE: 370 Catherine St., southwest of the Voyageur Bus Station, second floor.

WHEN: Open year round, Monday to Friday, 9 a.m. to 5 p.m. Public tours Wednesday, 10 a.m., 1:30 p.m. and 3 p.m. or by appointment.

WHAT: The Canada Council owns about 15,000 works of art by contemporary Canadian artists. Most of the collection is on loan throughout Canada; the rest is stored in a warehouse or on display in this small gallery. Wheelchair access, parking, washrooms.

CONTACT: 613-598-4331, Canada Council Art Bank.

Canadian Museum of Caricature

WHERE: 136 St. Patrick St., corner of St. Patrick St. and Sussex Dr., near the National Gallery of Canada.

WHEN: Open year round, Wednesday to Friday, 10 a.m. to 8 p.m.; Saturday to Tuesday, 10 a.m. to 6 p.m. Guided tours available daily, May through August.

WHAT: A permanent collection of Canadian cartoons is complemented by changing special exhibitions on various themes. Wheelchair access, washrooms, restaurants nearby.

CONTACT: 613-995-3145, Canadian Museum of Caricature.

Canadian Museum of Civilization

WHERE: 100 Laurier St., in Hull, Quebec, on the Ottawa River directly across from Parliament Hill.

WHEN: Year round. May through mid-September, open daily, 9 a.m. to 5 p.m.; Thursday, to 9 p.m. September through April, open daily except Monday, 9 a.m. to 6 p.m.; Thursday, to 9 p.m. Closed December 25. General admission free to all facilities on Thursdays. Admission charge to Cineplus and to Museum on all other days.

WHAT: The Canadian Museum of Civilization, opened in 1989, is architecturally unique. Inside, the latest in communications technology illustrates Canadian history and society from early Native culture to the present day. Cineplus is the world's only Imax-Omnimax film theatre. There's a 500-seat theatre for live performances and lectures, a restaurant, cafeteria, guides and audio-guides for rent. Wheelchair accessible.

CONTACT: 819-776-7000 (recorded information); 819-776-7006, Canadian Museum of Civilization.

Canadian Museum of Nature

WHERE: McLeod St. and Metcalfe St. Metcalfe Exit off the Queensway. Local bus #5 or #6.

WHEN: Year round, daily. May to Labour Day, open 9:30 a.m. to 5 p.m.; Sunday, Monday, and Thursday, to 8 p.m. September through April, open 10 a.m. to 5 p.m.; Thursday, to 8 p.m. Closed December 25. Admission free to all on Thursdays; admission charged at all other times. Parking fee.

WHAT: This building was used briefly by the Canadian Parliament after a fire in the capital building. The Museum presents a journey

---

through time covering the vanished world of dinosaurs as well as excellent displays of today's birds, mammals, plants and minerals. There are hands-on exhibits, live animals and a mini-theatre. The Discovery Den offers a range of exhibits and activities tailored especially for children. Cafeteria, museum shop, wheelchair accessible.

CONTACT: 613-996-3102, Canadian Museum of Nature.

Canadian War Museum

WHERE: 330 Sussex Dr.

WHEN: Open year round, daily, 9:30 a.m. to 5 p.m. Closed December 25. Admission free to Canadian veterans at all times and to the general public on Thursdays; admission charged at all other times.

WHAT: The Museum traces Canada's military history with displays of uniforms, vehicles and weapons of all types and vintages—from French colonial times to the Korean War. Self-guided tours, souvenir shop, wheelchair-accessible washrooms.

CONTACT: 613-992-2774, Canadian War Museum.

Central Experimental Farm

WHERE: Follow Queen Elizabeth Driveway southwest past Dows Lake and turn right at the traffic circle. The Central Experimental Farm is off Prince of Wales Dr.

WHEN: Grounds open year round, sunrise to dusk. Barns and greenhouse open daily, 9 a.m. to 4 p.m. Horse-drawn wagon rides available, weather permitting, May through September, Monday to Friday, 10 a.m. to 11:30 a.m. and 2 p.m. to 3:30 p.m.; Saturday and Sunday, 12:30 to 2:30 p.m. Sleigh rides available in winter months. Call for times.

WHAT: The Central Experimental Farm, established in 1886, is headquarters for the Canada Department of Agriculture and its Research Branch. On the 486-ha (1,200-a.) site visitors can tour flower beds, ornamental gardens, the arboretum and tropical greenhouse. There are showcase herds of dairy and beef cattle, sheep, swine and horses.

Large-scale experiments are conducted with field crops. Picnic areas on lawns. Wheelchair access to washrooms and barns.

CONTACT: 613-995-8963, Central Experimental Farm.

Chateau Laurier

WHERE: 1 Rideau St., beside the Rideau Canal locks, just down the street from Parliament Hill.

WHEN: Open year round, by appointment. One-hour guided tours offered daily in July and August, one in French, one in English. Telephone concierge to confirm times.

WHAT: If you're not staying in this grand old hotel while visiting Ottawa, consider one of the tours. Or, if you don't have time for a tour, at least pop into the lobby for a quick gawk. The Grand Trunk Railway Company built the 450-room hotel in 1912 to complement the train station across the street (now the Government Conference Centre). The hotel has been a temporary home for numerous cabinet ministers and members of Parliament. Prime Minister R. B. Bennett lived there from 1930 to 1935.

CONTACT: 613-232-6411, Chateau Laurier Hotel, ask for Concierge Desk.

City of Ottawa Archives

WHERE: 174 Stanley Ave., off Sussex Dr.

WHEN: Year round. June through Labour Day, open Monday to Friday, 8:30 a.m. to 4 p.m. Labour Day to end of May, open Monday to Friday, 8:30 a.m. to 4:30 p.m. Thanksgiving to end of May, open Tuesday evenings, 6:30 p.m. to 9 p.m. Closed on weekends and all statutory holidays.

WHAT: The Archives house municipal records, private document collections, historical photograph collections and published information on Ottawa's history. Washrooms, parking at rear, reference room, exhibit room. Not wheelchair accessible.

CONTACT: 613-564-1352, City of Ottawa Archives.

Capital Vignettes

WHERE: Parliament Hill beside Centre Block Bldg., near Infotent.

WHEN: Performances late June to late August, Wednesday to Sunday, 10:45 a.m. to 4 p.m.

WHAT: Outdoor theatrical presentations on the theme of Canada's past star historic figures such as Sir John A. Macdonald.

CONTACT: 613-239-5000, National Capital Commission.

Carillon concerts

WHERE: Parliament Hill.

WHEN: Concerts year round, weekdays, 12:30 to 12:45 p.m. June and July, additional performances Sunday and Thursday, 7:30 p.m. to 8:30 p.m. Times subject to change—call to confirm. Special concerts on Remembrance Day and other special occasions.

WHAT: The Dominion Carillonneur and guest performers play the fifty-three bronze bells in the Peace Tower.

CONTACT: 613-992-4793, Public Information Office, House of Commons.

Changing the Guard

WHERE: Parliament Hill in front of Parliament Buildings on the East Lawn.

WHEN: Late June through late August, daily, weather permitting, 10 a.m.

WHAT: A colourful, precise military ritual is performed by the Governor General's Foot Guards and the Canadian Grenadier Guards. The ceremony includes inspections of dress and weapons, the parading of the Colours through the ranks of the new guard and the exchange of compliments between the old and new guards. At the end, the guards march off, accompanied by the Band of the Ceremonial Guard, and the new guard takes over sentry duties at Rideau Hall. At Rideau Hall, sentries are posted daily from 10 a.m. to 6 p.m., and are relieved on the hour.

CONTACT: 613-992-3328, Public Information Office, House of Commons; 613-993-9977, Commanding Officer, Ceremonial Guard.

Currency Museum, Bank of Canada

WHERE: 245 Sparks St. Mall between Kent St. and Bank St.

WHEN: Year round. Labour Day to April, open Tuesday to Saturday, 10:30 a.m. to 5 p.m.; Sunday, 1 p.m. to 5 p.m. Closed Mondays. April through Labour Day, open daily, 10:30 a.m. to 5 p.m. Closed December 24, 25, 31, January 1, Good Friday, Thanksgiving and Remembrance Day. Free admission Tuesdays; small admission fee at all other times.

WHAT: The Museum depicts the evolution of money from its earliest beginnings to modern times, including whale's teeth, wampum, beads, bells, tea and salt blocks, Chinese tool money, the card money of the French regime, a three-ton Yap stone from the South Pacific and pre-historic currency from around the world. A short film explains the role of the Bank of Canada and the manufacture of paper money. Guided or self-guided tours. Wheelchair-accessible washrooms.

CONTACT: 613-782-8914, Currency Museum, Bank of Canada.

Discover the Hill

WHERE: Infotent on Parliament Hill.

WHEN: Late June to Labour Day weekend, tours from 9 a.m. to 4 p.m., every hour or more frequently.

WHAT: The forty-five-minute tours lead visitors to statues of Canadian prime ministers while the guide narrates Canada's first hundred years as a nation. The tour includes a description of Canada's government. Same-day reservations can be made at Infotent.

CONTACT: 613-239-5161, Co-ordinator, Discover The Hill.

Dows Lake Pavilion

WHERE: Northeast corner of Dows Lake.

WHEN: Open year round, 8 a.m. to 1 a.m.

WHAT: In winter, the pavilion is a changing and warming place for skaters; in summer, it is a marina with full facilities for boaters plus paddleboat and canoe rentals. Three ethnic restaurants, open all year, are the only restaurants situated on the canal in Ottawa. Wheelchair-accessible washrooms, gift shop, showers, laundry, skate sharpening and rentals.

CONTACT: 613-232-1001, Dows Lake Pavilion.

Garden of the Provinces

WHERE: Across from the National Library, Wellington St. and Bay St.

WHEN: Year round.

WHAT: Two symbolic fountains highlight a display of the arms and floral emblems of the provinces and territories of Canada. The upper fountain represents the many lakes and rivers of Canada.

Laurier House

WHERE: 335 Laurier Ave. E. at Chapel St. Nicholas St. Exit from Hwy. 417.

WHEN: October through March, open Tuesday to Saturday, 10 a.m. to 5 p.m.; Sunday, 2 p.m. to 5 p.m. April through September, open Tuesday to Saturday, 9 a.m. to 5 p.m.; Sunday, 2 p.m. to 5 p.m. Closed December 25, January 1 and Good Friday. Wheelchair accessible.

WHAT: This house was the residence of two former prime ministers, Wilfred Laurier and William Lyon Mackenzie King. The house contains some interesting historical exhibits and personal mementos of both men. The contents of the study of another Canadian prime minister, Lester B. Pearson, are also displayed. Wheelchair accessible.

CONTACT: 613-992-8142, Laurier House.

Mackenzie King Estate (Moorside and Kingswood)

WHERE: Old Chelsea, Quebec. Take Hwy. 5 north from Macdonald-Cartier bridge to Exit 12, turn left on Old Chelsea Rd. for 3 km (2 mi.). Turn left on to Gatineau Pkwy. and follow signs to the Mackenzie King Estate.

WHEN: Victoria Day weekend to Labour Day, open daily, 11 a.m. to 6 p.m. Labour Day through Thanksgiving, open Wednesday to Sunday, 11 a.m. to 6 p.m.

WHAT: The country estate of the former prime minister William Lyon Mackenzie King, located in the Gatineau Hills, features walking trails, lovely gardens, and period furniture in restored rooms and cottages. In the gardens you will encounter the mysterious "ruins" created by King. Tea room and restaurant, snack bar, washrooms, picnic grounds. Wheelchair access to gardens, grounds, washrooms, audio-visual shows, tea and snack room.

CONTACT: 613-239-5000, National Capital Commission.

Museum of Canadian Scouting

WHERE: 1345 Baseline Rd. From Queensway, south on Maitland, east on Baseline Rd.

WHEN: Open year round, Monday to Friday, 9 a.m. to 4:30 p.m. Closed all holidays. Scout shop open Saturday except July and August.

WHAT: The history of scouting in Canada and the life of the founder, Lord Baden-Powell of Gilwell, are depicted in photographs, charts, maps, artifacts, insignia, books and presentation pieces from around the world. There are random projectors and videos to assist those interested in learning about Baden-Powell and the scouting movement. Wheelchair-accessible washrooms.

CONTACT: 613-224-5131, Museum of Canadian Scouting.

National Archives of Canada

WHERE: 395 Wellington St. at Bay St., a ten-minute walk from the Parliament Buildings.

WHEN: Year round. Exhibitions are open daily, 9 a.m. to 9 p.m. Manuscript and Federal Archives reading rooms are open twenty-four hours a day, seven days a week. It is necessary, however, to request documents during regular working hours, Monday to Friday, 8:30 a.m. to 4:15 p.m.

WHAT: The National Archives acquires significant documents relating to Canada's development and provides research services and facilities to make this material available to the public. Books, paintings, water colours, engravings, photographs, manuscripts, sound recordings, films, maps and machine-readable records are maintained. Reproductions may be obtained at reasonable rates. Wheelchair accessible, special washroom facilities.

CONTACT: 613-992-3052, general inquiries, National Archives of Canada.

National Arts Centre

WHERE: Confederation Square, 53 Elgin St., near Parliament Hill.

WHEN: Tours held May through August, Tuesday, Thursday, Saturday and Sunday, noon, 1:30 p.m. and 3 p.m. September through April, tours held Saturday only, noon, 1:30 p.m. and 3 p.m. The twenty-to forty-minute tours are free. Performance ticket prices vary.

WHAT: The National Arts Centre is located in the heart of downtown Ottawa, overlooking the Rideau Canal and the Rideau Centre Complex. The Centre presents more than 900 performances each year, including English- and French-language plays, concerts by the NAC Orchestra and visiting orchestras and soloists, and dance and variety entertainment.

CONTACT: 613-996-5051 for information; 613-755-1111 for tickets by Ticketmaster.

National Aviation Museum

WHERE: Rockcliffe Airport. Follow Sussex Dr. past Rideau Hall to the Rockcliffe Pkwy. and follow signs for 4 km (2.5 mi.).

WHEN: Year round, Labour Day through April, open Tuesday to Sunday, 9 a.m. to 5 p.m.; Thursday, to 9 p.m. May through Labour Day, open daily, 9 a.m. to 5 p.m.; Thursday, to 9 p.m. Free admission after 5 p.m. Thursday, otherwise admission charged at all times.

WHAT: The Museum houses a collection of over one hundred historic aircraft plus a large collection of engines and other items linked to aviation history. The exhibits illustrate the evolution of the flying machine in peace and war, including the important role of aviation in Canada's development. The Walkway of Time in the main exhibit hall features aircraft that illustrate successive aviation eras from the turn of the century to the present. The Royal Canadian Air Force Hall of Tribute is found at the entranceway. Gift shop, free parking, wheelchair accessible, wheelchairs available.

CONTACT: 613-993-2010, National Aviation Museum.

National Gallery of Canada

WHERE: 380 Sussex Dr.

WHEN: Year round. May through August, open Wednesday to Friday, 10 a.m. to 8 p.m.; Saturday to Tuesday, 10 a.m. to 6 p.m. September through April, open Tuesday to Sunday, 10 a.m. to 5 p.m.; Thursday, to 8 p.m. Closed Monday and statutory holidays. Free admission on Thursdays; admission charged at all other times.

WHAT: This startling building features walls of glass, and skylights that introduce natural light to the galleries and interior courtyards and gardens. The Canadian galleries show Canadian art from 1800 to 1960, including works by the Group of Seven. The reconstructed Rideau Chapel, saved from demolition and declared a national historic site, displays works of ecclesiastical art and silver. Upper-level galleries feature works from the European, American and Asian collections, photographs, drawings, prints and Inuit art. There are changing exhibits of contemporary art on both levels. The building was designed to be barrier-free for disabled people. Restaurant, café, cafeteria, gallery shop. Charge for underground parking.

CONTACT: 613-990-1985, National Gallery of Canada.

National Library of Canada

WHERE: 395 Wellington St. at Bay St., a five-minute walk from Parliament Hill.

WHEN: Year round. Exhibition room open daily, 9 a.m. to 9 p.m. Service hours, Monday to Friday, 8:30 a.m. to 5 p.m.

WHAT: The National Library of Canada gathers, preserves and makes known Canada's literary and musical heritage, promotes the development of library services and resources in Canada and supports resource-sharing among Canadian libraries. There are exhibitions and music programmes.

CONTACT: 613-992-9988, National Library of Canada.

National Mineral Collection, Energy, Mines and Resources, Canada

WHERE: Logan Hall, 601 Booth St. Follow Queen Elizabeth Driveway southwest, turn right at Preston St. (Dows Lake), turn right on Carling Ave. and left on Booth St.

WHEN: Open year round, weekdays, 8 a.m. to 4:30 p.m. Closed on weekends and holidays.

WHAT: The National Mineral Collection began with the work of the Geological Survey of Canada, an organization authorized by Parliament in 1841 to investigate the geology and natural history of Canada. The small museum in Logan Hall has two galleries: an historical display of the people of the Geological Survey of Canada, and a collection of minerals and ores from around the world.

CONTACT: 613-995-4946, National Mineral Collection, Energy, Mines and Resources Canada.

National Museum of Science and Technology

WHERE: 1867 St. Laurent Blvd. at Lancaster Rd., 1.6 km (1 mi.) south of the Queensway.

WHEN: May through Labour Day, open Saturday to Tuesday, 9 a.m.

to 6 p.m.; Wednesday to Friday, to 8 p.m. Labour Day through April, open Tuesday to Sunday, 9 a.m. to 5 p.m. Evening astronomy programme, call for information. Closed December 25. Admission free to all on Thursday, otherwise admission charged at all times.

WHAT: Visitors can explore, push, pull, twist or just look at the exhibits, including locomotives, vintage automobiles and agricultural implements. The science hall features the Crazy Kitchen, printing equipment, model ships, communications and space equipment and computers. Special exhibitions and events are held all year. Cafeteria, gift shop, picnic grounds, wheelchair accessible.

CONTACT: 613-991-3044, National Museum of Science and Technology.

Nepean Museum

WHERE: 16 Rowley Ave., Ottawa, about ten minutes by car from Parliament Hill. Exit the Queensway at Woodroffe Ave. S., drive to Meadowland, east to Rowley Ave.

WHEN: Open year round, Tuesday to Saturday, 10 a.m. to 4 p.m.; Sunday, 1 p.m. to 4 p.m. Closed Mondays. NOTE: Collection of artifacts and some archival material available by appointment only.

WHAT: This historical museum features permanent displays and rotating exhibits of the history of Nepean, covering 1792 to the present. Free parking, picnic and play area, washrooms, wheelchair accessible.

CONTACT: 613-723-7936, Nepean Museum.

Nepean Point Park and Astrolabe Theatre

WHERE: North of St. Patrick St., behind the National Gallery.

WHEN: Open year round. The Cultures Canada Festival is held July through September.

WHAT: This site, a must for photographers, offers a splendid view of Parliament Hill and the Ottawa River. A statue in the park commemorates Samuel de Champlain. The Astrolabe amphitheatre seats

---

1,200 and is used in summer for a variety of shows, including the Cultures Canada Festival.

CONTACT: 1-800-465-1867 or 613-239-5000, National Capital Commission, Information Branch.

Nicholas Gaol International Hostel and Museum

WHERE: 75 Nicholas St.

WHEN: Open year round. Public tours held daily, 8 p.m. to 10 p.m. To arrange a tour during business hours, call 613-235-2595. Donations welcome.

WHAT: This limestone building, now a youth hostel, was a prison from 1862 to 1972. The last public hanging in Canada took place here in 1869, when Patrick Whelan was executed for the assassination of Thomas D'Arcy McGee, a Father of Confederation. The Museum contains a wealth of jail-related artifacts, including the gallows on which Whelan was hanged. Outdoor café in the jail graveyard. Gift shop. Not wheelchair accessible.

CONTACT: 613-235-2595, Nicholas Gaol International Hostel.

Noon Gun

WHERE: Major's Hill Park off Mackenzie Ave.

WHEN: Fired year round, weekdays at noon; Sundays and holidays, 10 a.m.

WHAT: In 1869, Sir John A. Macdonald authorized the firing of a noon gun to help regulate the postal service. Some would question the effect on postal service, but the nine-pound muzzle-loading ship's cannon is still fired.

Ottawa City Hall

WHERE: 111 Sussex Dr., on Green Island, Mann St. Exit from Queensway.

WHEN: Open year round, Monday to Friday, 9 a.m. to 3:30 p.m. Closed holidays.

WHAT: This modern structure overlooks the Ottawa and Rideau rivers and the Gatineau Hills. The council chamber, eighth floor balcony and foyer exhibit area are open to the public. Cafeteria, wheelchair access. In the riverside park behind the building visitors may catch a glimpse of the Royal swans, a Centennial year gift to Ottawa from Queen Elizabeth II.

CONTACT: 613-564-1128, Corporation of the City of Ottawa; 613-564-1400, Reception desk.

Ottawa Locks (Rideau Canal)

WHERE: Between Parliament Hill and the Chateau Laurier Hotel.

WHEN: Lock Station Commissariat Building and exhibits open mid-May to mid-October. Skating mid-December to mid-February, depending on ice conditions.

WHAT: This lock station, at the northern entrance to the Rideau Canal, features an impressive flight of eight locks that lift boats 24 m (79 ft.) from the Ottawa River. The locks are hand-operated, as they were when they were opened in 1832. There are exhibits of city artifacts in the Commissariat Building and associated Bytown Museum, picnic tables and washrooms.

CONTACT: 613-692-2581 or 613-283-5170, Northern Area Office, Rideau Canal, Canadian Parks Service.

Our Lady of Lourdes Shrine

WHERE: Montreal Rd., turn left on Cantin St. The shrine is at the corner of Cantin St. and Montford St. in Vanier.

WHEN: Year round.

WHAT: This reproduction of Our Lady of Lourdes Shrine in France, blessed in 1910, is a destination for pilgrimages. The shrine has outdoor masses and seating for 600 people.

CONTACT: 613-741-4175, Our Lady of Lourdes Shrine.

Parliament Buildings

WHERE: Parliament Hill, Wellington St.

WHEN: Open year round. September through May, guided tours daily, every thirty minutes, 9 a.m. to 4:30 p.m. Last week in May through August, tours every ten minutes, 9 a.m. to 8:30 p.m.; weekends, to 5:30 p.m. Closed December 25, January 1 and July 1. No reservations are necessary for individuals, but visitors wishing to view Question Period in the House of Commons, Monday to Thursday, 2:15 p.m., and Friday, 11:15 a.m., should arrive at least forty-five minutes in advance or obtain a pass from a member of Parliament.

WHAT: The Parliament Buildings, the seat of Canada's federal government, comprise three neo-Gothic Victorian buildings fronting on Wellington St., often collectively termed Parliament Hill. They are home to the House of Commons, the Senate Chamber, the Speaker's Chambers, offices for members and officials of both houses and the Library of Parliament. The Centre Block is crowned by the 92-m (302.5-ft.) Peace Tower with its carillon of fifty-three bells. The Tower, initially called the Victory Tower, was changed to the Peace Tower to honour those Canadians who lost their lives in the First World War. The Tower houses the Memorial Chamber with the Book of Remembrance that lists the names of those who died. In front of the Parliament Buildings, a Centennial Flame burns continuously as a symbol of Canada's first century of nationhood. Washrooms. Buildings, including Peace Tower, fully equipped for disabled visitors.

CONTACT: 613-996-0896, Co-ordinator, Parliamentary Guide Service.

Parliament Hill tours

WHERE: Departure from Infotent, Parliament Hill.

WHEN: End of June through August, daily.

WHAT: Free one-hour outdoor tours of Parliament Hill examine a century of history by focusing on five prime ministers. Role-playing activity programmes are also available for school groups aged eleven to eighteen.

CONTACT: 613-239-5161, National Capital Commission.

Pinhey Estate

WHERE: Northwest Kanata. From March Rd. turn right on Riddell Dr., to 6th Line, turn left and proceed to Pinhey's Point.

WHEN: Open Victoria Day weekend through Labour Day, 10 a.m. to 4 p.m.

WHAT: This limestone house, called Horaceville, is situated on 36 ha (88 a.) of grounds on the Ottawa River. The house was built during the first half of the nineteenth century by Hamnett Pinhey, whose descendants lived there until 1972. The estate features restored rooms, interpretive walks, an old grist mill, the ruins of a church and exhibits. Refreshments available.

CONTACT: 613-592-4281, City of Kanata Parks and Recreation.

Rideau Falls

WHERE: On Sussex Dr., beside the French Embassy and across from Ottawa City Hall.

WHEN: Year round.

WHAT: These lovely double falls were called rideau (curtain) by French-speaking voyageurs who saw them from the Ottawa River. The falls were an important industrial site. The first mill was built there in 1831; by the end of the century, water power from the falls had been harnessed for lumber, flour and textile mills as well as foundries, tanneries and breweries. The National Capital Commission has acquired the land and turned it into a park.

Rideau Hall

WHERE: 1 Sussex Dr., one long block past City Hall and opposite the Prime Minister's residence at 24 Sussex Dr.

WHEN: Tours available of public rooms year round, Monday to Friday, 9 a.m. to 4 p.m. By appointment only. Closed civic holidays. Outdoor walking tours offered from Victoria Day through Labour

Day, daily, hourly, 10 a.m. to 4 p.m. September through May, tours available weekends, 10 a.m. to 3 p.m. NOTE: Check first. All tours are cancelled when official functions are taking place in public rooms.

WHAT: Six rooms are available for public viewing in this 1865 mansion, the official residence of Canada's Governor General, representative of Her Majesty Queen Elizabeth II. Outdoor walking tours of the 36-ha (88-a.) grounds are available. The public rooms are wheelchair accessible. Wheelchairs and strollers are available free of charge for walking tours. Washrooms on grounds.

CONTACT: 613-993-0311, Rideau Hall.

Royal Canadian Mint

WHERE: 320 Sussex Dr.

WHEN: Open by appointment, weekdays, early May through August (except holidays), 8:30 a.m. to 11 a.m. and 12:30 a.m. to 2:30 p.m.

WHAT: The Royal Canadian Mint, built as a branch of the Royal Mint in London, struck its first coin in 1908. In 1931 it became an independent operation. Since 1976, circulating coinage, both foreign and domestic, has been produced in Winnipeg, but the Ottawa mint continues to strike special commemorative coins, tokens, medals and bullion investment coins. Gift shop, wheelchair accessible.

CONTACT: 613-993-5700, Royal Canadian Mint information.

Royal Canadian Mounted Police Stables

WHERE: North end of St. Laurent Blvd.

WHEN: Stables open year round, weekdays, 9 a.m. to 11:30 a.m. and 1 p.m. to 3:30 p.m.

WHAT: RCMP Rockcliffe is home to the Musical Ride, the RCMP Band and the Canadian Police College. The College provides advanced training to police forces from across Canada and abroad. Only the stables are open to the general public. The Band and Musical Ride are absent on tour for a considerable part of each year. However, public performances are presented from time to time when they are in Ottawa.

CONTACT: 613-993-2723, Royal Canadian Mounted Police Stables.

Sound and Light Show

WHERE: Parliament Hill.

WHEN: May through September, weather permitting, two forty-five-minute shows held nightly, one in English and the other in French. Shows are usually at 9:30 and 10:30 p.m. but schedules vary through the summer, so check first.

WHAT: Canada's history unfolds in a display of sound and light, including recorded music and historical commentary, against the backdrop of the Parliament Buildings. Wheelchair-accessible washrooms on Hill. Bleacher seating for approximately 750 people and lots of space to sit on the grass.

CONTACT: 1-800-465-1867 or 613-239-5000, National Capital Commission.

Sparks Street Mall

WHERE: Sparks St. between Elgin St. and Lyon St.

WHEN: Year round.

WHAT: This pedestrian street, closed to vehicles, is lined with flowers, exclusive shops and boutiques. Illuminated fountains, sidewalk cafés and open-air displays entertain strollers.

Supreme Court of Canada

WHERE: Wellington St. at Kent St.

WHEN: Year round. May through August, tours available daily, 9 a.m. to 5 p.m. (reservations recommended). Rest of the year, tours available Monday to Friday, 9 a.m. to 5 p.m. (reservations required). Court sittings: fall, winter and spring sessions, Monday to Friday, 10:30 a.m. to 12:30 p.m. and 2 p.m. to 4 p.m. During this period, court usually sits two weeks and adjourns for two weeks.

WHAT: A thirty-minute tour guided by law students provides information on the procedures of the Supreme Court, Canada's highest court, and the Federal Court, also housed in the building. Washrooms, wheelchair accessible.

CONTACT: 613-995-4330, Supreme Court of Canada.

Tin House Court

WHERE: Across from Jeanne d'Arc Court, entrances on Clarence St. and Murray St.

WHEN: Year round.

WHAT: This unusual work of art was created by tinsmith Honore Foisy, who lived in Lower Town between 1902 and 1916. He and his relatives worked for years to embellish his house with hundreds of hand-shaped pieces of tin, meticulously soldered to form an elaborate decoration.

Tulips

WHERE: Commissioner's Park and other city parks.

WHEN: Spring. Tulip Festival held each year for ten days in mid-May.

WHAT: In 1943, Princess Juliana of the Netherlands fled the German invasion and took refuge in Ottawa. When her baby was born, the Dutch flag was flown from the Peace Tower and Parliament declared a portion of the hospital to be Dutch territory, thus entitling the "Dutch-born" Princess Margriet to ascend the Dutch throne. A grateful Holland sent thousands of tulip bulbs to Ottawa, and every year another 10,000 are sent. Three million bulbs now bloom during the Festival of Spring each year, 250,000 of them in Commissioner's Park.

CONTACT: 1-800-267-7285, 1-800-267-0450 or 613-239-5000, Canada's Capital Visitor Information Centre.

Ontario's Near North

Includes: Algonquin Park, Burk's Falls, Cache Bay, Callander, Magnetawan, Marten River, Mattawa, North Bay, Powassan, Sundridge, Temagami and Trout Creek.

Ontario's Near North helps put the vastness of Ontario in perspective. It is one of the smallest tourist regions yet it contains Algonquin Provincial Park (about 150 per cent larger than Prince Edward Island), Lake Nipissing (900 km²/-350 sq. mi.) and Lake Temagami (260 km²/90 sq. mi.).

Festivals, Carnivals, Celebrations, Special Events:

FEBRUARY: North Bay, *Carnaval et Semaine Française;* North Bay, *Winter Carnival.*

MARCH: Mattawa, *Mt. Antoine Winter Carnival* (donut eating contest, golf tournament, family challenge race); North Bay, *Laurentian Winter Carnival* (challenge ski race, donut eating contest, dance).

MAY: Mattawa, *Spring Fling* (arts and crafts show, boat show, clowns); North Bay, *Near North Golden Pickerel Derby.*

JUNE: Temagami, *Grey Owl's Temagami* (wilderness festival, art festival, heritage displays, Canada Day picnic); North Bay, *Tradi-*

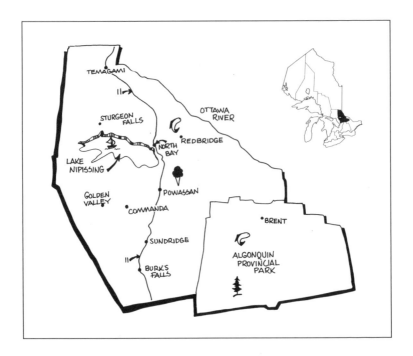

tional Youth and Elders Gathering (arts and crafts, traditional teachings, music, legends and customs, dancing and singing).

JULY: North Bay, *Super Saturdays;* Mattawa, *Mattawa River Canoe Race* (64-km/40-mi. marathon canoe race).

AUGUST: Kearney, *Annual Regatta* (Bavarian gardens, land and water competitions, hayride); Temagami, *Bass Tournament;* South River, *Challenge Run* (sanctioned 5 km/3 mi. and 10 km/6.25 mi. runs, all age categories); North Bay, *Gateway Heritage Festival* (midway, petting zoo, concessions, salute to seniors); Mattawa, *Summer Festival* (fishing derby, fish fry, mayor's play day, North Eastern Fiddling and Step Dancing Championships).

NOVEMBER: North Bay, *Symphony Orchestra special programs.*

DECEMBER: Mattawa, *Christmas in Mattawa* (sleigh rides, craft fair, skating, carollers).

More detailed information on the festivals, carnivals, celebrations and other attractions of Ontario's Near North is available from: Almaguin Nipissing Travel Association Regional Information Centre, Seymour St. and the North Bay Bypass, Box 351, North Bay, Ontario P1B 8H5, 705-474-6634.

Brent

The Brent Crater

WHERE: About 6 km (3.7 mi.) northeast of the Village of Brent near the northern edge of Algonquin Park, about 32 km (20 mi.) south of Hwy. 17.

WHEN: Year round.

WHAT: The crater is a circular depression approximately 3 km (1.9 mi.) in diameter, believed to have been formed by the high-speed impact of a giant meteorite 450 million years ago. The crater can be seen from a look-out tower on its eastern rim.

Burks Falls

The Cutter's Edge—Manivalde Woodworking

WHERE: 4 km (2.5 mi.) north of Burk's Falls, then 5 km (3 mi.) east on North Pickerel Lake Rd.

WHEN: Year round. July to September, open Monday to Saturday, 10 a.m. to 5 p.m.; Sunday, 1 p.m. to 5 p.m. October to June, closed Sunday. Phone ahead for off-season hours.

WHAT: Original handcrafted articles, including many gift items, pine and oak furniture, are displayed in an early Canadian barn workshop. Folk art, supplies and classes available. Wheelchair accessible with assistance. No washrooms.

CONTACT: 705-382-2026, The Cutter's Edge—Manivalde Woodworking.

Commanda

Commanda General Store Museum

WHERE: In the hamlet of Commanda on Hwy. 522, 22 km (13.7 mi.) west of Trout Creek, about 64 km (40 mi.) southwest of North Bay.

WHEN: Open Victoria Day to Labour Day, daily, 8 a.m. to 6 p.m.

WHAT: In the 1880s, Commanda stood at the crossroads of two major government colonization roads. Toronto lawyer James Arthurs, who arrived in 1885 to cash in on the lumber harvesting boom, built the Commanda General Store, a two-storey structure with a false front lavishly embellished with Victorian gingerbread. The building — a rare example of High Victorian commercial architecture — has been restored by the non-profit Gurd and Area Historical Corporation as a museum-cum-tea-room selling baked goods and local handcrafts. Wheelchair-accessible washrooms.

CONTACT: 705-729-2113, Commanda General Store Museum.

Golden Valley

Loring Deer Herd

WHERE: Near Golden Valley on Hwy 522, about 40 km (25 mi.) west of Trout Creek, 70 km (43.5 mi.) south of North Bay. Just east of Golden Valley, take Little River Rd. south from Hwy. 522. Parking area on the right. Trail leads to the viewing platform. Skis or snowshoes may be required, depending on snow conditions.

WHEN: January through March.

WHAT: One of Ontario's largest herds of whitetail deer winters in the Loring-Restoule area near Golden Valley. To combat the hazards of deep snow and aggressive predators, a partnership has been established between hunt clubs, tourist associations and the Ministry of Natural Resources to provide feed lots for the deer. An enclosed, unheated platform offers a vantage point to view the deer. Be quiet when coming in the trail from the parking lot. When there is still snow in the bush but it is melting from fields, look for deer at the edge of farm fields along Hwy. 522.

CONTACT: 705-474-5550, Ministry of Natural Resources, North Bay office.

North Bay

Allison The Bookman

WHERE: 342 Main St.

WHEN: Open year round, daily, 10 a.m. to 9 p.m. Closed December 25, 26, and January 1.

WHAT: This store in downtown North Bay claims to have Canada's largest selection of used paperback books, magazines, children's books and comics, as well as many hard cover books.

CONTACT: 705-476-1450, Allison The Bookman.

Homestead of the Dionne Quintuplets

WHERE: On the North Bay Bypass at Seymour St., beside the North Bay Regional Tourism Information Centre.

WHEN: Year round. Open Victoria Day through Thanksgiving, daily.

WHAT: A small admission fee is charged to enter the log cabin in which the Dionne Quintuplets were born on May 28, 1934, but outdoor sightseeing is free. The building houses Dionne family artifacts, including the bed in which the quints were born, some baby clothes and the frilly white dresses the girls wore in 1939 to meet King George VI in Toronto. Free parking, washrooms, tourist information centre next door.

North Bay Arts Centre, W.K.P. Kennedy Art Gallery

WHERE: 150 Main St. E.

WHEN: Open year round, Tuesday to Friday, 11 a.m. to 5 p.m.; Saturday, noon to 4 p.m.

WHAT: The Gallery features a wide range of contemporary and historical Canadian and international art and a range of media, from sculpture to printmaking and drawing. Workshops, lectures, films, audio-visual programmes. Wheelchair accessible.

CONTACT: 705-474-4747, North Bay Arts Centre.

Powassan

Powassan Funny Farm

WHERE: Hwy. 534, 2 km (1.2 mi.) west of Hwy. 11 near Powassan.

WHEN: Victoria Day through Labour Day, open Wednesday to Sunday, noon to 7 p.m. July and August, open daily, noon to 9 p.m.

WHAT: A petting zoo and family variety shows are the free attractions. A teahouse in a greenhouse setting claims to offer the world's largest selection of ice cream, yoghurt, and home-made chocolate treats. The tea room serves hundreds of flavours of tea. Gift shop specializes in jokes and gags. Not wheelchair accessible.

CONTACT: 705-724-3315, Powassan Funny Farm.

Redbridge

North Bay Fish Culture Station

WHERE: Hwy. 63 at Redbridge, 37 km (23 mi.) northeast of North Bay.

WHEN: Open year round, daily, 9 a.m. to noon and 1 p.m. to 4 p.m. Closed holidays.

WHAT: The hatchery is classified as an intensive fish culture operation. Brook trout, lake trout and splake may be seen in the fry and yearling stages. Picnic tables. Wheelchair-accessible washrooms.

CONTACT: 705-663-2311, North Bay Fish Culture Station.

Sturgeon Falls

Sturgeon River House Museum

WHERE: 250 Fort Rd., 5 km (3 mi.) west of Sturgeon Falls.

WHEN: Mid-May to mid-September, open daily, 10 a.m. to 7 p.m. Donations welcomed.

WHAT: Antique furniture, machinery and artifacts are displayed. Washroom, picnic tables, gift shop. Wheelchair accessible.

CONTACT: 705-753-0570 or 705-753-4716, Sturgeon River House Museum.

Sundridge

Sundridge Maple Sugar House

WHERE: Hwy. 11, 2 km (1.2 mi.) south of Sundridge.

WHEN: Year round, daily. October to June, open 9 a.m. to 6 p.m. July to September, open 8 a.m. to 8:30 p.m. Closed December 25 to 27. Maple syrup demonstrations mid-March to early April.

WHAT: Displays illustrate the history and manufacture of maple syrup. A pioneer log home portrays domestic life a hundred years ago. Antiques and live animals. Store sells maple products, honey, jams, Native crafts and gift items, including Canadian books. Washrooms, picnic area, nature trails, wheelchair accessible.

CONTACT: 705-384-7764, Sundridge Maple Sugar House.

Temagami

Grey Owl plaque

WHERE: In Finlayson Point Provincial Park just south of Temagami.

WHEN: Summer.

WHAT: The plaque honours Grey Owl, a conservationist, author and lecturer who was also an unrepentant fraud. He claimed to have been born in Mexico of an Apache Indian mother, but is believed to have been born in England in 1888, the son of George Belaney, a Scot. He emigrated to the Temagami and Biscotasing area in 1906 and became a trapper, guide and forest ranger. He adopted Indian ways and in 1925 married an Iroquois woman. He became well known through his writing and as a lecturer who used his woods lore to further the cause of wildlife conservation in Canada.

CONTACT: 705-569-3344, Temagami and District Chamber of Commerce.

Temagami Area Fish Hatchery

WHERE: Adjacent to the Welcome Pavilion in downtown Temagami.

WHEN: Daily tours available in July and August.

WHAT: The Temagami Area Fish Improvement Programme was initiated by Temagami residents and cottagers with an interest in preserving walleye habitat and giving nature a hand in walleye reproduction. Volunteers gather spawn each spring on area lakes and rivers and hatch up to two million eggs, releasing them as fingerlings in about six weeks. A tour of the hatchery includes the spawning tanks and a video describing the process.

CONTACT: 705-569-3344, Tourism Temagami.

Temagami Canoe Company

WHERE: Lakeshore Rd., just past Ministry of Natural Resources office.

WHEN: Year round, by appointment.

WHAT: The company has been handcrafting canvas-covered cedar strip canoes since 1929 and still uses many of the early techniques, such as steaming ribs in wooden tanks. Small gift shop.

CONTACT: 705-569-3777, Temagami Canoe Company.

Temagami Look-out, Caribou Mountain Tower Trail

WHERE: From the Ontario Northland Railway Station in the centre of town take O'Connor Dr. until it ends at a right hand turn onto Ski Club Rd. Follow Ski Club Rd. for 1.5 km (.9 mi.) to the ski chalet and follow a trail for about fifteen minutes to the base of a look-out tower.

WHEN: Spring through fall.

WHAT: The fire look-out tower is rickety, no longer in use and unsafe to climb, but from its base there's a wonderful panorama of the lakes, rivers and hills of the district. No washrooms. Not wheelchair accessible.

CONTACT: 705-569-3344, Temagami and District Chamber of Commerce.

Welcome Centre and Pavilion

WHERE: Lakeshore Dr. on the waterfront.

WHEN: Interpretive programmes and displays July and August, daily, 9 a.m. to 5 p.m. Open in May, June and September by request.

WHAT: The Centre offers daily film presentations in a 100-seat theatre, Ministry of Natural Resources interpretive displays and a satellite collection of twenty canoes from the Kanawa International Museum. Tourist information. Washrooms. Wheelchair accessible.

CONTACT: 705-569-3344, The Welcome Centre, Chamber of Commerce.

Rainbow Country

Includes: Manitoulin Island, Espanola, French River, Little Current, Massey, Parry Sound and Sudbury.

Rainbow Country includes the world's largest freshwater island, Manitoulin, and on it the 777 km² (300-sq. mi.) Wikwemikong Indian Reservation, which is technically not a part of Canada since the land was never ceded. The region also includes Killarney Provincial Park and the Thirty Thousand Islands along the east side of Georgian Bay.

Festivals, Carnivals, Celebrations, Special Events:

JANUARY: Pointe au Baril, *Annual Winter Whirl* (sledding, darts, races); Sudbury, *Women on Snow* (ride for women).

FEBRUARY: Levack-Onaping Falls, *Winter Carnival* (queen pageant, casino night, talent contest, fish derby); Sudbury, *Snowflake Festival* (jug curling, tug-o-war, snowshoe golf); Sudbury, *Professional and Amateur Competition of Snowmobile Racing;* Carling, *Winter Carnival* (snowmobile races, tea boiling, log sawing); Dowling, *Winter Carnival* (quiz games, social, hockey tournaments); Humphrey, *Winter Frolic* (dog sled mail run from Humphrey to Rousseau, barbecue).

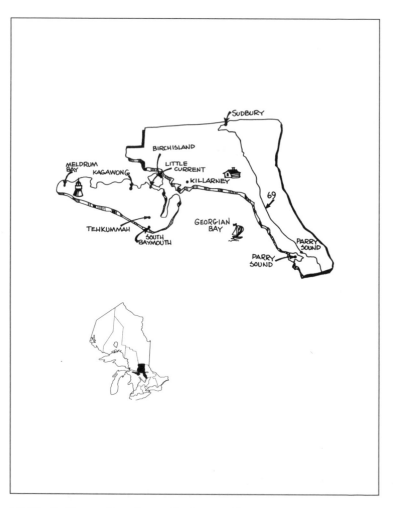

MAY: Sudbury, *Symphony Orchestra Concert.*

JULY: Sudbury, *Canada Day Celebration;* Sudbury, *Northern Lights Festival*, (rhythm and blues, jazz, country, ethnic music).

AUGUST: Wikwemikong, *Indian Pow Wow.*

DECEMBER: Sudbury, *Symphony Orchestra Christmas Concert.*

More detailed information on the festivals, carnivals, celebrations and other attractions of Rainbow Country is available from:

Rainbow Country Travel Association, Sudbury Welcome Centre, Hwy. 69 S. at Whippoorwill Rd., R.R. 3, Sudbury, Ontario P3E 4N1, 705-522-0104.

Birch Island

Dreamer's Rock

WHERE: In Whitefish River Indian Reserve near Birch Island Lodge Rd., east of Hwy. 6, about 12 km (7.5 mi.) northwest of Little Current.

WHEN: Year round.

WHAT: A shallow depression at the summit of a tall quartzite rock was used for a rite of passage for Indian youths approaching puberty. The boy would recline in solitude in the elongated hollow and fast, receiving visions of the future in dreams from his guardian spirit.

Ojibway Trading Post

WHERE: Off Hwy. 6, 14 km (8.7 mi.) north of Little Current on Manitoulin Island.

WHEN: Victoria Day through Thanksgiving, open daily, 8 a.m. to 9 p.m. July through August, open 8 a.m. to 11 p.m.

WHAT: Items on sale include Indian handcrafts in bark, quills, beads, soapstone and deerhide. Jewelry, vests, moccasins.

CONTACT: 705-285-7265, Ojibway Trading Post; 705-285-4585, off-season.

Kagawong

Bridal Veil Falls

WHERE: At the entrance to the Village of Kagawong on Hwy. 540 on Manitoulin Island.

WHEN: Year round. Best seen in spring or fall.

WHAT: A trail leads to the falls—a delicate, lacy cascade which drops over a limestone ledge. You can walk behind the falls. Picnic area. (The Village of Kagawong has a turn-of-the-century mood. Drop into the Anglican Church to see the pulpit fashioned from the planks of a wrecked ship.)

Killarney

Killarney Museum

WHERE: Commissioner's St., Killarney, at the end of Hwy. 637, 115 km (71.5 mi.) southwest of Sudbury.

WHEN: July and August, open Tuesday to Sunday, noon to 4 p.m. and 6 p.m. to 8 p.m. June and September to Thanksgiving, open weekends only, 1 p.m. to 4 p.m. Closed rest of the year.

WHAT: A pine log cabin displays household artifacts and old tools from Killarney's past. Items are included from the homes of the Roque and the De La Morandiere families, the original settlers who came to Killarney in the early 1800s. A twelve-minute slide show presents area history from 1820 to modern times. Self-guided tours; washrooms across street in Town Centre Bldg.

CONTACT: 705-287-2283, Curator, Killarney Museum; 705-287-2424, Township of Rutherford and George Island.

Little Current

Cup and Saucer Hiking Trail

WHERE: 19 km (11.8 mi.) west of Little Current at the junction of Hwy. 540 and Bidwell Rd., on Manitoulin Island.

WHEN: Spring through fall.

WHAT: The hiking trail is so named because of the little hill, the cup, which sits atop the bigger hill, the saucer. Budget three hours for this trek, which takes you to the edge of the Niagara Escarpment. Budget more time if you decide to take the Adventure Trail from that point, up ladders through a natural rock chimney.

Meldrum Bay

Mississagi Lighthouse

WHERE: About 11 km (6.8 mi.) west of Meldrum Bay at the west end of Manitoulin Island.

WHEN: Open daily Victoria Day weekend through September.

WHAT: Visitors can climb an 1870 lighthouse that overlooks the treacherous Mississagi Strait. Historians believe this is where the *Griffon* came to grief. The ship, built at Niagara for Sieur de Rene Cavelier LaSalle, disappeared on her maiden voyage and was never seen again. Iron and wood samples taken from a wreck in the area are of the approximate antiquity, but divers have yet to recover any of the seven brass cannon that were on board.

Parry Island

Ghost town

WHERE: On Parry Island, about 5 km (3 mi.) south of Parry Sound.

WHEN: Year round. Best seen in spring before the leaves are out, or in fall after the leaves have fallen.

WHAT: Depot Harbour on Parry Island was once a booming railway terminus and Great Lakes port with a population of 3,000 people. Today it is the largest of Ontario's 300 ghost towns. Visitors can wander the ruins of more than a hundred houses, three churches, a school, railway yards and roundhouse and two huge grain elevators. The town was founded about a hundred years ago by timber baron John Rudolphus Booth, who pushed a rail line from Ottawa through Algonquin Park to Georgian Bay. When the railway reached Parry Sound, Booth refused to pay the inflated prices Parry Sounders demanded for their property, so he built his own town at Depot Harbour on nearby Parry Island. Canadian National Railways eventually acquired Booth's assets, and in 1928 moved the railhead. The community began its decline, which ended abruptly in 1945 when the elevators, in which cordite was stored, accidentally blew up.

Parry Sound

Parry Sound Observation Tower

WHERE: On Tower Hill, overlooking Parry Sound.

WHEN: Spring through fall.

WHAT: The first look-out tower, built in 1927, became the town's trademark. In the early 1970s, when the first tower became unsafe, the Ontario Ministry of Natural Resources built a 29.9-m (98-ft.) replacement. Today's visitor commands a superb view of Parry Sound and some of Georgian Bay's 30,000 islands. In July and August, washrooms, a snack bar and picnic area are provided. A grand new museum of community artifacts, to which a modest admission is charged, is found at the foot of the tower. Museum and washrooms are wheelchair accessible.

CONTACT: 705-746-5365, West Parry Sound District Museum.

South Baymouth

South Baymouth Fish Research Station

WHERE: 5 km (3 mi.) north of South Baymouth, off Hwy. 6.

WHEN: Display room open June through September, Monday to Friday, 8:15 a.m. to 4:30 p.m.

WHAT: View local fish species in four aquaria. Other displays explain the work of the research station. No public washrooms, not wheelchair accessible.

CONTACT: 705-859-3137, South Baymouth Fish Research Station.

Sudbury

Big Nickel

WHERE: Lorne St. and Big Nickel Mine Rd., 5 km (3 mi.) west of downtown Sudbury.

WHEN: Year round.

WHAT: A 9.1-m (30-ft.) nickel coin marks the Big Nickel Mine. Mine tours are offered in spring through fall for an admission charge. Visitors can mail a postcard from Canada's only underground postal box.

CONTACT: 705-522-3701, Science North, promotion officer.

Copper Cliff Museum

WHERE: Balsam St. and Power St., Copper Cliff. Take Balsam St. Exit from Hwy. 17 W.

WHEN: Open June through Labour Day, Tuesday to Sunday, 11 a.m. to 4 p.m.

WHAT: A pioneer log cabin, built in the early 1930s, is furnished to the period of early settlement in Copper Cliff. Guided tours, picnic tables. No washrooms. Not wheelchair accessible.

CONTACT: 705-674-3141, Community Recreation Programme Co-ordinator, Copper Cliff Museum.

Ellero Stone Art

WHERE: 983 Lorne St.

WHEN: Open year round, Monday to Friday, 9 a.m. to 6 p.m.; Saturday, 9 a.m. to 5 p.m.

WHAT: See stone sculptures hand carved in Canadian stones, including nickel-copper ore from Sudbury and marble from the Ottawa Valley, by master sculptors Peter and Fred Ellero. Studio tours, washrooms, gift shop. Wheelchair accessible with assistance.

CONTACT: 705-674-4704, Ellero Stone Art Manufacturers and Distributors Inc.

Farmers Festival Market

WHERE: Parking lot of Sudbury Theatre Centre on Shaughnessy St.

WHEN: Open mid-May through October, Saturday and Sunday, 7 a.m. to 7 p.m.

WHAT: In addition to fresh farm produce, some stalls offer arts and handcrafts and baked goods. Wheelchair accessible.

CONTACT: 705-674-7477, Farmers Festival Market.

Flour Mill Heritage Museum

WHERE: At the St. Charles Pumphouse, St. Charles St. off Notre Dame.

WHEN: Open mid-June to Labour Day, Monday to Friday, 10 a.m. to 4 p.m.; Sunday 1 p.m. to 4 p.m.

WHAT: This pioneer house displays early Canadian furnishings and implements. Not wheelchair accessible.

CONTACT: 705-674-2110, Museum, during operating hours; 705-674-3141, City of Sudbury Recreation Dept.

La Galerie Du Nouvel-Ontario

WHERE: 20 St. Anne's Rd.

WHEN: Open year round, Monday to Thursday, noon to 5 p.m.; Saturday, 11 a.m. to 2 p.m. Closed holidays.

WHAT: The Gallery displays Franco-Ontarian visual arts, including photographs, paintings, sculpture and ceramics. Wheelchair-accessible washrooms.

CONTACT: 705-675-6493, La Galerie du Nouvel-Ontario.

Laurentian University Museum and Arts Centre

WHERE: John St. at Nelson.

WHEN: Open year round, Tuesday to Sunday, noon to 5 p.m. Other times by appointment. Closed Mondays and holidays. Donations welcome.

WHAT: The Centre is housed on the estate of W. J. Bell, an early Sudbury area lumber baron, in the home and coach house, built 1906. A continuously changing programme of exhibits is displayed in three galleries. Wheelchair access to main floor gallery. Gift shop.

CONTACT: 705-674-3271, Museum and Arts Centre, Laurentian University.

Laurentian University Tour

WHERE: Laurentian University, Ramsey Lake Rd.

WHEN: Tours offered year round, Monday and Friday, 10 a.m. to 1 p.m. Ten days' advance notice required. Small fee for planetarium show, which must be arranged with the Office of the Planetarium.

WHAT: General campus tours take about two hours. The planetarium tour and show takes one hour.

CONTACT: 705-675-1151, Ext. 3100 Liaison Office, Laurentian University; 705-675-1151, Ext. 2222, Office of the Planetarium.

Slag-dumping spectacle

WHERE: International Nickel Company.

WHEN: Night-time, year round.

WHAT: Rail cars of molten slag (the waste left over after ore is smelted) are shunted out on a dump high above your observation point and, one by one, tipped by remote control so their molten loads cascade down like lava from a volcano. INCO no longer discloses where and when slag is being dumped. Scout a night-time dump-site from the Big Nickel, get closer to it—if company security people don't have the roads blocked off—and hope there will be another dump. But don't get too close!

Sudbury Civic Square Tour

WHERE: Brady St., downtown.

WHEN: Year round. Tours offered June through August, Monday to Friday, 8:30 a.m. to 4:30 p.m. Closed holidays.

WHAT: Visitors can tour the modern administration and activity centre for the Regional Municipality and the City of Sudbury. Wheelchair-accessible washrooms.

CONTACT: 705-673-2171, Ext. 514, Regional Municipality of Sudbury.

Tehkummah

Blue Jay Creek Fish Culture Station

WHERE: In Tehkummah, 16 km (10 mi.) northwest of South Baymouth on Manitoulin Island.

WHEN: Open year round, daily, 9 a.m. to 4 p.m.

WHAT: See the development of several trout species from fry to adult stock. Learn the complexities of hatching, feeding and rearing trout and walleye. Washrooms wheelchair accessible.

CONTACT: 705-859-3006, Blue Jay Creek Fish Culture Station.

Algoma Country

Includes: Agawa Canyon, Blind River, Chapleau, Elliot Lake, Hornepayne, Sault Ste. Marie, St. Joseph Island, Spanish, Thessalon, Wawa, White River.

Granite cliffs, seascapes across the largest of the Great Lakes and a tangible link with the early explorers are found in this region. In the southwest corner are the ruins of the 1796 Fort St. Joseph, a key link in the early fur trade, and at the northwest corner is White River, claiming distinction as both the coldest place in Canada and the home of Winnie-the-Pooh.

Festivals, Carnivals, Celebrations, Special Events:

JANUARY: Sault Ste. Marie, *Ontario Winter Carnival Bon Soo* (snow sculpturing, polar bear swim, sleigh rides).

FEBRUARY: Blind River, *Winter Carnival* (ice sculpture, timber village, jack rabbit ski races); Chapleau, *Pub Night*.

MAY: Sault Ste. Marie, *Lock Cities Chorus Harmony International* (ladies barbershop chorus).

JUNE: Thessalon, *Seniors' Day* (bingo, poker walk, entertainment); Sault Ste. Marie, *Kids' Day* (fishing for trout, pony and wagon rides, farm tours); Elliot Lake, *Uranium Festival* (baby

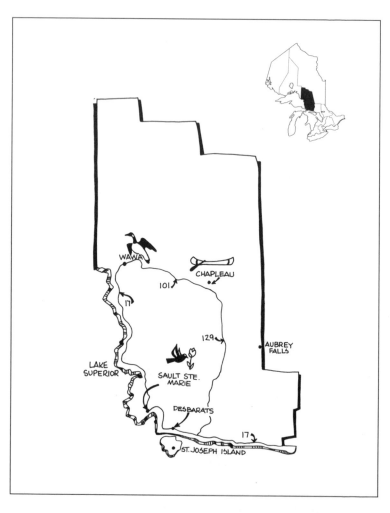

show, senior citizen rally, parade); Sault Ste. Marie, *Coming of Summer Festival* (tugboat parade and races, international bridge walk, Can Am live release bass tournament); Bruce Mines, *Plummer Additional Centennial Celebrations* (square dance, buggy rides, fashion show, turkey shoot); Blind River, *Voyageur Day* (live entertainment, pioneer cuisine); Thessalon, *Sea to Sea Voyageur* (kids' games, picnic, display and skit); Sultan, Wakami Lake Provincial Park, *Woodsmen's Day* (the spirits of lumberjacks reminisce about life in the logging camps, log cutting, burling, splitting contests); Blind River, *Mississauga First Nations Annual Pow Wow* (arts and crafts display, traditional Native food, dancing, music and costumes); Elliot Lake, *D-Day Parade* (veterans, cadets, drum head service).

JULY: Blind River, *Community Days* (talent show, fiddlers' contest, beer garden, sky divers); Sault Ste. Marie, *Steelton Stampede* (pony rides, face painting, duck and fish ponds, cloggers); Sault Ste. Marie, *Rotary Community Day* (parade, games, food); Blind River, *Annual Olde Tyme Fiddling Contest* (open competition, novelty); Sault Ste. Marie, *Canada Day* (music, theatre, dance, fireworks).

AUGUST: Thessalon, *Community Day* (parade, radio-controlled boats, games of chance); Richards Landing, *Cornfest* (fun run, horseshoe contest, arts and crafts).

SEPTEMBER: Algoma, *Fall Festival* (comedy, readings, recitals).

NOVEMBER: Sault Ste. Marie, *Santa's Party* (lucky fish pond, candy canes).

DECEMBER: Sault Ste. Marie, *Christmas Concert with the Sault Symphony Orchestra.*

More detailed information on the festivals, carnivals, celebrations and other attractions of Algoma Country is available from: Algoma Kinniwabi Travel Association, Suite 203, 616 Queen St. E., Sault Ste. Marie, Ontario P6A 2A4, 705-254-4293.

Aubrey Falls

Aubrey Falls

WHERE: About 2 km (1.2 mi.) off Hwy. 129, 114 km (71 mi.) south of Chapleau, and 113 km (70 mi.) north of Hwy. 129, signposted as "Scenic Lookout."

WHEN: Victoria Day through Thanksgiving, daily, dawn to dusk. (Water diverted remainder of year.)

WHAT: The waters of the Mississagi River tumble over jagged rocks into a gorge 39 m (129 ft.) below. Parking and picnic area.

Chapleau

Centennial Museum

WHERE: Monk St.

WHEN: Open Victoria Day through Labour Day, daily, 10 a.m. to 6 p.m. Off-season by appointment.

WHAT: The Museum depicts life in Chapleau, featuring sports, logging and trapping. The lower level houses a trapper's log cabin and a 30.5-m (100-ft.) mural displaying a winter scene. The upper level features a mural of the first fort in Chapleau as well as an early 1800s living room, Chapleau's first store, a 3.7-m (12-ft.) birchbark canoe and other interesting regional artifacts. Tourist information centre. Washrooms and picnic tables.

CONTACT: 705-864-1122, Museum.

Desbarats

Ripple Rock

WHERE: Near the rock outcropping on Hwy. 17, about 2.5 km (1.6 mi.) west of Desbarats and 4 km (2.5 mi.) east of Hwy. 548.

WHEN: Year round.

WHAT: The prominent ripple marks on this large rockcut were created by shoreline waves about two billion years ago. Subsequent compression of the earth's crust tilted the sandstone formation to its present 60-degree angle.

St. Joseph Island

Fort St. Joseph National Historic Site

WHERE: On St. Joseph Island, 51 km (38 mi.) south of Hwy. 17 on the south shore. Follow the Canadian Parks Service beaver logo.

WHEN: Victoria Day to June, open daily, 10 a.m. to 5 p.m. July 1 through Labour Day, open daily, 10 a.m. to 6 p.m. Labour Day to Thanksgiving Day, open daily, 10 a.m. to 5 p.m.

WHAT: The most westerly British military post in Upper Canada, built 1796, was an important trading station and military post in the War of 1812. Today, the fort is located on a 336-ha (830-a.) wilderness area and bird sanctuary. Films and numerous displays can be viewed in the reception centre. Staff are available to answer questions. Wheelchair-accessible washrooms, barbecue pits, picnic tables, dock and mooring.

CONTACT: 705-246-2664, Superintendent, Fort St. Joseph National Historic Site; off-season, 705-942-6262, Environment Canada, Canadian Parks Service.

Sault Ste. Marie

Bellevue Park

WHERE: Off Queen St., east end of city, past Great Lakes Forestry Research Centre.

WHEN: Year round. Marina open Victoria Day weekend through Labour Day weekend.

WHAT: The park contains flower gardens, a greenhouse, bird and indigenous wild animal displays, a marina and a children's playground. Band concerts may be held in summer. Telephone for dates and times. Food concession and washrooms open May through August. Picnic tables.

CONTACT: 705-759-5223, City Park Director, City of Sault Ste. Marie.

Ermatinger Old Stone House

WHERE: 831 Queen St. E. Free parking off Bay St.

WHEN: April through May, open Monday to Friday, 10 a.m. to 5 p.m. June through September, open daily, 10 a.m. to 5 p.m. October and November, open Monday to Friday, 1 p.m. to 5 p.m. or by appointment. Donations accepted. Children under fourteen must be accompanied by an adult.

WHAT: Canada's oldest stone house west of Toronto was built in 1814 for a Swiss fur trader and his wife, the daughter of an influential chief of the Ojibwa Tribe. Exhibits depict regional history and the fur trade. Cooking, baking and nineteenth-century crafts are demonstrated in the reproduction summer kitchen. Gift shop. Washrooms. Not wheelchair accessible.

CONTACT: 705-759-5443, Ermatinger Old Stone House.

Great Lakes Forestry Centre

WHERE: 1219 Queen St. E.

WHEN: Tours offered late June through August, Monday to Friday, 2 p.m.

WHAT: A one-hour guided tour of Canada's largest forest research complex includes live insects, greenhouses, laboratories and displays. Washrooms, wheelchair-accessible centre, picnic area in nearby municipal park.

CONTACT: 705-949-9461, Great Lakes Forestry Centre.

Municipal Fish Hatchery

WHERE: 35 Canal Dr.

WHEN: June through August, open daily, 10 a.m. to 4 p.m. September to May, open Monday to Friday, 9 a.m. to 4 p.m. Donations welcome.

WHAT: Ontario's first municipally operated hatchery, built in 1987, raises and releases Chinook salmon, brown trout and rainbow trout. Wheelchair accessible.

CONTACT: 705-759-5446, Community Services Dept., City of Sault Ste. Marie.

Northern Breweries Ltd.

WHERE: 503 Bay St.

WHEN: July and August, tours offered Monday to Thursday. Telephone ahead to book times. Tour participants must be nineteen years or older.

WHAT: A tour of one of Canada's oldest breweries follows the brewing processes and outlines the different kinds of beer and the basic ingredients used in brewing ale and lager. Tasting included. Not wheelchair accessible.

CONTACT: 705-254-7373, Northern Breweries Ltd.

St. Mary's Paper Inc.

WHERE: 75 Huron St., next to the locks.

WHEN: Victoria Day through Thanksgiving Day, tours offered Tuesday and Thursday, 1:30 p.m. Register for tour at security gate. Flat shoes required, no children under twelve allowed. No cameras allowed.

WHAT: Guided tours of this recently modernized plant demonstrate the process of producing supercalendar paper. The product, used for advertising flyers, is largely exported to the U.S. Not wheelchair accessible.

CONTACT: 705-942-6070, Ext. 265, St. Mary's Paper Inc.

The Sault Star

WHERE: 145 Old Garden River Rd.

WHEN: Year round. Closed statutory holidays. Arrange tours one week in advance.

WHAT: Visitors will follow the production of a daily newspaper from start to finish, including the press room, newsroom and composing room. Slide presentation. Not wheelchair accessible.

CONTACT: 705-759-3030, Ext. 274, The Sault Star.

Sault Ste. Marie Museum

WHERE: Downtown at corner of Queen St. and East St., at entrance to Queenstown. (Eastside, Riverside and McNabb buses.)

WHEN: Open year round, Monday to Saturday, 9 a.m. to 4:30 p.m.; Sunday, 1 p.m. to 4:30 p.m. Closed statutory holidays. Donations welcome. Appointment required for archival research.

WHAT: The Museum, located in a heritage building, contains displays recreating the history of Algoma over the past ten thousand years. The Discovery Gallery features hands-on activities. Circulating exhibits occupy galleries on the first and third floors. Washrooms, full wheelchair access, free parking at rear.

CONTACT: 705-759-7278, Sault Ste. Marie Museum.

Wawa

The Wawa Goose

WHERE: At the entrance to Wawa from Hwy. 17. Can be seen from the highway.

WHEN: Year round.

WHAT: The word Wawa in Ojibwa means wild goose—hence the town's trademark metal goose, with its 5.8-m (19-ft.) wingspan. A new tourist information building with parking, washrooms and picnic tables is found adjacent to the goose.

High Falls

WHERE: 1.6 km (1 mi.) south of Wawa on Hwy. 17 and 3 km (2 mi.) west by gravel road.

WHEN: Year round. Particularly impressive when frozen solid in winter and accessible by snowmobile or cross-country skis.

WHAT: The scenic falls on the Magpie River are 23 m (75 ft.) high and 38 m (125 ft.) wide. Parking, wheelchair-accessible washrooms, picnic shelter, barbecue pit, boat launch, hiking trails.

CONTACT: 705-856-2244, Director of Leisure and Community Services, Township of Michipicoten.

James Bay Frontier

Includes: Cobalt, Cochrane, Englehart, Hearst, Iroquois Falls,
Kapuskasing, Kirkland Lake, Latchford, Moose Factory, Moosonee,
New Liskeard, Smooth Rock Falls, Timmins.

This region, which includes some of the richest mineral deposits in Canada, ranges north to the watershed of James Bay and tidewaters of the North Atlantic Ocean. Much of the northern expanses are largely unexplored and are the private domain of sports hunters, fishermen and modern-day adventurers.

Festivals, Carnivals, Celebrations, Special Events:

FEBRUARY: Cochrane, *Winter Carnival* (princess pageant, torch-light parade, hockey tournaments); Haileybury, *Lions Winter Carnival* (cross-country skiing, horse-drawn sleigh rides, hockey competitions); South Porcupine-Porcupine, *Winter Carnival* (snowshoe golf tournament, tough guy-tough gal contest, snowshoe golf); Moonbeam, *Moonbeam Carnival* (sporting activities); Timmins, *Carnaval* (Laronde contest, monster bingo).

MARCH: Larder Lake, *Firemen's Fish Derby*; Timmins, *National Ski Week at Kamiskotia Ski Resort*; *South Porcupine Loppet* (18-km/11.2 mi. and 25-km/15.6-mi. cross-country ski races);

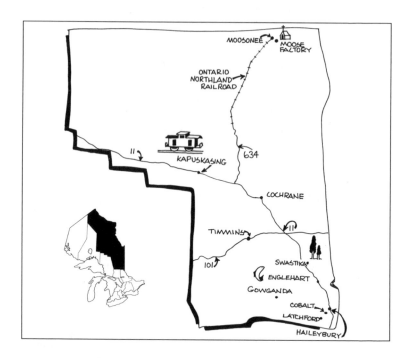

Timmins, *Ontario Ski Championships*.

MAY: Hearst, *Wado-Kai Karate Championships*; Timmins, *Promenade* (walk downtown with health check-up spots at different locations).

JUNE: *South Porcupine Multicultural Festival* (food, music, costumes, dance, crafts); Timmins, *Downtown Canada Birthday Party* (parade, games, birthday cake); Larder Lake, *Lions Annual Fish Derby*; Haileybury, *Heritage Festival* (arts and crafts, costume judging, talent show, ceremonial canoe arrival, bathtub races).

JULY: Timmins, *Downtown Sidewalk Sale Days* (dog and cat shows, mining theme, limbo contest); Timmins, *Schumacher Day* (major fastball tournament, beer garden); Kirkland Lake-Larder Lake, *Canada Day*; Timmins, *Day in the Park* (games, food, celebrity dunking); Timmins, *Prospector's Rendez-vous* (Great Porcupine Gold Rush Triathlon, Prospector's Claim Staking competition, arts competition); Timmins, Northern College of

---

Applied Arts and Technology, *Gaelic Arts Recital*; Timmins, *The Great Mattagami Canoe Race* (20-km/12.5-mi. loop for men, ladies, mixed and family).

AUGUST: Cobalt, *Miner's Festival* (amusement rides, foot race around Cobalt Lake, kiddies parade); Elk Lake, *Annual Civic Holiday and Annual Western Jamboree* (parade, square dance and fiddle competition, mud bog moto-cross, teddy bear's picnic, bathtub races).

OCTOBER: Timmins, *Downtown Hallowe'en Party* (children dress in costume, colouring contest, apple dunking).

NOVEMBER: Timmins, *Santa Claus Parade*; Timmins, *Symphony Orchestra* (special performance).

More detailed information on the festivals, carnivals, celebrations and other attractions of James Bay Frontier is available from: Cochrane Timiskaming Travel Association, Box 1162, Timmins, Ontario P4N 7H9, 705-264-9589.

Cobalt

Heritage Silver Trail

WHERE: Tours originate at Cobalt Mining Museum, 24 Silver St.

WHEN: Open June through August, daily, 9 a.m. to 5 p.m. Call ahead for guided tours.

WHAT: A free map is provided at the Cobalt Mining Museum to guide visitors on a 6-km (3.7-mi.) tour of five mines around the town that have interesting histories. The route is well marked and at each mine site there are explanatory signs. If arrangements are made in advance, a guide can accompany you in your car to the Colonial mine, last worked in the 1950s, but now used on occasion as a classroom by the Haileybury School of Mines. You can borrow a hard hat from the Museum and, on a level, dry, 152-m (500-ft.) circle tour, you can see just about all phases of silver or gold mining. There's a small admission fee to the Cobalt Mining Museum, one of the most interesting and well organized small museums in Ontario.

CONTACT: 705-679-8301, Cobalt Mining Museum.

Highway Book Shop

WHERE: Hwy. 11, just south of the turnoff to Cobalt.

WHEN: Year round, seven days a week.

WHAT: This book shop boasts more than 500,000 titles, many of them out of print. If you know the title or the author, chances are owner Doug Pollard can find a used copy of that book you'd like to read again, and sell it to you.

CONTACT: 705-679-8375, Highway Book Shop.

Cochrane

Norbord Industries Ltd., plywood manufacturing

WHERE: Follow Railway St. off Hwy. 11 to 70 Thirteenth Ave.

WHEN: Open July through Labour Day. Guided tours Monday and Wednesday, 3 p.m. No children under five allowed.

WHAT: In one of the largest poplar plywood plants in Canada, you can observe the manufacturing process in all stages—from logs to the finished product. Thirty- to forty-five-minute tour. Not wheelchair accessible.

CONTACT: 705-272-4210, Norbord Industries Ltd.

Englehart

Hills Lake Fish Culture Station

WHERE: 22 km (13.7 mi.) west of Englehart off Hwy. 560.

WHEN: Open year round, daily, 9 a.m. to 4 p.m.

WHAT: This hatchery raises lake, brook trout, and Aurora trout and splake. A new visitor centre houses fish tanks, a slide show and tourist information. Wheelchair-accessible washrooms, picnic tables, fishing.

CONTACT: 705-544-8006, Manager, Ministry of Natural Resources, Hills Lake Fish Hatchery.

Kap-Kig-Iwan Falls

WHERE: In Kap-Kig-Iwan Provincial Park, 2 km (1.2 mi.) south of Englehart off Hwy. 11.

WHEN: Late spring through early fall.

WHAT: Spectacular falls can be seen on the Englehart River, where the river is forced into a deep, cliff-lined ravine. There are rough trails from the parking lot down both sides of the river to vantage points overlooking the falls. The hiker is well rewarded. Picnic facilities near the parking area.

Gowganda

Gowganda and Area Museum

WHERE: In Gowganda.

WHEN: Mid-May to mid-September, open daily, 8 a.m. to 8 p.m. Other times, open by appointment.

WHAT: The 1918 "One Big Union" Union Hall houses artifacts from the early settlers of the area, with an emphasis on mining. There are displays of outdoor mining equipment and a log cabin. The Museum also houses archives relating to mining and prospecting. Counter with maps, postcards, books. No wheelchair access.

CONTACT: 705-624-3171, Gowganda and Area Museum.

Haileybury

Haileybury School of Mines Geological Displays

WHERE: In Haileybury.

WHEN: Open in summer, Monday to Friday, 8 a.m. to 4 p.m.

WHAT: The school of mining technology and related subjects uses these displays of mineral and ore samples in its teaching programme. The samples are identified by name and geographic origin. The collection also includes teaching displays of ancient and modern mining techniques, diamond drilling and chemical core analysis. One case contains timbers from a copper mine in Cyprus which operated 2,400 years ago. Wheelchair-accessible washrooms.

CONTACT: 705-672-3376, Haileybury School of Mines.

Temiskaming Art Gallery

WHERE: Public Library in Haileybury, 545 Lakeshore Rd. (Hwy. 11B).

WHEN: Open year round, Tuesday to Friday, 2 p.m. to 8 p.m.; Saturday, 2 p.m. to 6 p.m.

WHAT: This gallery, emphasisizing Northern artists, also hosts a variety of shows, including travelling exhibits from the Art Gallery of Ontario and the Ontario Crafts Council. One level is wheelchair accessible.

CONTACT: 705-672-3706, Curator, Temiskaming Art Gallery.

Kapuskasing

Ron Morel Memorial Museum

WHERE: CNR Via Station Park, adjacent to Hwy. 11.

WHEN: Open Victoria Day to Labour Day, Monday to Friday, 9 a.m. to 5 p.m. Donations welcomed.

WHAT: The Museum is housed in two railway coaches and a caboose headed by a steam locomotive. The coaches contain pioneer and railway memorabilia from the late nineteenth and early twentieth centuries, including articles from Kapuskasing's First World War Internment Camp. Washrooms, picnic area, gift shop.

CONTACT: 705-335-5443, Museum; 705-335-2341, off-season, Kapuskasing Town Hall.

Latchford

Latchford Covered Bridge

WHERE: In Latchford just off Hwy. 11, 11 km (6.8 mi.) south of Cobalt.

WHEN: Year round.

WHAT: The bridge is a large culvert over Latchford Creek which the town has covered with a wooden structure to earn the title World's Shortest Covered Bridge. The bridge is 3.4 m (11 ft., 3 in.) long. It's surprising to see how many travellers dutifully turn off the highway, stop to take a photograph, and then go on their way, probably wondering why they bothered to stop.

House of Memories

WHERE: Hwy. 11 in Latchford, 11 km (6.8 mi.) south of Cobalt.

WHEN: Mid-May to mid-October, open Tuesday to Sunday, 1 p.m. to 4 p.m. July and August, open 10 a.m. to 7 p.m. Donations welcome.

WHAT: This ten-room house is chock-a-block with regional artifacts from the early 1900s. Souvenir counter. Washroom. Wheelchair access to first floor.

CONTACT: 705-676-2110, House of Memories.

Moose Factory

NOTE: Moose Factory Island, in the mouth of the Moose River, can be reached only by water taxi from Moosonee on the mainland. Moosonee may be reached only by air or rail—there is no road connection with the rest of the province. The Polar Bear Express, operated by Ontario Northland Railroad, makes a round trip from Cochrane, 300 km (186 mi.) south, every day of the week except Friday, from late June through Labour Day weekend.

Moose Factory Centennial Museum and Park

WHERE: Moose Factory Island (reached by boat taxi from Moosonee).

WHEN: Open last week of June through Labour Day.

WHAT: The Museum depicts the history of the settlement of this area by the Hudson's Bay Company in 1670 and the story of the fur trade and development of the area. Featured are traps, snowshoes, musket balls and moosehide leather work. The blacksmith shop nearby dates from 1740. On the ancient tombstones in the adjoining graveyard the graphic tales of lost struggles are told. The old powder magazine, the only stone building on the island, is also located in the park. Washrooms, picnic tables. Light lunches and souvenirs available in adjacent Anglican parish hall.

St. Thomas Church

WHERE: Moose Factory Island, 500 m (550 yd.) from the water taxi dock.

WHEN: Year round, daily.

WHAT: The square-log church, built in 1860 for the Anglican Church and the Hudson's Bay Company, was the original cathedral for the Diocese of Moosonee and served the entire Arctic community until 1905. It is still an active parish church. It contains beautiful beadwork-moosehide altar cloths, fine silk embroidery on white deerhide and Cree language prayer books. Washrooms, picnic area, restaurant in parish hall down the street.

CONTACT: 705-658-4800, St. Thomas Church.

Moosonee

James Bay Education Centre
(Campus of Northern College)

WHERE: On the road between the railway station and the river.

WHEN: Tours offered July and August, daily except Friday, 11 a.m. to 5 p.m.

WHAT: The complex includes a gymnasium, cafeteria and kitchen, library, workshops and skill training centre. The motto, "Be taught here so that you might follow a new path," is written in Cree syllabics mounted in concrete between the pillars flanking the front entrance. A new interpretive centre features Cree artifacts and exhibitions of Native art and crafts. Washrooms, food services, cafeteria. No wheelchair access.

CONTACT: 705-336-2913, Director of Native Services, James Bay Education Centre.

Revillon Museum

WHERE: 25 Revillon St.

WHEN: Open late June through Labour Day, daily, 1 p.m. to 5 p.m.

WHAT: The Museum, one of the oldest buildings in Moosonee, was once a Revillon staff house. Moosonee's history is closely related to the story of the French Company, which was the Hudson's Bay Company's chief rival in the James Bay area for three decades during the early part of this century. Most of the Museum deals with early twentieth-century life on the James Bay Frontier.

CONTACT: 705-336-2993, Revillon Museum.

Swastika

Swastika Tree Nursery

WHERE: West of Kirkland Lake on Hwy. 66 towards Matachewan. Well signposted.

WHEN: Open year round, Monday to Friday, 8 a.m. to 2:30 p.m. Best seen between May and September. Closed on statutory holidays.

WHAT: The Tree Nursery is Ontario's largest. Individual visitors are welcome but two-hour organized tours are available only for groups by reservation. Wheelchair access to buildings, but not the van used for tours.

CONTACT: 705-567-3372, Swastika Tree Nursery.

Timmins

Timmins Museum—National Exhibition Centre

WHERE: 70 Legion Dr. off Hwy. 101, South Porcupine.

WHEN: Open year round, Monday to Friday, 9 a.m. to 5 p.m.; Wednesday and Thursday, 7 p.m. to 9 p.m.; Saturday and Sunday, 1 p.m. to 5 p.m. Closed December 25, 26, January 1 and 2. Donations accepted.

WHAT: The history of Timmins and the evolution of the mining industry are depicted through mineral and geological exhibits. The Museum includes local history displays, changing arts and crafts displays and films from an extensive collection. Minerals from around the world are shown in the Costain Mineral Gallery. The outdoor mining court has a display of pre-1940 mining machinery. Picnic tables, gift shop, washrooms, wheelchair access.

CONTACT: 705-235-5066, Curator, Timmins Museum.

Ukrainian Historical and Cultural Museum

WHERE: One block south of the Senator Hotel on Mountjoy St. S. in the 1922 Ukrainian Labour Temple.

WHEN: Year round. June to Labour Day, open Wednesday to Sunday, 1 p.m. to 4:30 p.m. After Labour Day, open weekends only, 1 p.m. to 4:30 p.m. Donations accepted.

WHAT: The Museum houses historical and cultural artifacts which demonstrate the contribution of Ukrainian immigrants in the mining areas of northern Ontario. A large doll collection features ethnic dolls of all nations. Kobzar Parkette next door to the Museum contains antique mining, lumbering and farming equipment. Gift shop. Not wheelchair accessible.

CONTACT: 705-267-1772, Ukrainian Historical and Cultural Museum.

North of Superior

Includes: Armstrong, Beardmore, Geraldton, Longlac, Marathon, Nipigon, Rossport, Terrace Bay, Thunder Bay.

This vast region of Northern Ontario contains Lake Nipigon, Ontario's largest lake exclusive of the Great Lakes, only 813 km² (314 sq. mi.) smaller in area than Prince Edward Island. Thunder Bay, created by the 1970 amalgamation of Port Arthur and Fort William, can claim to be the birthplace of the three-martini lunch. It was the site of the annual Great Rendezvous when more than a thousand North West Company agents, Indians, trappers, adventurers and voyageurs met to trade beaver pelts for blankets and alcohol.

Festivals, Carnivals, Celebrations, Special Events:

JANUARY: Thunder Bay Symphony Orchestra, *A Salute to Terry Fox;* Thunder Bay, *Confederation College Candlelight Series;* Thunder Bay, *New Year's Ski Jump Meet at Big Thunder.*

FEBRUARY: Thunder Bay Symphony Orchestra, *Mozart and Friends;* Thunder Bay, *International Soo* (snowmobile race to Minneapolis); Thunder Bay, *Ontario Provincial College Alpine Ski Championships at Big Thunder.*

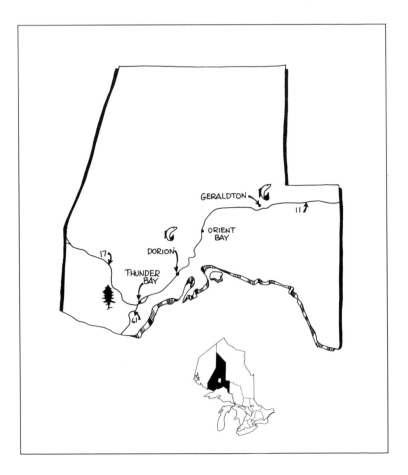

MARCH: Thunder Bay, *Provincial Broomball Championships.*

MAY: Thunder Bay, *Marina Park, Kite Day* (kite-making workshops, demonstrations, competitions); Thunder Bay, Canada Games Complex, *Thunderboat Invitational Swim Meet;* Thunder Bay, Old Fort William, *Season Launch;* Thunder Bay, *Multicultural Association Folklore Festival* (food, dance, song, exhibits).

JULY: Longlac, *Summerfest* (children's mini-festival, industrial and forestry tours, wheelbarrow weightlifting competition, parade); Thunder Bay, *Big Thunder National Ski Training Centre, Plastic Summer Jumping* (ski-jumping on plastic mat); Thunder Bay,

Wind Jamboree (sailboat and sailboard competitions); Thunder Bay, *Harbourfest* (music, crafts, fashion show, sports competitions); Thunder Bay, *Canada Day* (music and stage show, amusement park, fireworks).

AUGUST: Pass Lake, *Festival of the Giant* (kids bicycle and running races, corn roast, loon- and moose-calling contests, no-talent show); Marathon, *Neys Nostalgia Days* (campfire programme with spirits of the past, voyageur logging games, dances and activities).

NOVEMBER: Longlac, *Super Bowl Curling Classic;* Thunder Bay, Big Thunder, *World Cup of Ski Jumping.*

DECEMBER: Thunder Bay, *Central Canadian Figure Skating Championships.*

More detailed information on the festivals, carnivals, celebrations and other attractions of North of Superior is available from: North of Superior Tourism, 79 North Court St., Thunder Bay, Ontario P7A 4T7, 807-345-3322.

Dorion

Dorion Fish Culture Station

WHERE: 8 km (5 mi.) north of Hwy. 11-17 at Dorion, about 74 km (46 mi.) northeast of Thunder Bay.

WHEN: June through mid-September, open daily. Guided tours available 9 a.m. to noon and 1 p.m. to 4 p.m. October through May, no tours without prior arrangements, but the facility is open for visits.

WHAT: The station raises brook trout, lake trout and splake from fingerlings to adults. A video and the tour takes thirty to forty minutes. Visitor centre, viewing walkway, picnic area, washrooms. Wheelchair accessible with assistance.

CONTACT: 807-857-2322, Manager, Dorion Fish Culture Station.

Ouimet Canyon

WHERE: About 10 km (6 mi.) north of Hwy. 11-17 near Dorion and 56 km (35 mi.) east of Thunder Bay. Well signposted.

WHEN: May through Thanksgiving, open daily, depending on weather. The road isn't plowed in winter and opens when the snow has melted in the spring.

WHAT: The canyon is a natural fault approximately 150 m (500 ft.) in depth and width. The roadway in from the highway is steep and narrow and unsuitable for hauling trailers, but it is paved. Viewing platforms are cantilevered out over the precipice for spectacular views up and down the canyon. Definitely not recommended for those with vertigo! The trails from the parking lot to the viewing platforms are wheelchair accessible. Picnic tables, toilets.

CONTACT: 807-475-1531, Parks Superintendent, Ouimet Canyon, Ministry of Natural Resources.

Geraldton

MacLeod Mine Headframe and the Glory Hole

WHERE: The MacLeod Mine headframe is just south of Geraldton at the junction of Hwy. 11 and Hwy. 584. The Glory Hole is .6 km (.4 mi.) east of the junction on the south side of Hwy. 11.

WHEN: Year round.

WHAT: MacLeod Mine No. 1 produced more than two million ounces of gold between 1936 and 1970 before the ore vein petered out. The Glory Hole is a large, deep crater created by MacLeod goldminers from underneath. The hole is fenced off but draws a number of visitors each year.

The Million Dollar Bridge to Nowhere

WHERE: On the Ogoki River about 160 km (100 mi.) north of Geraldton. Follow Hwy. 584 to junction with Hwy. 643, continue to the logging road at the end. Drive another 88 km (55 mi.) more on first-class gravel roads owned and maintained by Kimberly Clark Canada Inc.

WHEN: Year round.

WHAT: Approximately 64 km (40 mi.) of road and the bridge were built between 1977 and 1980 to provide access to untouched timber resources. The construction was funded largely by the federal government under a regional economic development programme. The precise amount of public money thus wasted is not known, but the current costs of building a similar road are about $50,000 per kilometre. The bridge, made of steel and concrete, is believed to have cost $1 million. The driving surface is about 12 m (40 ft.) above the Ogoki River—high enough that a helicopter reportedly flew under it about three years ago. You can drive your vehicle onto the bridge and across the river, but on the other side the road ends abruptly. There is only enough cleared space to turn your vehicle around.

Orient Bay

The Palisades of the Pijitawabik

WHERE: At the scenic look-out on Hwy. 11 near Orient Bay, about 38 km (24 mi.) north of Nipigon.

WHEN: Year round.

WHAT: The sheer cliffs at several points along the Lake Nipigon shoreline are the dramatic result of erosion and glacial activity that began more than a thousand million years ago.

Thunder Bay

Amethyst Factory Centre

WHERE: 400 East Victoria Ave.

WHEN: Open year round, Monday to Saturday, 8:30 a.m. to 5 p.m.

WHAT: This complete lapidary manufacturing plant uses Thunder Bay amethyst. Tours demonstrate the production of clocks, gemstones and jewelry. Rock and gift shop. Wheelchair accessible.

CONTACT: 807-622-6908, Amethyst Factory.

Centennial Botanical Conservatory

WHERE: Behind Chapples Park at Balmoral and Dease St. Exit from Hwy. 11-17B at Waterloo St. N. Turn left onto Dease St.

WHEN: Open year round, daily, 1 p.m. to 4 p.m. Closed December 25 and 26, January 1 and Good Friday.

WHAT: The Conservatory offers a world-wide variety of plant life and attractive displays of exotic tropical plants and cacti. Washrooms not wheelchair accessible.

CONTACT: 807-622-7036, Conservatory; 807-625-2351, Parks Dept.

Centennial Park, 1910 Logging Camp

WHERE: Near Boulevard Lake in the heart of the city at Centennial Park Rd. Exit from Hwy. 11-17 via Hodder Ave. to Arundel St. W.

WHEN: Logging Camp open mid-June to Labour Day, daily, 10 a.m. to 8 p.m. Park open year round.

WHAT: The 57-ha (140-a.) park on the Current River features a complete 1910 logging camp where visitors can see how lumberjacks lived and worked as they harvested the forest. The Museum contains photographs and artifacts of the surrounding camps and a collection of logging tools. A blacksmith's shop, stable, Finnish steam bath and bunkhouse are also featured. Playground, domestic animal farm, 19 km (12 mi.) of hiking and cross-country ski trails. CONTACT: 807-683-6511, Centennial Park; 807-625-3166, Parks Service Supt., Centennial Park.

Chippewa Park

WHERE: East of Hwy. 61 at the end of City Rd., south end of city.

WHEN: Open late June through Labour Day. Alcohol ban in effect July 1 weekend.

WHAT: This park comprises 120 ha (300 a.) of land on the shores of Lake Superior. An exhibit of animals indigenous to northwestern Ontario can be viewed from an overhead walkway. Small fee may be charged. Camping, picnic tables, restaurant, groceries, souvenirs, cabins, beach. Amusement rides for adults and children (charge applies).

CONTACT: 807-623-3912, Chippewa Park; 807-625-2351, Parks Dept.

International Friendship Gardens

WHERE: Thunder Bay south in Chapple's Park off Victoria Ave.

WHEN: In growing season.

WHAT: During Centennial Year, Canadians from different ethnic backgrounds were invited to create a garden representing their native land. More than eighteen such gardens were created around two small lakes. The Dutch built a full-sized windmill in their garden. Free parking.

Kakabeka Falls

WHERE: 32 km (20 mi.) west of Thunder Bay, Hwy. 11-17 at entrance to Kakabeka Falls Provincial Park.

WHEN: Year round for falls viewing. Water flow is regulated by dam allowing a higher flow rate on weekends. The falls are most picturesque in spring and fall when water flows with full force.

WHAT: The "Niagara of the North" on the Kaministiquia River drops 39 m (128 ft.) into a cliff-lined gorge. Both sides of the falls are accessible from a parking lot just inside the provincial park. Boardwalk and viewing platforms all year, pedestrian bridge across the river adjacent to the falls, camping mid-May to mid-September, beach area, picnic areas, playgrounds, visitor centre with tourist information and naturalist programmes open during camping season. Cross-country skiing in winter.

CONTACT: 807-475-1531, Kakabeka Falls Provincial Park, Ministry of Natural Resources; 807-473-9231, Park Office, mid-May to mid-September.

Little Suomi

WHERE: Downtown Thunder Bay around Bay St. and Algoma St.

WHEN: Year round.

WHAT: This district of Thunder Bay boasts the largest population of Finns outside Finland. Settled by Finnish immigrants in 1872, the area has a distinctive European appearance. Private houses and stores are often side by side, and signs are in both English and Finnish.

Mount McKay

WHERE: Turn off Hwy. 61 at the airport, cross the Kaministikwia River and follow the signs. Park in the gravel lot just past the last hairpin turn and follow the trail.

WHEN: Mid-May to end of September.

WHAT: Visitors can enjoy a great view of Thunder Bay and area from a look-out atop Mt. McKay, the highest mountain in the Northwestern chain. Mt. McKay is a mesa which juts 320 m (1,050 ft.) above the surrounding terrain.

Northwestern Ontario Sports Hall of Fame

WHERE: 435 Balmoral St., top floor of the Twinhaven School. Exit from Hwy. 11-17B at Waterloo St., north of Dease St., turn left into Twinhaven School parking lot.

WHEN: Open year round, Monday to Friday, 10 a.m. to 4:30 p.m.; Sunday, 1 p.m. to 4 p.m. Closed all statutory holidays.

WHAT: The galleries highlight accomplishments by area citizens in skiing, hockey, bowling, soccer, cycling, curling, golf, tennis, swimming and track and field events. Washrooms. Not wheelchair accessible.

CONTACT: 807-622-2852, Northwestern Ontario Sports Hall of Fame.

Terry Fox Monument

WHERE: Just east of Thunder Bay beside the Terry Fox Courage Hwy., the official name of the Trans-Canada Hwy. between Nipigon and Thunder Bay.

WHEN: Year round.

WHAT: Most Canadians know the story: in 1980, twenty-one-year-old Terry Fox of British Columbia dipped his foot in the Atlantic Ocean at St. John's, Newfoundland, and started what he called the Marathon of Hope. He planned to run across Canada that summer—on one leg, since his other leg had been lost to cancer—to raise money for cancer research. By a sort of running hop, he managed 42 km (26 mi.) a day and covered 5,372 km (3,338 mi.) to Thunder Bay. By then cancer had spread through his body and he had to stop. He returned home and died the following June. The Province of Ontario has honoured him by erecting a statue to his memory at Thunder Bay look-out, close to the end of his Marathon of Hope.

Thunder Bay Art Gallery

WHERE: Confederation College Campus. Enter off Balmoral Ave. and keep right, or enter off Edward St. and keep left.

WHEN: Open year round, Tuesday to Thursday, noon to 8 p.m.; Friday to Sunday, noon to 5 p.m.

WHAT: This non-profit public gallery, with three exhibition areas, features contemporary Canadian Indian art, touring exhibits from major art museums and works by regional artists. Displays change every four to six weeks. Art classes, lectures, concerts and special exhibit openings. Gift shop, wheelchairs, washrooms, wheelchair accessible.

CONTACT: 807-577-6427, Thunder Bay Art Gallery.

Thunder Bay Auditorium

WHERE: 450 Beverly St., corner of Winnipeg Ave.

WHEN: Open year round. One-hour tours available in July or August or at other times by appointment. Admission charge for performances.

WHAT: This 1,500-seat multi-purpose facility includes three licensed lounge areas. Washrooms, fully accessible to wheelchairs. Boutique.

CONTACT: 807-343-2310, Thunder Bay Community Auditorium.

Thunder Bay Historical Museum

WHERE: 219 South May St.

WHEN: Year round. Mid-June to Labour Day, open daily, 11 a.m. to 5 p.m. Rest of year, open Tuesday to Sunday, 1 p.m. to 5 p.m.

WHAT: The Museum contains a collection of Indian artifacts, marine and military material, photographs, documents and maps. Washrooms. Not wheelchair accessible.

CONTACT: 807-623-0801, Director, Thunder Bay Historical Society Inc.

Thunder Bay Model Rail Association Exhibit

WHERE: Marina Park.

WHEN: Open mid-June through Labour Day, daily, noon to 8 p.m. Donations welcome.

WHAT: Northwestern Ontario's largest model rail exhibition has been mounted by the Thunder Bay Model Railroad Association

---

in the upstairs section of the old CN depot in Marina Park, a heritage building.

CONTACT: 807-625-2149, Thunder Bay Public Affairs.

Thunder Bay Thermal Generating Station

WHERE: At the mouth of the Kam River on Mission Island, a short drive over the Jackknife Bridge near Walsh St. and Syndicate Ave.

WHEN: Tours available by appointment, July and August, Tuesday and Friday, 10:30 a.m. Ages twelve and over.

WHAT: The Thunder Bay Public Visitors and Convention Bureau provides Guest Ambassadors to conduct ninety-minute tours through all areas of this 150-megawatt coal-fired generating station. Parts of the tour are wheelchair accessible.

CONTACT: 807-623-2701, Thunder Bay Thermal Generating Station.

Sunset Country

Includes: Atikokan, Dryden, Ear Falls, Fort Frances, Ignace, Kenora, Pickle Lake, Rainy River, Red Lake, Sioux Lookout, Vermilion Bay.

In this most sparsely settled region of Ontario is found some of Ontario's most luxurious wilderness lodges, and some of the best fishing and hunting on the continent. The major communities have museums to trace their pasts and festivals and celebrations whose entertainments remind residents and visitors of the many recreational advantages available in the vast outdoors.

Festivals, Carnivals, Celebrations, Special Events:

MARCH: Dryden, *Pub Night;* Sioux Lookout, *Band Concert;* Sioux Lookout, *Annual Northern Banks Hockey Tournament* (teams from northern communities).

MAY: Atikokan, *Trade Show;* Fort Frances-Rainy Lake, *Multicultural Association Culturama Festival* (song, dance and crafts); Kenora, *Lake of the Woods Multicultural Festival* (food, entertainment, displays).

JUNE: Kenora, *Lake of the Woods Canada Day Festival* (crafts, demonstrations, exhibits, music); Sioux Narrows, *Canada Day*

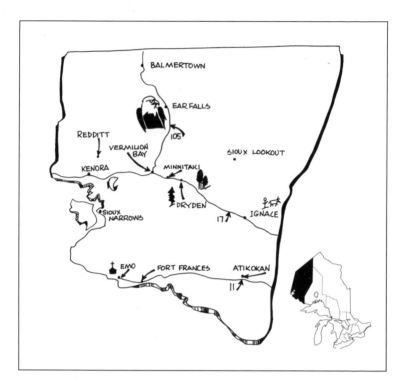

(boat races, bicycle parade, fireworks); Kenora, *Children's Festival.*

JULY: Rainy River, *Railroad Daze* (barbecue, talent show, fish fry, games); Vermilion Bay, *Canada Day* (art market, children's events); Sioux Narrows, *Whitefish Bay Pow Wow* (dance, singing and drumming competitions, Native food and crafts).

AUGUST: Sioux Narrows, *Annual Sioux Narrows Arts Festival* (exhibition, show and sale of original artwork and crafts); Atikokan, *Sports Days;* Vermilion Bay, *Children's Festival* (arts and crafts, jugglers and clowns); Dryden, *Dog Fanciers Club Dog Show* (conformation and obedience competition); Vermilion Bay, *Village Relay Race* (paddle canoe, bike, run or walk, putt one hole, fish fry, dance); Kenora, *Bass Invitational* (catch and release tournament).

NOVEMBER: Dryden, *Christmas Parade.*

More detailed information on the festivals, carnivals, celebrations and other attractions of Sunset Country is available from: Ontario's Sunset Country Travel Association, 102 Main St., 2nd Floor, Box 647, Kenora, Ontario P9N 3X6, 807-468-5853.

Atikokan

Atikokan Centennial Museum

WHERE: Civic Centre, off Burns St. and Sykes St.

WHEN: Open year round, Monday to Friday, 1 p.m. to 5 p.m.; Tuesday to Thursday, also 6:30 p.m. to 8:30 p.m.; Saturday, noon to 5 p.m. Closed Sunday and holidays.

WHAT: The Museum's gallery features a variety of art exhibits which change monthly. A nominal admission fee is charged to the adjacent historical park and museum, which contains interesting and unusual community and iron ore mining artifacts. On the park grounds you will find a restored logging engine and train and other large logging and mining relics. Gallery not wheelchair accessible.

CONTACT: 807-597-6585, Curator, Atikokan Centennial Museum and Historical Park.

Balmerton

Campbell Gold Mine Tour

WHERE: Northeast of Red Lake at Balmertown on Hwy. 125. Tours leave Recreation Centre.

WHEN: Tours offered June through August, Thursday, 1 p.m. to 3 p.m. Open until last Thursday in August, weather permitting.

WHAT: The tour shows visitors the surface and mill operations of an underground mine. Suitable clothing such as flat shoes and slacks are recommended. Washrooms and recreational facilities. Not wheelchair accessible.

CONTACT: 807-735-2075, Campbell Mine-Placer Dome Inc.

Dryden

Canadian Pacific Forest Products Ltd. (Dryden Operations)

WHERE: Duke St.

WHEN: Tours offered June through August, Monday to Friday, 9 a.m., 10:30 a.m., 1 p.m. and 2:30 p.m. Minimum age, twelve years. Telephone in advance to be sure there's room on the tour you want.

WHAT: This mill produces bleached kraft pulp and white papers. One-hour tours take visitors through the paper- and lumber-making operations in the plant, which underwent a $550 million modernization and expansion programme in 1989. Not wheelchair accessible.

CONTACT: 807-223-9376, Canadian Pacific Forest Products Ltd., summer; 807-223-9233, winter.

Dryden and District Museum

WHERE: 15 Van Horne Ave.

WHEN: Year round, Monday to Friday, 10 a.m. to 5 p.m.; Saturday, 10 a.m. to 4 p.m. Closed statutory holidays. Donations welcome.

WHAT: The Museum houses a collection of 9,000 artifacts from the early 1800s to the present. Wheelchair-accessible washrooms.

CONTACT: 807-223-4671, Dryden and District Museum.

Dryden Tree Nursery

WHERE: 6 km (3.7 mi.) north of Hwy. 17, 1 km (.6 mi.) west of Wabigoon.

WHEN: Year round. Tours offered Monday to Friday, 8 a.m. to 4 p.m.

WHAT: The 1,050-ha (2,600-a.) nursery contains over thirty million seedlings of various species in different stages of growth. Ten production greenhouses produce four million seedlings per year. Tours take about two hours. Washrooms. Not wheelchair accessible.

CONTACT: 807-938-6326, Nursery Superintendent, Ministry of Natural Resources.

Maximillian Moose

WHERE: Hwy. 17 beside the Tourist Information Bureau.

WHEN: Year round.

WHAT: A 6-m (18-ft.) statue of a moose.

Northwestern Fire Management Centre

WHERE: 5 km (3 mi.) east of town on Hwy. 17, north on Hwy. 601 (follow airport signs) then right on Ghost Lake Rd. just before the airport.

WHEN: Year round, by appointment only.

WHAT: The Centre is responsible for planning and coordinating the fire management programme for about 19 per cent of Ontario's total land mass. Guided tours include the co-ordination centre for fire suppression and prescribed burn activities, the lightning location system used to help predict fires, warehouse and maintenance facilities and, depending on the season and current fire hazard, detection and water-bombing aircraft. Washrooms, first aid, wheelchair accessible.

CONTACT: 807-937-4402, Ontario Ministry of Natural Resources.

Ear Falls

Bald Eagle Capital of North America

WHERE: Around Ear Falls, a major centre for wilderness fishing and hunting on Hwy. 105, 100 km (62 mi.) north of Vermilion Bay on Hwy. 17.

WHEN: Late spring through fall.

WHAT: This is a likely spot to sight the Bald Eagle, a magnificent carnivore that is increasingly scarce.

Emo

Norlund Chapel

WHERE: Beside Hwy. 11 just west of Emo.

WHEN: Year round, daily.

WHAT: One of the smallest churches in the world was built in 1973 from the spire of St. Patrick's Catholic Church. In 1971 lightning struck an iron cross atop St. Patrick's Church and fire broke out. At the height of the blaze the wooden steeple, complete with cross, fell into the blazing church but didn't burn. The steeple forms the roof of a 2.4-by-3-m (8-by-10-ft.) non-denominational house of prayer built by Elmer Norlund.

Rainy River District Women's Institute Museum

WHERE: In Emo, junction of Hwy. 11 and Hwy. 71, across from the Ontario Provincial Police station.

WHEN: Open Victoria Day weekend through August, daily, 11 a.m. to 5 p.m. Other times by appointment.

WHAT: The Museum houses a collection of pioneer artifacts relating to the history of settlers in the Rainy River District. Souvenirs and local crafts are available. Washroom, picnic tables, tourist information.

CONTACT: 807-482-2007, Rainy River District Women's Institute Museum.

Fort Frances

Boise Cascade Canada Ltd.

WHERE: Tours start from Post 8, Scott St. and Central Ave.

WHEN: June through August, tours offered Monday to Friday, 10 a.m. and 1:30 p.m., except statutory holidays. Reservations required. Children under twelve not admitted.

WHAT: The paper-making process from pulp to specialty papers is explained on this one-hour tour. Washrooms. No wheelchair access.

CONTACT: 807-274-5311, Manager, Regional Communications, Boise Cascade Canada Ltd.

Ignace

Ignace Museum

WHERE: 36 Main St. in the new library.

WHEN: Open year round, Monday to Thursday, 10 a.m. to noon, 1 p.m. to 5 p.m. and 7 p.m. to 9 p.m.; Friday, 1 p.m. to 5 p.m. September to June, also open Saturday, 1 p.m. to 5 p.m. Closed Sunday and holidays.

WHAT: This museum houses a modest collection of tools, photographs, Indian paintings and carved artifacts gathered from the community. Wheelchair-accessible washrooms.

CONTACT: 807-934-2548, Ignace Museum.

Pictographs

WHERE: In the Ignace area.

WHEN: Late spring through early fall.

WHAT: Within the Ignace area are twenty known sites of Ojibwa pictographs. These rock paintings are messages to the supernatural beings known as manitous, whose favour the Ojibwa considered essential to survival. You'll need a canoe, boat or float plane to reach most of them. They are located on the shores of Indian, Paguchi, Barrel, Mameigwess, Arethusa, Bending, Red Paint, Flat Rock and White Otter Lakes.

White Otter Castle

WHERE: On the shores of White Otter Lake, 40 km (25 mi.) south of Ignace, 48 km (30 mi.) northwest of Atikokan. The castle can be reached only by water, float plane or snowmobile.

WHEN: Year round.

WHAT: This massive, three-storey log house with four-storey tower is the legacy of James Alexander McQuat, subject of many legends. McQuat was 1.7 m (5 ft., 7 in.) tall, and weighed 66 kg (145 lb.) Yet he built the castle single-handedly between 1903 (when he was 57) and 1912. Many of the red pine logs he used are 11 m (37 ft.) long and weigh over a ton. How he managed to raise them into position and hold them while he dove-tailed them remains a mystery. A $1.5 million restoration programme is being carried out by the Ontario government.

CONTACT: 807-597-6971, District Manager, Ministry of Natural Resources, Atikokan.

Kenora

Boise Cascade Canada Ltd.

WHERE: 504 Ninth St. N.

WHEN: Open July and August, Monday, Wednesday, Thursday, Friday. One-hour tours offered at 9:30 a.m. and 1:30 p.m. Visitors must be over twelve years old and wear sturdy, closed-toed shoes. No cameras allowed. Advance reservations required.

WHAT: Visitors can follow the newsprint manufacturing process from pulpwood to the finished product. The plant produces 862 tonnes (950 tons) of high grade newsprint daily. Washrooms. Not wheelchair accessible.

CONTACT: 807-467-3000, Boise Cascade Canada Ltd.

Devil's Gap Rock

WHERE: At the narrowest point of Devil's Gap Channel south of Kenora. There is no road to the "spirit rock," as some call it, but it may be seen from the M.S. *Kenora* boat cruise.

WHEN: Year round.

WHAT: There is no romantic or touching Native legend attached to this large rock. In 1894 three visitors to the area painted a face on the rock as a joke. Residents liked its features and over the years it has been repainted a number of times.

Husky the Muskie

WHERE: In McLeod Park at the end of Lake of the Woods.

WHEN: Year round.

WHAT: This 12.2-m (40-ft.) leaping fibreglass muskellunge is the symbol of Kenora. The town used to be called Rat Portage (as in muskrat) until the Maple Leaf Flour Company said it wouldn't go ahead with a proposed mill if the word "rat" would have to appear on its flour bags. The town was rapidly named Kenora, a name derived from the first two letters of three area communities: Keewatin, Norman and Rat Portage.

Keewatin Boat Lift

WHERE: North on Ottawa St., across railway tracks, west along the tracks.

WHEN: Open Victoria Day weekend through Labour Day. Hours of operation vary.

WHAT: Lake of the Woods and the Winnipeg River meet—almost—just west of Kenora. This ingenious lift carries boats the 10.7-m (35-ft.) vertical distance between the lake and the river. The lift, believed the only one of its kind, lowers a cradle into which the boat floats. Boats as long as 9.1 m (30 ft.), weighing as much as 9 tonnes (10 tons), are then lifted. The cradle is rolled along a short section of track and lowered to the other side. Picnic area, washrooms.

CONTACT: 807-547-2881, Town of Keewatin.

Mather Walls House

WHERE: 1116 Ottawa St. in downtown Keewatin, at the top of Main St. hill.

WHEN: Open July through Labour Day, Monday to Friday, 10 a.m. to 4 p.m. Donations welcome.

WHAT: The house was built in 1889 by David L. Mather, who operated the Woods Lumber Mill. The main floor has been restored to turn-of-the-century appearance. Displays by the Historical Society occupy the second floor. Gift counter. Washrooms. Not wheelchair accessible.

CONTACT: 807-547-2870, The Mather Walls House, Lake of the Woods Historical Society.

Minnitaki

Egli's Sheep Farm

WHERE: At Minnitaki on Hwy. 17 about 18 km (11 mi.) west of Dryden.

WHEN: Farm show July through Labour Day, Monday to Friday, 11 a.m. The show lasts about an hour. The retail store is open year round, daily in summer. Closed Sunday in winter and December 25 and 26 and January 1.

WHAT: This large commercial sheep farm produces meat, wool and sheepskins. Tours of the 500-head operation and manufacturing facilities are available. An indoor live farm show demonstrates all aspects of sheep farming. A large gift shop offers a wide variety of merchandise derived from the sheep. Wheelchair-accessible washrooms.

CONTACT: 1-800-465-2966 or 807-755-5231, Egli's Sheep Farm.

Redditt

The Bottle Houses

WHERE: In the Village of Redditt, 25 km (15.5 mi.) north of Kenora on County Rd. 658 (a gravel road).

WHEN: Year round.

WHAT: A collection of houses has been built out of empty liquor bottles. The largest, 3.7 by 4.3 m (12 by 14 ft.) contains a doll collection. There's a house for Snow White and the Seven Dwarfs, another for Goldilocks and the Three Bears, a windmill, wishing well and water fountain, all made from bottles. No signs have been posted to direct you to the bottle houses, which are found behind the home of Hank Deverell. When he's at home, visitors are welcome and he enjoys chatting with them. Anyone in the village can show you the way.

Sioux Lookout

Sioux Lookout Museum

WHERE: At Sioux Lookout on Wellington St.

WHEN: Mid-May to mid-June, open weekends, 9 a.m. to 6 p.m. Mid-June through Labour Day, open daily, 9 a.m. to 6 p.m. Donations welcome.

WHAT: The Museum portrays the history of Sioux Lookout, Hudson and area. Themes include transportation and communications, mining, military, domestic activities and Native heritage. Washrooms, picnic tables. Wheelchair access to museum, but not washrooms.

CONTACT: 807-737-1562, Sioux Lookout Museum; 807-737-2700, in off-season.

Sioux Narrows

Sioux Narrows Bridge

WHERE: At the Village of Sioux Narrows on Hwy. 71, 60 km (37 mi.) south of Kenora.

WHEN: Year round.

WHAT: This is the longest single-span wooden bridge in the world. The 32-m (105-ft.) central spans of Douglas fir are made from British Columbia trees that pre-date European settlement of Canada. When it was built in 1935, the 64-m (210-ft.) bridge was designed to last forty years and carry a maximum load of 18 tonnes (20 tons). Tests conducted in 1980 found the timbers to be as sound as when the bridge was built and the load limit to be 110 tonnes (120 tons).

Vermilion Bay

Clark's Wildlife Museum

WHERE: Vermilion Bay, junction of Hwy. 17 and Hwy. 647, 43 km (26.7 mi.) west of Dryden.

WHEN: Year round. In summer, open 6 a.m. to 10 p.m. Off-season, open 7 a.m. to 7 p.m.

WHAT: This small museum features beautifully wrought displays of animals and birds in lifelike poses in their natural habitat— including beavers in a pond. With the exception of a huge polar bear, all sixty-odd specimens are indigenous to the area. The museum is designed to draw visitors into an outfitting store but there's no pressure to buy. Friendly staff are happy to abandon the sales area to answer questions. Washrooms, gift shop, wheelchair access.

CONTACT: 807-227-2099, Clark's Wildlife Museum.

Fort Vermilion

WHERE: On Hwy. 17 in Vermilion Bay, about 43 km (26.7 mi.) west of Dryden.

WHEN: Year round. May through September, open daily, 9 a.m. to 8 p.m. October through April, open Monday to Thursday, 9 a.m. to 3 p.m.

WHAT: A replica of an early log fort, based on Old Fort William in Thunder Bay, houses a travel information centre and community display rooms. A variety of special events are held during the summer. Washrooms, picnic area, playground, barbecues, wheelchair accessible.

CONTACT: 807-227-2640, Fort Vermilion Tourism Association.

Red Eagle Totem

WHERE: Northeast corner of Hwy. 17 and Hwy. 105 at Vermilion Bay.

WHEN: Year round.

WHAT: This 15.2-m (50-ft.) totem pole carved by Shaman Chief Kitpou of British Columbia includes nine figures, each representing an Indian legend. The totem pole was dedicated to the children of Vermilion Bay in a 1977 ceremony in which 300 children helped to raise it into place with ropes.

More Ontario For Free

A wealth of well researched and professionally produced travel and tourism information is available from the Ontario Ministry of Tourism and Recreation—*and it's all free!*

To order the material, dial 1-800-668-2746 between 8 a.m. and 6 p.m. Toronto time from within Canada or the continental United States (except Yukon, NWT and Alaska). The office is open seven days a week mid-May to Labour Day and Monday through Friday the rest of the year. When requesting information, specify your areas of interest: antiquing, boating, camping, fishing, dining, hiking, etc. In every recognized category of travel or recreation the Ministry has excellent, up-to-date resource material to help you do your thing in Ontario.

The Ministry produces the best available road map of Ontario, the *Ontario Canada Official Road Map*. There's a thick book called *Accommodations* with detailed information about every hotel, motel, lodge, inn, resort or rental cabin in the province. A four-colour magazine-format booklet called *Travel Ontario Canada* lists all major points of interest, community by community throughout the province.

Camping tells you everything about more than 200 provincial parks, 304 conservation areas and hundreds of privately owned campgrounds. *Country Inns* provides detailed information about establishments, seventy-five years and older, that serve food or offer accommodation. Similar catalogues are available listing marinas, cruises, antique markets, fishing, hunting, flea markets, etc. Each year the Ministry publishes summer and winter catalogues of festivals and special events across the province.

The map and booklets are also available on request at Travel Information Centres at every major entry point to the province by road and at dozens of Regional Travel Information Centres province-wide.

Two additional guidebooks are available at book stores across Ontario.

The Ontario Getaway Guidebook, by David E. Scott, is the only comprehensive guide to the province. It describes all points of touristic interest in the province and suggests dining spots and accommodations in each area, all of which were inspected by the author.

A Taste of Ontario Country Inns describes sixty of author David E. Scott's best culinary finds on his extensive travels. Each listing includes the chef's favorite recipe scaled down to serve one, two or four. T*he Ontario Getaway Guidebook* and *A Taste of Ontario Country Inns* are both published by Whitecap Books Ltd.

Ontario Holidays

Many attractions in Ontario are seasonal. Opening and closing dates are often tied to statutory holidays.

American readers should note that Canada celebrates Thanksgiving Day on the second Monday in October. (When most Americans celebrate Thanksgiving Day in November, most Canadian crops have already been harvested—or they're frozen solid!)

Here's a list of some Canadian holidays and festivals:

Easter, Good Friday, Easter Monday: usually third weekend in April

Victoria Day: mid-May

Canada Day: July 1

Civic Holiday: In Ontario, Monday of the weekend closest to August 1

Labour Day: First Monday in September

Thanksgiving: Second Monday in October

Index

About the Author

D avid E. Scott has been a writer, photographer, or editor for the past three decades; with a brief reprieve in the early seventies as the owner of a disco in Andorra. A great lover of travel, he has lived in many countries and toured almost a hundred. His travel books and articles have brought him much acclaim; in 1989 he won an outstanding award from the southwestern Ontario Travel Association. His other works include *A Taste of Ontario Country Inns, The Ontario Getaway Guidebook,* and several travel guides to Canada.

Photo: Wendy Scott